G
TRAI

LIGHTHOUSE MUSEUM, ST SIMONS ISLAND

Golden Isles VB

TRAVEL ✦ SMART®
GEORGIA

First Edition

Donald O'Briant

AVALON
TRAVEL

TRAVEL ✦ SMART: GEORGIA

1st EDITION

Donald O'Briant

Published by
Avalon Travel Publishing
5855 Beaudry St.
Emeryville, CA 94608, USA

Please send all comments, corrections,
additions, amendments, and critiques to:

TRAVEL ✦ SMART: GEORGIA
AVALON TRAVEL PUBLISHING
5855 BEAUDRY ST.
EMERYVILLE, CA 94608, USA
e-mail: info@travelmatters.com
www.travelmatters.com

Printing History
1st edition— August 2000
5 4 3 2 1

ISBN: 1-56261-531-9
ISSN: 1530-8316

Editors: Marybeth Griffin Macy, Suzanne Samuel
Graphics Coordinator: Erika Howsare
Production: Amber T. Pirker
Design: Marie J.T. Vigil
Index: Leslie Miller
Cover Design: Janine Lehmann/Marie J.T. Vigil
Maps: Mike Ferguson, Mike Morgenfeld

Front cover photo: large—© John Elk III (Swan House, Atlanta), small—© Leo de Wys (Davenport
House, Savannah)
Back cover photo: © Leo de Wys (Atlanta)

Distributed in the United States and Canada by Publishers Group West.

Printed in the United States by Publishers Press.

GEORGIA TRAVEL·SMART: A GUIDE THAT GUIDES

Most guidebooks are primarily directories, providing information but very little help in making choices-you have to guess how to make the most of your time and money. *Georgia Travel•Smart* is different: By highlighting the very best of the state and offering various planning features, it acts like a personal tour guide rather than a directory.

TAKE THE STRESS OUT OF TRAVEL

Sometimes traveling causes more stress than it relieves. Sorting through information, figuring out the best routes, determining what to see and where to eat and stay, scheduling each day-all of this can make a vacation feel daunting rather than fun. Relax. We've done a lot of the legwork for you. This book will help you plan a trip that suits you-whatever your time frame, budget, and interests.

SEE THE BEST OF THE STATE

Author Donald O'Briant has lived in Georgia for 27 years. He has hand-picked every listing in this book, and he gives you an insider's perspective on what makes each one worthwhile. So while you will find many of the big tourist attractions listed here, you'll also find lots of smaller, lesser-known treasures, such as the wild horses on Cumberland Island off the Georgia coast or a nighttime swamp tour of the Suwannee Canal Recreation Area. And each sight is described so you'll know what's most-and sometimes least-interesting about it.

In selecting the restaurants and accommodations for this book, the author sought out unusual spots with local flavor. While in some areas of the state chains are unavoidable, wherever possible the author directs you to one-of-a-kind places. We also know that you want a range of options: One day you may crave Charleston-style crab cakes at Atlanta's City Grill, while the next day you would be just as happy (as would your wallet) with barbecue from Fat Matt's Rib Shack. Most of the restaurants and accommodations listed here are moderately priced, but the author also includes budget and splurge options, depending on the destination.

CREATE THE TRIP YOU WANT

We all have different travel styles. Some people like spontaneous weekend jaunts, while others plan longer, more leisurely trips. You may want to cover as much ground as possible, no matter how much time you have. Or maybe you prefer to focus your trip on one part of the state or on some special interest, such as history, nature, or the outdoors. We've taken these differences into account.

Though the individual chapters stand on their own, they are organized in a geographically logical sequence, so that you could conceivably fly into Atlanta, drive chapter by chapter to each destination in the book, and end up close to where you started. Of course, you don't have to follow that sequence, but it's there if you want a complete picture of the state.

Each destination chapter offers ways of prioritizing when time is limited: In the Perfect Day section, the author suggests what to do if you have only one day to spend in the area. Also, every Sightseeing Highlight is rated, from one to four stars:

★★★★   must see
★★★   highly recommended
★★   worthwhile
★   see if you have time

At the end of each sight listing is a time recommendation in parentheses. User-friendly maps help you locate the sights, restaurants, and lodging of your choice.

And if you're in it for the ride, so to speak, you'll want to check out the Scenic Routes described at the end of several chapters. They take you through some of the most scenic parts of state.

In addition to these special features, the appendix has other useful travel tools:
- The Planning Map and Mileage Chart help you determine your own route and calculate travel time.
- The Special Interest Tours show you how to design your trip around any of five favorite interests, ranging from the Civil War to outdoor recreation.
- The Calendar of Events provides an at-a-glance view of when and where major events occur throughout the state.
- The Resource Guide tells you where to go for more information about national and state parks, individual cities and counties, local bed-and-breakfasts, and more.

HAPPY TRAVELS

With this book in hand, you have many reliable recommendations and travel tools at your fingertips. Use it to make the most of your trip. And have a great time!

WHY VISIT GEORGIA?

When Georgia invited the world to visit in 1996, a few million people accepted the invitation. Some went to watch the Olympic Games, but many others stayed long after the torch was extinguished to explore the state's numerous natural and man-made wonders.

Each year the 30 million or more visitors discover the state's diversity. In the north, tumbling waterfalls and the foothills of the Blue Ridge Mountains beckon hikers and campers. In the south, the Okefenokee Swamp offers an unrestricted view of alligators and other wildlife. On the coast, a chain of golden isles welcomes sportsmen and sun worshippers with miles of pristine beaches, dozens of golf courses, and a historic five-star resort on an island that once was the playground of the Rockefellers and Carnegies.

In between the mountains and the coast, vacationers can drive through picturesque rural villages and modern cities, spend a night in a towering hotel or at a rustic campsite, dine at country cafés and world-class restaurants, browse through village shops and sprawling malls, and tour Civil War battlefields and civil rights landmarks. History buffs can visit the remnants of Spanish forts along the coast or tour the streets and cemeteries of Savannah, a city made famous in John Berendt's best-selling book, *Midnight in the Garden of Good and Evil*.

And, of course, there is Atlanta, the city that emerged from the ashes of the Civil War like the mythical bird, the Phoenix. *Gone With the Wind* fans who come here looking for Scarlett O'Hara's beloved Tara will be disappointed to discover that the white-columned mansion existed only on the movie screen and in Margaret Mitchell's imagination, but they still can walk through the small apartment where Mitchell composed her masterpiece and tour authentic antebellum mansions on the outskirts of the city.

A cosmopolitan blend of the past and the present, Atlanta offers fine dining; cultural attractions such as the symphony, ballet, theater, and art galleries; and professional sporting events ranging from baseball's Atlanta Braves to ice hockey's new Atlanta Thrashers.

As with most big cities, however, the real pleasures of Atlanta are found in the small restaurants, nightclubs and blues and barbecue joints that are tucked away off the main thoroughfares, or in the numerous ethnic eating places in the Asian, Hispanic, and African American neighborhoods. Yes, Atlanta is an international city with a booming business district, but like the rest of the state, it is a place where Southern hospitality still thrives and where even sushi chefs say, "Y'all come back, now!"

LAY OF THE LAND

Known as the Empire State of the South, Georgia claims the largest land mass east of the Mississippi River. Its 58,930-square-mile area is 20 percent larger than New York and nearly twice as big as Virginia. Within that vast territory is a wide range of geography. In the north, the Blue Ridge, the Appalachian Plateau, and the Appalachian Ridge and Valley regions of the Appalachian Mountains form a natural boundary between Georgia and its neighbors, Tennessee and North Carolina.

In the northeast, the pine and hardwood-covered slopes of the Blue Ridge rise from 2,000 feet to nearly 5,000 feet above sea level.

Between the peaks are a number of clear mountain lakes, tumbling waterfalls, and rushing trout streams bordered by rhododendron, mountain laurel, and hardwood forests. White-water enthusiasts are attracted to the wild and scenic Chattooga River, made famous in the movie based on James Dickey's novel, Deliverance. The highest point in the Blue Ridge is Mt. Enotah, or Brasstown Bald, which soars to 4,784 feet. In contrast, the spectacular Tallulah Gorge is nearly 1,000 feet deep and two miles long. One of the Tallulah River's three waterfalls plunges more 700 feet to the floor of the canyon.

In the extreme northwest corner of the state, the Appalachian Plateau, with its narrow valleys and sandy soil, ranges from 1,800 feet to 2,000 feet above sea level. The adjoining Appalachian Ridge and Valley region is a greener region of fertile valleys dotted with farms and orchards.

Just south of the mountains, the Piedmont, with its rolling hills, slopes gently toward the coastal plains. The state's major metropolitan centers of Atlanta, Athens, Augusta, Columbus and Macon are located in this region. Geographic landmarks include the Savannah River on the eastern border, Lake Lanier north of Atlanta, and the Chattahoochee River, which winds through the Piedmont on its way to the Gulf of Mexico. Sixteen miles east of Atlanta is Stone Mountain, a 1,683-foot peak that is the largest piece of exposed granite east of the Mississippi.

Separating the Piedmont from the East Gulf Coastal Plain and the Atlantic Coastal Plain is the Fall Line, a narrow strip that marks the beginning of what was the coastline millions of years ago.

The Atlantic Coastal Plain and the East Gulf Coastal Plain are prime agricultural areas of the state with thousands of acres yielding peanuts, soybeans, cotton, corn, tobacco, peaches and pecans. The middle, fertile region, known as the Black Belt, is where antebellum plantations thrived. As the soil becomes sandier farther south in the pine barrens, farmland has been converted to pine forests that are primarily owned by pulpwood and lumber companies.

At the southern end of the Atlantic Coastal Plain lies the Okefenokee Swamp, the nation's largest wildlife refuge. The Okefenokee, which translates as "Land of the Trembling Earth" in Seminole, was created when the eastern ridge rose suddenly and isolated a vast pocket of coastal water. As vegetation spread and cypress trees grew, the area became one big peat bog.

The Seminoles have a more romantic version of the Okefenokee's origin. According to legend, the swamp was created when the beavers and the people fought over the land. In anger, the beavers broke all of their dams, flooded the area, and then departed. The Okefenokee is full of wildlife, from alligators to wildfowl, but there are no beavers. The headwaters of the Okefenokee are the source of Stephen Foster's famous Suwannee River.

Other natural landmarks include Providence Canyon south of Columbus on the western border of the state. Called "Georgia's Little Grand Canyon," its colorful red-and-white walls plunge steeply from a forest floor crowded with plum-leaf azaleas and rare wildflowers.

The Atlantic Coast, famous for the historic port city of Savannah, is 100 miles of barrier islands, beaches and marshlands. Jekyll, St. Simons, Sea Island, and Tybee have become popular resorts, but there are still natural areas such as Cumberland Island that are protected by the National Park Service. On Cumberland, wild horses run freely and loggerhead turtles lay their eggs on an unspoiled beach.

FLORA AND FAUNA

From the air, one would think Georgia is covered in kudzu, the ubiquitous vine imported from Japan to control erosion. While it's true that kudzu has taken over thousands of acres of farmland and even swallowed up abandoned barns and houses, it is only one of many species of vegetation in the state.

In the mountainous regions of the north, the forests are dominated by oaks, pines, red spruce, sugar maples, hickories, and beeches. Laurels and rhododendrons fill the gaps in valleys and along mountain streams. Botanists say there are more species of trees in the Appalachians than there are in Europe.

In the middle and southern part of the state, dogwoods, magnolias, crape myrtle, chinaberry and redbud trees produce a colorful and aromatic sea of blossoms beginning in March and April.

Pines are predominant in the coastal plains, but you will also find huge live oaks with tendrils of gray Spanish moss hanging from their branches. Saw palmettos, with their fan-shaped fronds, fill in the gaps between the pines and the oaks. In the swamps, knobby-kneed bald cypresses loom out of the black water.

Wildflowers are plentiful all over the state, especially since the Department of Transportation began a project to sow wildflower seeds along the medians of the interstate highways. Daisies, Queen Anne's lace, and Cherokee roses are found everywhere, but the dominant flowering vines are honeysuckle and wisteria. Almost as tenacious as kudzu, honeysuckle blooms throughout the summer and fills the air with a heavy, sweet aroma. Hanging clusters of purple blossoms of wisteria can be seen in forests and on backyard trellises every spring.

Wildlife in the state remains abundant despite the spreading suburbs and industrial development. Game birds include wild turkeys, doves, quail, marsh hens, ruffed grouse and ducks. White-tailed deer, once rare in the South, are now so plentiful they can be seen grazing along the shoulders of highways on moonlit nights.

Black bears roam the mountains and an occasional Florida panther can be seen. Other wildlife includes bobcats, beavers, coyotes, foxes, rabbits, squirrels, minks, otters, and wild hogs. Snakes are plentiful, too, so hikers should watch for the poisonous copperheads, water moccasins, rattlesnakes, and coral snakes.

A fisherman's paradise, the lakes and rivers of Georgia teem with trout, bass, bream, catfish, eels, crappie, and shad. The coastal waters are alive with alligators, crabs, turtles, shrimp, oysters, flounder, mullet, mackerel, and mussels.

Because it is situated on the eastern flyway migration route, Georgia is a great place for birdwatching. More than 350 different species, from bluejays to woodpeckers, can be seen throughout the year. Among the native birds are mockingbirds, cardinals, ruby-throated hummingbirds, brown thrashers, catbirds, wrens, owls, purple martins, whippoorwills (or goatsuckers), hawks, buzzards, ospreys, herons, woodstorks, egrets, and an occasional bald eagle. Georgia has made the preservation of wildlife and its habitats a priority in the face of increased development. It was one of the first states to pass legislation protecting tidal marshlands. The Georgia Conservancy has taken an active role in preserving natural areas and, in addition, thousands of acres of woodlands are protected as national forests.

HISTORY AND CULTURES

Long before white settlers arrived, Georgia was the home of prehistoric Indians called Mound Builders. These aborigines built earth dwellings as high as three stories. Some of these earthworks are still visible today. The Etowah Mounds near New Echota in northwest Georgia, the Ocmulgee Mounds near Macon in mid-Georgia and the Kolomoki Mounds in southwest Georgia are among the most incredible archaeological sites in the country. Traces of pottery and other artifacts from the Archaic period nearly 11,000 years ago have been found near Augusta on the Savannah River.

Following the Archaic period, the Woodland period of 1000 B.C. to 900 A.D. was characterized by farming, trading, and a more civilized culture. With the Mississippian period that began in 900 A.D., larger villages sprang up and communities were built around lodges where meetings took place. Sporting events with makeshift balls were held on nearby fields. A glimpse of this life can be seen at the Etowah Mounds north of Atlanta near Cartersville.

When the mound builders disappeared some 300 years later, other Indian tribes such as the Creeks and Cherokees moved into the area. The Creeks settled in the south and the Cherokees went into the mountains of North Georgia and North Carolina.

In 1540, the Native American culture was disrupted by the invasion of Spanish explorer Hernando de Soto and his soldiers. The Spaniards were not interested in settling the area; they were searching for gold. Overlooking the rich deposits near Dahlonega, de Soto moved on, leaving behind smallpox and influenza. With no natural resistance to the European diseases, entire tribes were wiped out.

After de Soto departed, the islands along the coast of Georgia became a battleground between the British, Spanish, and French. French Huguenots, who arrived in the 1560s, were soon pushed out by the Spanish. In 1566, the Spanish built a fort on St. Catherines Island to protect against future invaders.

The British arrived in 1733, when General James Oglethorpe founded the colony and named it after King George II. Spain protested the move, but Oglethorpe persisted and landed with 120 colonists on Yamacraw Bluff, the future site of Savannah. The original plan was to send mostly imprisoned or newly released debtors to the colony, but in the end only a few debtors were sent.

In the beginning, Oglethorpe intended to found a kind of Utopia in Georgia, a place where there was no slavery and no imbibing of hard liquor. But the colonists soon envied the easier life of slave owners across the river in South Carolina, and 16 years later, the ban on slavery was lifted. Alcoholic prohibition, too, proved as unenforceable as that of the 1920s.

On a positive note, the colonists were aided by the Creek Indian chief Tomochichi, who helped persuade other tribes to allow the British to settle peacefully. But life did not remain peaceful for long. As illegal trading and smuggling increased, England and Spain went to war.

Oglethorpe's attempt to capture Florida was thwarted, but in 1742, British troops decisively defeated the Spanish in the Battle of Bloody Marsh on St. Simons Island. The victory ended the war in America between the British and Spanish.

In the Revolutionary War, Georgia escaped much of the fighting until 1778, when British troops captured Savannah. With the help of the French navy, the Americans laid siege to the city for three weeks. A subsequent attack failed, however, and by the end of the war, the British controlled most of the state.

After the war, Georgia became the fourth state to ratify the United States Constitution. Five years later, in 1793, Eli Whitney invented the cotton gin near Savannah and farming was forever changed. Plantations that had grown a variety of crops now devoted all their land to the cash crop of cotton. Still, most of the farms in the state were 100 acres or smaller and operated without slave labor.

A dismal period in Georgia's history occurred in the years before the Civil War when unscrupulous politicians and corrupt speculators tried to sell 50 million acres—most of which they didn't own—for huge profits. The scheme, which came to be known as the Yazoo Land Fraud, was exposed by the federal government. As punishment, the state of Georgia was forced to give up part of its western territory to Alabama and Mississippi. The politicians agreed to this only if the federal government would remove the Native Americans from other territory that Georgia claimed to own. As a result, in 1827, the Creek Indians were moved to the Arkansas Territory and, in 1838, the remaining Cherokees were relocated to Oklahoma. White settlers quickly moved in and cleared the land for farming.

Shortly after Abraham Lincoln was elected president in 1860, Georgia Governor Joseph E. Brown called for secession from the Union. Former congressman Alexander H. Stephens led the opposition, but when Georgia voted to secede from the union, Stephens became vice president of the Confederacy. Not everyone who supported secession favored slavery, however. Also at issue in the minds of many Southerners was states' rights, or the belief that the states were not under the control of the federal government and had the right to withdraw from the union at any time.

The resulting war scarred Georgia perhaps more than any other state. In the early years of the war, the Union navy blocked the port of Savannah and conducted frequent raids along the coast. The Rebels won their first great victory in Georgia at Chickamauga in 1863, but a year later General William T. Sherman began his devastating march to the sea. After bloody encounters at Kennesaw Mountain, Sherman surrounded the city of Atlanta. The city finally surrendered after four fierce battles. Sherman then ordered the city burned— a scene familiar to any who saw the film *Gone With the Wind*—and then began his destructive March to the Sea. Enraged at the conditions of the Union troops at the Confederate P.O.W. camp at Andersonville, Sherman showed no mercy. More than $100 million worth of property was destroyed as Sherman's army cut a path 60 miles wide across the state. Only when he reached Savannah did he relent and spare the beautiful houses. The destruction and humiliation left a bitter taste in the mouths of Southerners for decades. Some would say it lingers today.

That bitterness was especially evident in Reconstruction. Georgia was readmitted to the Union in 1868 but was expelled a year later when it refused to ratify the 15th Amendment to the Constitution, which made it illegal to deny the right to vote on the basis of race. The state finally ratified the amendment in 1870 and was permanently readmitted to the Union.

The rest of the century saw continued resistance to racial equality. Jim Crow laws were passed; separate restrooms, schools and churches were established for whites and blacks; and the Ku Klux Klan grew in numbers.

In Atlanta, however, enlightened visionaries such as newspaper editor Henry Grady set out to change the image of the South and make it more racially progressive. Appearing together on the same platform at the 1895 International Cotton States Exposition in Atlanta, Grady and respected black educator Booker T. Washington offered encouraging and conciliatory messages aimed at bridging racial differences.

World War II brought prosperity to the state and the postwar boom made Atlanta one of the business capitals of the South. But there were other, more important changes afoot. Georgia, like other Southern states, had resisted racial integration. It would take the combined efforts of civil rights leader Martin Luther King Jr. and moderate white politicians such as Atlanta mayor

Ivan Allen Jr. and Georgia Governor Jimmy Carter to bring equality. The process was slow and painful, but by 1973 Atlanta had elected Maynard Jackson mayor, the first black mayor of a major Southern city.

Since then, Georgia has made great strides economically, culturally and politically. Major corporations have joined Coca-Cola and Delta Airlines in moving their headquarters to Atlanta, Hartsfield International Airport continues to be one of the busiest in the world, and Ted Turner's Cable News Network has put the city on the global communications map. Meanwhile, two other African American mayors were elected in Atlanta, Jimmy Carter became president in 1976, and the International Olympic Committee chose Atlanta as the site of the 1996 Olympic Games.

Not all the problems of racial and economic division have been solved, but as the state moves forward, more Georgians than ever are focused on the future instead of the past.

THE ARTS

Whether you are interested in modern art, old masters, or folk art, Georgia has a museum or gallery for every taste. The High Museum in Atlanta has exhibited everything from Renoir to Norman Rockwell. The Museum of Art in Albany has an outstanding collection of African art, and the Morris Museum of Art in Augusta displays works by Southern artists as well as contemporary folk artists.

Folk art and Appalachian crafts are an important part of the cultural scene in Georgia. Dozens of festivals each year feature some of the best work of the Appalachian Southern Highlanders. The unique pottery by the Meaders family in north Georgia has become prized creations for serious collectors. Other mountain craftsmen create works of art in quilts, furniture, baskets woven from vines, and dulcimers carved from native trees.

Perhaps two of the most famous Georgia folk artists are Howard Finster and the late Eddie Owens Martin. Finster's Paradise Gardens in northwest Georgia is a whimsical array of religious-themed sculptures created from used automobile parts and other scrap materials. Martin, a former fortune-teller who called himself St. EOM, created a unique four-acre exhibit of strangely colored figures in south Georgia.

CUISINE

When most visitors from outside of the region think of Southern cuisine, they have barbecue and fried chicken in mind. There's plenty of both in Georgia, but that's only a sampling of the food you can find. Meat-and-threes—traditional country cafés that serve a choice of a meat and three vegetables—are good places to try the local cooking. Look for the local mom-and-pop establishments that have been in business for several years and you won't be disappointed. In addition to fried chicken and barbecue, the standard fare at these restaurants are country-fried steak and sawmill gravy (a white cream gravy), country fried ham, fried catfish, turnip or collard greens, black-eyed peas, stewed squash, and belt-busting desserts such as pecan pie and banana pudding.

With an influx of immigrants from other parts of the world, the cuisine in Georgia has lately taken on more of an international flavor. In Atlanta, for example, it is not unusual to find a number of Chinese, Thai, French, Greek, Middle Eastern, Mexican, Cuban, Vietnamese, and Korean restaurants.

The menu changes as you travel to the coast, however, and restaurants in Savannah and the Golden Isles specialize in freshly caught seafood. Some restaurants, such as Elizabeth on 37th, feature gourmet dishes with crab, shrimp, red snapper, and flounder; others provide heaping platters of fried shrimp, oysters, fish, and hush puppies.

Wherever you eat at breakfast, you are bound to come face to face with a Southern delicacy called grits. The coarsely ground hominy is as ubiquitous in Georgia as kudzu and, to some Northerners, about as unpalatable. Granted, grits are an acquired taste, but with enough salt, pepper, butter, grated cheese or red-eye gravy (the gravy made from fried country ham drippings), grits are quite delicious.

OUTDOOR ACTIVITIES

Georgia's mild climate and diverse geography make it an ideal place for outdoor activities. The mountains offer hundreds of miles of trails for hiking; dozens of trout streams and lakes for trout fishing; and numerous campgrounds for family outings. In the Chattahoochee-Oconee National Forest alone, there are more than 300 miles of trails for hikers and backpackers. Among the most popular are the Appalachian Trail, a 2,036-mile path that begins in north Georgia and ends in Maine; the 30-mile William Bartram Trail in the Blue Ridge Mountains; and the 50-mile Benton MacKaye Trail in north Georgia.

Wild, scenic rivers such as the Chattooga provide a challenge for serious rafters, while the more gentle Chattahoochee is a favorite rafting route for the less adventurous. Skiers can enjoy the winter sport on the slopes of man-made snow at Sky Valley in northeast Georgia.

The opportunities for water sports in the state are endless. Lake Lanier,

Lake Oconee and Lake Hartwell, among others, are havens for boating, fishing, jet-skiing, and water skiing. Georgia's beaches are some of the best in the world and attract thousands of sun-worshippers every summer.

Georgia offers golfers a chance to play on courses designed by sports legends such as Bobby Jones and Greg Norman. And, while the Augusta National Golf Course, home of the famous Masters, is available to members only, Augusta has several public courses. Other fine courses can be found in Callaway Gardens, Stone Mountain, and numerous state parks in Georgia.

Those who truly want to escape civilization can find solitude and adventure in the Okefenokee Swamp National Wildlife Refuge in south Georgia. Boaters and canoeists can explore the natural habitat of alligators, bears, and other wildlife on day trips or overnight excursions. Boat rentals are available, or you can furnish your own.

Whatever your choice of outdoor activity, you are likely to find it in Georgia. More details are provided in the Fitness and Recreation sections of each destination chapter that follows in this book.

PLANNING YOUR TRIP

Before you set out on your trip, you'll need to do some planning. Use this chapter in conjunction with the tools in the appendix to answer some basic questions. First of all, when are you going? You may already have specific dates in mind; if not, various factors will probably influence your timing. Either way, you'll want to know about local events, the weather, and other seasonal considerations. This chapter discusses all of that.

How much should you expect to spend on your trip? This chapter addresses various regional factors you'll want to consider in estimating your travel expenses. How will you get around? Check out the section on local transportation. If you decide to travel by car, the Planning Map and Mileage Chart in the appendix can help you figure out exact routes and driving times, while the Special Interest Tours provide several focused itineraries.

The chapter concludes with some reading recommendations, both fiction and nonfiction, to give you various perspectives on the region. If you want specific information about individual cities or counties, use the Resource Guide in the appendix.

WHEN TO GO

The time of year you decide to visit Georgia will depend on what activities you like. Sports fans, of course, will want to schedule their visits when the

Braves, Falcons, Hawks or Thrashers are playing at home. The Masters Golf Tournament is held in Augusta every April, but only those who have inherited tickets (or who are willing to pay hundreds of dollars) are admitted.

Hunting and fishing enthusiasts need to check on the dates the appropriate seasons are open. Trout season is limited in some parts of the state, as is the wild game season. A fishing license is required for anyone over 16 years of age. Licenses for residents and temporary permits for non-residents are sold at bait-and-tackle shops and sporting goods stores. Or you can buy them on line at www.permit.com.

No matter what time of year it is, somewhere in Georgia there is some kind of festival taking place. Among the more popular annual events are the St. Patrick's Day festivities in Savannah, a celebration that draws more than 100,000 revelers; the Georgia Renaissance Festival, a re-creation of a six-teenth-century English country fair, held in the spring and fall; the Georgia Mountain Fair, a gathering of mountain musicians and craftsmen in Hiawassee every August; the Scottish Games and Highland Gathering at Stone Mountain in October; and the Atlanta Dogwood Festival in April.

In Atlanta and much of Georgia, there is an old saying: "If you don't like the weather, just wait a couple of hours and it will change." While this is a slight exaggeration, weather in the spring and summer can be unpredictable. Thunderstorms can appear out of nowhere and subside just as quickly.

Spring and fall are the best times to visit Georgia because the temperatures are milder. Winters are rarely severe with only an occasional ice storm south of the mountains. In north Georgia, snowfalls of five or six inches occur a few times each winter. Summers can be shocking for visitors more accustomed to temperate climes. Temperatures often hover in the 90s in July and August and high humidity creates the feeling of a steam bath. Many locals take refuge from the sweltering summers by traveling to the mountains and coast. Not surprisingly, water sports are very popular throughout the state in the summer.

HOW MUCH WILL IT COST?

Trips to Georgia can be tailored to fit any budget. Families who enjoy camping and cooking their own meals can spend a week for a few hundred dollars or less. Those with more expensive tastes can live like royalty for $300 a night in luxury hotels in Atlanta or in the elegant Greyfield Inn on Cumberland Island. In between is a wide range of possibilities. Motels can be booked for as little as $39 a night, and bed-and-breakfasts start at around $60. Gasoline is still relatively inexpensive, but motorists need to remember that Georgia is a big state and mileage can add up fast.

Most businesses in Georgia accept all major credit cards and traveler's checks and automatic teller machines are plentiful. If you're using an ATM other than one belonging to your financial institution, you will be charged a fee of $1.50 or more. Some grocery stores, however, allow you to make purchases and get cash back without a fee.

Sales tax in Georgia varies, depending on which county you're in. Generally the tax is six or seven percent, with hotels charging a tax of around 13 percent.

If you're driving to Georgia from another state, be sure to stop at the welcome centers on the interstate to check out some of the free publications with discount coupons for motels and restaurants. Savings can be substantial, particularly if you're not staying during the weekend. Free highway maps are also available there. Otherwise, many motels give 10 percent discounts to AAA or AARP members.

WHAT TO BRING

Because of the unpredictability of the weather, wise travelers to Georgia should be prepared for almost anything. Yes, you can be assured that summers will be hot, but sometimes so are winters. Temperatures have been known to rise above 70 between Thanksgiving and Christmas. And several times the northern part of the state has been blanketed with snow in late March and early April. Even if you're planning to visit in the spring, taking along a light windbreaker or sweater is a good idea.

What to wear the rest of the time is pretty much up to you. Casual dress such as khakis or jeans is the rule for most attractions in Georgia, with exceptions at some of the finer restaurants or cultural events. Sleeveless shirts are a no-no at some restaurants, and signs reading "No Shirt, No Shoes, No Service" are posted at nearly every dining establishment. It goes without saying that good, comfortable shoes are a necessity if you plan to do any walking. And bring along old sneakers for rafting or canoeing. The bottoms of Georgia's creeks can be treacherous with sharp stones and broken bottles. Whenever you go, take rainwear and an umbrella. Summer thunderstorms are as unpredictable as the outcome of an Atlanta Falcons' game.

If you plan to engage in outdoor adventures, a good supply of insect repellent is recommended. South of Macon is an imaginary demarcation known as the "Gnat Line," which separates the southern and northern parts of the state according to insect population. And while the pesky bugs are more plentiful in South Georgia, you'll still encounter some of them even in the mountains. Mosquitoes, of course, are everywhere, and ticks and chiggers (redbugs) are a constant problem for anyone walking in wooded areas. Be sure to check yourself or your children each night for ticks and carry a good supply of Benadryl for the itching.

In addition to insect repellent, bring along a good first-aid kit, sunscreen, matches, a flashlight, a compass, and a waterproof bag for spare clothing. Unless you're venturing into the Okefenokee or planning to walk a lot of remote trails, a snake-bite kit is probably not necessary.

CRIME AND SAFETY

Crime is not a major problem, but visitors to Georgia's major urban areas need to be aware of the dangers. Check with the local visitor centers to learn which parts of the city you should avoid. There seem to be very few cases of pickpocketing in Georgia cities, but travelers still should take precautions. Don't wear expensive jewelry and do not leave any packages or valuables in plain view, even in locked cars. Put everything in the trunk. Car break-ins are common, even in presumably secure parking lots.

ORIENTATION AND TRANSPORTATION

No matter where you want to go in Georgia, if you arrive by plane you will probably land at Atlanta's Hartsfield International Airport, the headquarters for Delta Airlines. There are also airports for smaller planes in Savannah, St. Simons, Augusta and other cities in the state. Rail service via MARTA (Metropolitan Atlanta Rapid Transit Authority) is available from the airport and around the city. Most of the visitors to the state, however, drive their own vehicles. Three major interstate highways cross Georgia: I-85 and I-75 north and south, and I-20 east and west. Several limited-access scenic highways wind through the state as well, and most of the backroads are well-maintained. Car rentals are available in metropolitan areas from around $30 a day and up. Foreign visitors need to have an international driver's license and agencies generally require the renter to be at least 25 years of age and have a valid credit card. Except for the occasional winter storm and huge traffic jams in Atlanta during rush hours, driving conditions in Georgia are ideal.

Speed limits in Georgia are confusing at times. Interstate limits range from 70 miles per hour in rural areas to 55 on urban expressways. Georgia law requires seat belts to be buckled at all times and lights must be turned on whenever windshield wipers are used.

Interstate travel is fast and relatively trouble-free, but some of these routes are extremely boring. If you don't have a tight schedule to keep, you can make

---

your trip more enjoyable and adventurous by taking some of the scenic routes suggested in this book. Here you will find small towns that time forgot, an occasional gem of a mom-and-pop restaurant, inviting shops with antiques and local crafts, and the ubiquitous roadside stands selling everything from boiled peanuts to apples and fried pies. In addition, you'll gain an intimate acquaintance with the true sights, sounds, and scents of the state, instead of the diesel fumes on the interstates.

As in other states, Georgia requires a valid driver's license and proof of insurance. Tougher DUI laws have led to more frequent checkpoints, particularly on weekends, and the Highway Patrol makes random checks for drugs along the coastal roads and highways leading to and from Florida.

Visitors from other countries may be surprised at the lack of passenger rail service around the state. Plans to change that are in the works, but no improvements are expected for the next five to ten years. Check AMTRAK schedules (800-872-7245) for the two rail lines that pass through the state. The Silver Meteor runs along the Atlantic Seaboard from Boston to Miami, with stops in Savannah and Jacksonville, Fla. Visitors headed to the Okefenokee Swamp can get off in Jacksonville and rent a car.

AMTRAK's Crescent begins in New York and connects with Washington, D.C., Atlanta, Birmingham and New Orleans, with a stop in Gainesville. Located about 55 miles north of Atlanta, Gainesville is the gateway to the Lake Lanier recreation area, the Blue Ridge Mountains and the beginning of the Appalachian Trail.

CAMPING, LODGING, AND DINING

The proliferation of state parks in Georgia makes it a perfect destination for campers. But for those who prefer a few more comforts, there are hotels and motels for every taste or budget. From the luxury Ritz-Carlton in Atlanta to the basic mom-and-pop motels in south Georgia, travelers should be able to find suitable accommodations.

Locating quaint inns or historic bed-and-breakfasts is easier in the cities and countryside outside of Atlanta, however. Atlanta is teeming with highrise hotels and chain motels, but the city offers few choices for charming Victorian cottages.

In other cities, such as Savannah, spending several nights in one of the numerous historic inns is the best way to get a true sense of the city. And, just south of Savannah in the Golden Isles, the experience of staying in Cumberland Island's atmospheric Greyfield Inn or in the Jekyll Island Club Hotel is well worth the price.

Those planning to stay in major cities or visit parts of the state during peak tourist seasons, however, should make reservations well in advance. During major conventions, festivals or college spring break, hotels and motels can fill up quickly.

Finding places to eat in Georgia is no problem. Fast food franchises dot every interstate exit, and any town of any size has a barbecue restaurant or a country cafe. Atlanta offers some of the best gourmet restaurants with national reputations as well as dozens of fine ethnic restaurants. Wherever you go, it is wise to dine on the specialties of the area. In north Georgia restaurants, for example, the mountain trout normally will be fresher and more succulent than shrimp shipped in from the coast.

It is difficult to spend any time in Georgia without sampling something fried. There are fried green tomatoes, fried chicken, fried catfish, country-fried steak, fried okra, and more. Don't be lured into some of the more popular tourist restaurants to partake of any of these delicacies. It's best to venture out into the countryside where family-owned restaurants still offer real mashed potatoes, skillet-fried chicken and garden-fresh vegetables.

If you prefer a cocktail or a glass of wine with your meal, be prepared for some confusion, depending on where you are in the state. Some counties are "dry," others have restaurants that serve only wine and no hard liquor. The legal drinking age in Georgia is 21 and anyone under that age cannot enter nightclubs that do not serve food. Unlike New Orleans, Atlanta and other Georgia cities do not allow open containers of alcohol to be carried or consumed in cars or on public property. Restaurants can serve alcohol on Sundays, but you cannot buy liquor, beer or wine in stores after midnight on Saturday.

DISABLED TRAVELERS

Most of Georgia's cities have responded well to those with special needs. Hartsfield International Airport is one of the most accessible in the country. MARTA, the rapid rail transit system, has elevators and special seating for those with disabilities, and car rental agencies provide vans equipped with lifts. All of the major hotels and restaurants offer special accommodations for those in wheelchairs, but be sure to check in advance when making reservations. These rooms fill up quickly. And state parks and historic sites also provide services for those with special needs.

For more information, contact the Mayor's Action Center in Atlanta at 404/330-6026, or the Society for the Advancement of Travel for the Handicapped, 212/447-7284, or www.sath.org on the Internet.

RECOMMENDED READING

While Georgia has not produced as many acclaimed writers as, say, Mississippi and North Carolina, it is the home of several notable authors. The most famous is Margaret Mitchell, whose novel *Gone With the Wind* created an image of a gracious and elegant South that lingers today. At the other end of the spectrum, Erskine Caldwell's *Tobacco Road* portrayed the South as a land of poverty, hookworms and incest. The truth lies somewhere in between. In addition to Mitchell's and Caldwell's works, here are some other books that may be helpful to visitors to the state and region.

Fiction

For a glimpse of Atlanta after *Gone With the Wind* (MacMillan, 1936), pick up a copy of Anne Rivers Siddons' *Peachtree Road* (HarperCollins, 1989). Siddons' novel portrays the city as it was in the 1950s and '60s, when Atlanta still had a small-town atmosphere. A more recent picture of Atlanta and south Georgia emerges in Tom Wolfe's novel, *A Man in Full* (Farrar, Straus and Giroux, 1998), a chronicle of the downfall of real estate baron Charlie Croker. In the book, Wolfe brilliantly describes the racial and social aspects of the city as well as the world of wealthy businessmen who own private jets and 20,000-acre quail hunting plantations.

Poet James Dickey's novel, *Deliverance* (Houghton Mifflin, 1970), depicted the violent results when four Atlanta men on a white-water canoeing adventure in North Georgia encounter some mountain men.

Milledgeville author Flannery O'Connor's collection, *The Complete Stories* (Farrar, Straus and Giroux, 1946), portrays the Gothic nature of the post-World War II South.

And, in her Pulitzer Prize-winning novel, *The Color Purple* (Simon & Schuster, 1982), Eatonton native Alice Walker tells of a black woman's struggle in rural Georgia.

Nonfiction

For a comprehensive overview of the state, Kenneth Coleman's *A History of Georgia* (University of Georgia Press, 1991) is a good place to start. A complementary book is *Atlanta Rising* (Longstreet Press, 1996) by Frederick Allen, a lively historical account of the city from 1946 to the present.

There are a number of Civil War books available, but Burke Davis' *Sherman's March* (Random House, 1980), is one of the best. Davis follows the Union general mile-by-mile as he cuts a destructive swath through Georgia.

Taylor Branch's *Parting the Waters: America in the King Years* (Simon &

Schuster, 1988) is an excellent history of Dr. Martin Luther King Jr.'s role in the civil rights movement in the 1950s and early 1960s.

For a history of Atlanta as seen from the parallel viewpoints of an affluent black family and a powerful white family, Gary Pomerantz's *From Peachtree to Sweet Auburn* (Scribner's, 1996) is an interesting story well told about the families of former mayors Maynard Jackson and Ivan Allen.

Georgia has more than its share of eccentrics, and National Public Radio contributor Bailey White finds a number of them in her essays in *Mama Makes Up Her Mind* (Addison-Wesley, 1993).

More eccentrics can be found in Melissa Fay Greene's *Praying for Sheetrock* (Addison-Wesley, 1991), an account of clip joints and corruption in coastal McIntosh County, and in John Berendt's *Midnight in the Garden of Good and Evil* (Random House, 1994). Berendt's gossipy book about the characters surrounding the murder trial of a colorful Savannah antiques dealer is a classic.

1
ATLANTA

Tom Wolfe's portrayal of Atlanta in his 1998 novel, *A Man in Full*, is fairly close to the mark. Wolfe saw the city as a vibrant, bustling business center surrounded by ethnic neighborhoods and predominantly white suburbs. As the corporate headquarters of Delta Airlines, Coca-Cola, CNN, UPS, Holiday Inn, and others, Atlanta exudes an image as a booming Sun Belt city on the go. Like other major metropolitan centers, Atlanta has grappled with traffic gridlock and an exodus of residents from downtown. After the Olympic Games in 1996, however, the downtown and midtown areas of Atlanta underwent a renaissance as singles and young couples moved back into the city in droves. Real estate prices soared, many apartment buildings were converted to condominiums, and once-vacant lofts in the business district are now trendy apartments.

In the midst of all the commercial activity, however, Atlantans still take time to participate in sports or watch the professionals perform. The Atlanta Braves draw huge crowds to Turner Field, the former Olympic Stadium, and the Atlanta Falcons now play before a packed house at the Georgia Dome after their 1998-99 Super Bowl season. And with basketball's Atlanta Hawks and the Atlanta Thrashers of the National Hockey League at home in the new Phillips Arena, there is usually a sports activity happening every weekend.

Nightlife has improved in downtown with the opening of new restaurants and The Tabernacle, an old Baptist Church that is now the site of blues, jazz,

GREATER ATLANTA

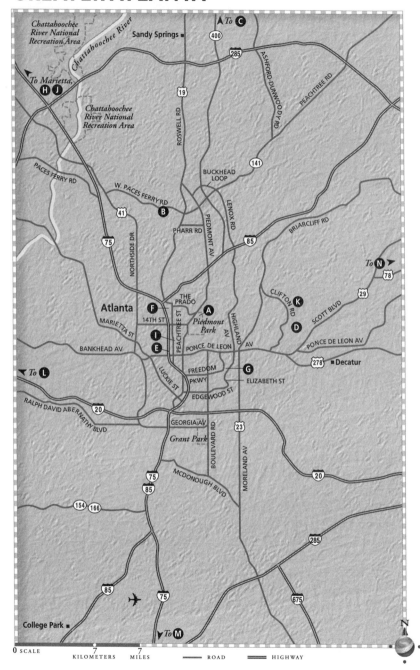

Chattahoochee River National Recreation Area

Chattahoochee River

Sandy Springs

▲ To C

400

285

ASHFORD-DUNWOODY RD

PEACHTREE RD

To Marietta,

H J

Chattahoochee River National Recreation Area

19

ROSWELL RD

141

PACES FERRY RD

W. PACES FERRY RD

BUCKHEAD LOOP

41

B

LENOX RD

BRIARCLIFF RD

PHARR RD

PIEDMONT AV

85

To N

78

75

NORTHSIDE DR

29

CLIFTON RD

K

SCOTT BLVD

Atlanta

F

THE PRADO

A

D

14TH ST

Piedmont Park

HIGHLAND

MARIETTA ST

PEACHTREE ST

I

AV

PONCE DE LEON AV

BANKHEAD AV

E

PONCE DE LEON AV

278

Decatur

To L

LUCKIE ST

FREEDOM PKWY

G

ELIZABETH ST

EDGEWOOD ST

RALPH DAVID ABERNATHY BLVD

20

GEORGIA AV

BOULEVARD RD

23

Grant Park

MORELAND AV

75

85

MCDONOUGH BLVD

20

154 166

285

85

75

675

College Park

To M

N

0 SCALE

7
KILOMETERS

7
MILES

ROAD

HIGHWAY

and rock concerts. But most visitors seeking a wider range of entertainment and dining experiences have to drive to Buckhead or to one of the neighborhoods such as Little Five Points or Virginia-Highlands, where funky clubs and restaurants offer everything from Irish music and Delta blues to Asian cuisine and low-country barbecue.

A PERFECT DAY IN ATLANTA

There are many options for perfect days in Atlanta. One choice would be to begin the day with a walk through Centennial Olympic Park. After that, line up across the street for a tour of CNN and shopping at the Turner store. If there's time before lunch, walk six blocks to Underground Atlanta, browse among the shops, and refresh yourself at the World of Coca-Cola. Following lunch at Thelma's Kitchen, head to Auburn Avenue and a tour of the Martin Luther King Center for Nonviolent Social Change. In the late afternoon, drive to Grant Park and visit the pandas at ZooAtlanta. Watch the sunset over drinks at the Sundial atop the Westin Peachtree Plaza before dinner at The Pleasant Peasant.

Another perfect day could include a morning at the High Museum of Art, an afternoon at the Atlanta History Center, and dinner at one of Buckhead's fine restaurants.

ORIENTATION

It is possible to explore Atlanta without a car, but the city is so spread out into different neighborhoods, it really is a driving town. The city is divided north to south by I-75/I-85, and by I-285, a perimeter highway that encircles Atlanta and sets off the main commercial districts from the suburbs. Downtown streets are designated NW or NE depending which side of Peachtree Street they are on. Downtown Atlanta is geared toward conventions and 9-5 businesses with a few attractions

SIGHTS

- ⓐ Atlanta Botanical Garden
- ⓑ Atlanta History Center
- ⓒ Bulloch Hall
- ⓓ Fernbank Museum of Natural History
- ⓓ Fernbank Science Center
- ⓔ Fox Theatre
- ⓕ High Museum of Art
- ⓖ Jimmy Carter Library and Museum
- ⓗ Kennesaw Mountain National Battlefield
- ⓘ Margaret Mitchell House
- ⓙ Marietta Square
- ⓚ Michael Carlos Museum
- ⓛ Six Flags Over Georgia
- ⓜ Stately Oaks Plantation
- ⓝ Stone Mountain Park

Note: Items with the same letter are located in the same area.

DOWNTOWN ATLANTA

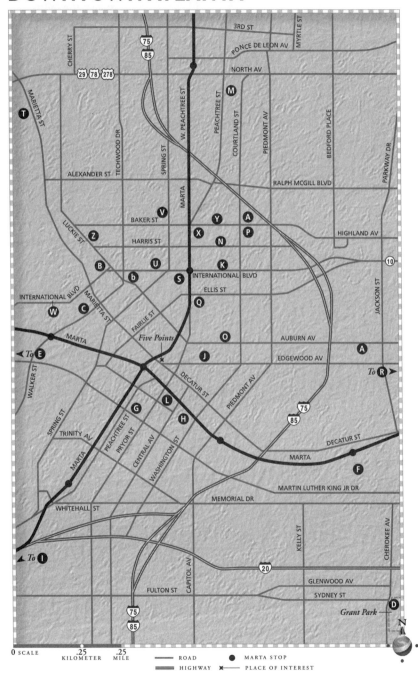

available after dark. Most of the nightlife and restaurants are centered in the Midtown, Virginia-Highlands and Buckhead neighborhoods north of downtown.

Atlanta is served by most major airlines at Hartsfield International Airport about 15 minutes from downtown. Shuttle service, **MARTA,** 404/848-4711, the metro rapid transit system, and taxis are available. MARTA is a convenient way to move around the city, within limits. Fares are $1.50 and rail lines run east and west, and north and south. At some stations you will have to transfer to buses, and the routes can be confusing. Taxi fares are comparable to those of other big cities, usually a $5 flat rate within the downtown area and an additional 20 cents a mile outside that zone. All the major car rental agencies have offices at the airport and at some downtown hotels. **Greyhound-Trailways,** 800/231-2222, offers national and statewide bus service, and **Amtrak,** 800/872-7245, provides service from Atlanta to Washington, Philadelphia, New York, Gainesville, Macon, Birmingham, and New Orleans.

Group tours are available through **Gray Line of Atlanta,** 2541 Camp Creek Pkwy., 404/767-0594, **Special Tours,** 620 Peachtree St., 404/724-9244, and **White Horse Tours, Inc.,** 2840 NE Expwy., 404/320-9026.

DOWNTOWN ATLANTA SIGHTSEEING HIGHLIGHTS

★★★★ **CYCLORAMA**
880 Cherokee Ave., 404/624-1071

SIGHTS

- **A** Auburn Avenue Historic District
- **B** Centennial Park
- **C** CNN Center
- **D** Cyclorama
- **E** Herndon Home
- **F** Oakland Cemetery
- **G** Underground Atlanta
- **H** World of Coca-Cola
- **I** Wren's Nest
- **D** ZooAtlanta

FOOD

- **J** City Grill
- **K** Dailey's Restaurant
- **L** Lombardi's
- **M** Mick's
- **N** Morton's of Chicago
- **O** Mumbo-Jumbo
- **P** Nikolai's Roof
- **M** Pleasant Peasant
- **C** Reggie's British Pub and Restaurant
- **Q** Restaurant at the Ritz-Carlton Atlanta
- **R** Son's Place
- **S** Sundial Restaurant
- **T** Thelma's Kitchen

LODGING

- **P** Atlanta Hilton
- **U** Comfort Inn
- **V** Days Inn Downtown
- **W** Embassy Suites Hotel
- **X** Hyatt Regency
- **Y** Marriott Marquis
- **C** Omni Hotel
- **Z** Quality Hotel
- **Q** Ritz-Carlton Atlanta
- **G** Suite Hotel
- **a** TraveLodge
- **S** Westin Peachtree Plaza
- **b** Wyndham Atlanta

Note: Items with the same letter are located in the same area.

Near ZooAtlanta is one of the most amazing art exhibits you will ever see. The dramatic Civil War images of the Battle of Atlanta are re-created in a circular painting and diorama 42 feet high and 358 feet in circumference. Visitors view the painting from a revolving platform and listen to a narration enhanced with music, sound effects, special lighting, and music. The diorama features 128 figures, including one fallen soldier who is a dead ringer for Clark Gable. The exhibit also has many Civil War artifacts and memorabilia. The most interesting is the steam locomotive Texas that was used by Confederates to pursue the General after it was seized by Andrews Raiders in the great locomotive chase of 1862.

Details: *Open daily 9:30-4:30. Closed major holidays. $6 adults, $4 children 6-12, $5 seniors. (1-2 hours)*

★★★★ WORLD OF COCA-COLA
55 Martin Luther King Jr. Dr., 404/676-5151

Perhaps the most refreshing stop on your downtown tour is this four-story pavilion celebrating the world's most popular soft drink. A 13-minute high-definition video shows just how far-reaching Coke is, from the Pyramids of Egypt to the Imperial Palace of Thailand. Other exhibits take visitors on a tour of 100 years of the beverage's history, beginning with the creation of the soft drink by Atlanta pharmacist Dr. John Pemberton. In the Barnes Soda Fountain area, you can visit a replica of a 1930s soda fountain and listen to songs from that era about Coke. And, finally, you can pause to refresh yourself at the Taste of the World exhibit by sampling Coca-Cola products from around the globe.

Details: *Open Mon-Sat 10-9:30, Sun 12-6. $3.50 adults, $2.50 children 6-12, $3 seniors. (1 hour)*

★★★★ ZOOATLANTA
800 Cherokee Ave., 404/624-5600

With more than 1,000 animals living in surroundings as close to their natural habitats as possible, ZooAtlanta is one of the finest facilities in the country. Some of the favorite attractions are the Ford African Rain Forest inhabited by four primate families, the Sumatran Tiger Exhibit modeled after an Indonesian forest, the children's OK-to-Touch Corral, and the Birds of Prey Amphitheater. It's best to visit the zoo during the more temperate seasons, but the steamy jungle climate of July and August can make the experience more realistic.

PANDAMONIUM AT ZOOATLANTA

Until recently, the main attraction at ZooAtlanta was a gorilla, Willie B., named after former mayor William B. Hartsfield. Now that the beloved ape has gone on to that great jungle in the sky, ZooAtlanta's stars are Lun-Lun and Yang-Yang, two pandas on loan from China. The pandas are free to roam a $7 million habitat, complete with gray boulders and bamboo. The habitat has indoor and outdoor facilities, a private place called a cubbing den, and a birthing den should the animals decide to mate.

Thousands of visitors have already flocked to ZooAtlanta since the 200-pound pandas arrived in November 1999. The gift shop, Pandamonium, has also been a big hit with its assortment of panda bears, panda flashlights, panda key chains, and other panda souvenirs. For more information about ZooAtlanta, see "Sights."

Details: Open Mon-Fri 10-4:30; Sat-Sun 10-5:30 during daylight savings time. Closed on major holidays. $7.50 adults and children 12-18, $6.50 seniors, $5 children 3-11. (2 hours)

★★★ **AUBURN AVENUE HISTORIC DISTRICT**

Sweet Auburn, as it is known locally, was Atlanta's thriving black entertainment and business district from 1890 until the 1930s. The area began deteriorating during the Depression, but recently it has enjoyed a revival. Among the landmarks of interest are the historic **Ebenezer Baptist Church,** where Martin Luther King Jr. and his father preached; the **Martin Luther King Center for Nonviolent Social Change;** and the **King Birthplace.** The King Center, built as a memorial to the slain civil rights leader, features photographs and memorabilia from King's public and private life along with his Nobel Peace Prize. An eternal flame burns at the gravesite with the inscription "Free at last." The King Birthplace a block away is an 1894 two-story frame house that contains many photographs and furnishings belonging to the family.

Details: Sweet Auburn begins at Woodruff Park and Edgewood Ave. Ebenezer Baptist Church is located at 407 Auburn Ave., 404/688-7263. Open Mon-Fri 9-4:30, Sat 11-2. Free. Martin Luther King Center for Nonviolent Social Change is located at 449 Auburn Ave., 404/524-1956. Open daily 9-5:30. Free. King Birthplace is located at 501 Auburn Ave., 404/331-1590 or 404/331-3919. Open daily 9-5. Free. (2-3 hours)

★★★ CNN CENTER
1 CNN Center (International Blvd. at Marietta St.), 404/827-2300

You probably won't run into Ted Turner, but you will get an opportunity to sit in the audience of *Talk Back Live* and watch how reporters react to fast-breaking world events during a 45-minute tour of the Cable News Network studios. Kids will love browsing exhibits of Cartoon Network and MGM memorabilia. And, of course, there is an abundance of souvenirs for sale in the Turner Store.

Details: Tours daily 9-5, except holidays. $6 adults, $3.50 children under 13, $4 seniors. (1-2 hours)

★★ CENTENNIAL PARK
Techwood Dr. and Marietta St.

Just across the street from CNN Center, the park is one of the lasting legacies of the 1996 Olympic Games. Designed around a dancing fountain with five interlocking Olympic rings, the park is paved with engraved commemorative bricks that were sold to help finance the Olympics. Concerts are held periodically in the amphitheater.

Details: Open year-round. (1 hour)

★★ OAKLAND CEMETERY
Martin Luther King Jr. Dr. at Oakland Ave., 404/688-2107

When Margaret Mitchell was buried here on August 17, 1949, she joined other famous Atlantans, from governors and generals to golfing great Bobby Jones, who have been laid to rest in Oakland Cemetery since 1850. The cemetery was a favorite spot for nineteenth-century Atlantans who often spent Sunday afternoons tending family plots and picnicking under the tall oaks. The park, with its statuary and marble mausoleums adorned with stained glass, offers an opportunity to dip into local history and Victorian art while strolling under some of Atlanta's oldest magnolia trees.

Details: Open daily 8-6. Free. Brochures for walking tours sold at cemetery office for $1.25. (1 hour)

★ HERNDON HOME
587 University Pl. NW, 404/581-9813
Born a slave in 1858, Alonzo F. Herndon went on to become one of the most successful African American businessmen in America. After working as a farm laborer, he became a barber, opened several barbershops in Atlanta, and later founded the Atlanta Life Insurance Company. He and his wife, Adrienne, designed their Beaux Arts Classical mansion using architectural styles they observed on a trip to Europe. A unique example of an upper-middle class residence, the Herndon Home is listed on the National Register of Historic Places.
Details: *Open Tue-Thu 10-11:30 a.m. Free. (1 hour)*

★ UNDERGROUND ATLANTA
50 Upper Alabama St., 404/523-2311
This 12-acre entertainment and shopping center is located on what used to be the street level of Atlanta. A zero-mile post erected in 1850 marked the terminus of the town's first rail line. As Atlanta grew, however, viaducts and buildings were constructed over the area. Many of the buildings were razed when the MARTA rail line was routed through the district, but in 1989 the vacant shops were renovated and reopened as an enclosed, air-conditioned mall. New shops were built above ground around Peachtree Fountains Plaza and a 138-foot light tower that is the center of Christmas and New Year's Eve celebrations. The new Underground is a collection of shops and carts with an entertainment section of nightclubs and restaurants known as Kenny's Alley.
Details: *Open Mon-Sat 10-9:30, Sun 12-6. (1-2 hours)*

★ WREN'S NEST
1050 Ralph David Abernathy Blvd., 404/753-8535
This Victorian home of Joel Chandler Harris, chronicler of the Uncle Remus tales, has been preserved much as it was when Harris lived here in the late nineteenth and early twentieth centuries. Each of the nine rooms contains photographs and memorabilia such as a stuffed great horned owl presented to Harris by Teddy Roosevelt. A slide show and regular storytelling sessions bring the African folklore characters of Br'er Rabbit and Br'er Fox to life.
Details: *Open Tue-Sat 10-4, Sun 1-4. $4 adults, $1 children 4-12, $2 seniors and teenagers. (1 hour)*

GREATER ATLANTA SIGHTSEEING HIGHLIGHTS

★★★★ ATLANTA HISTORY CENTER
130 West Paces Ferry Rd., 404/814-4000

Looking for Tara? Well, you won't find the Hollywood version of Scarlett O'Hara's home here, but you will see what Margaret Mitchell had in mind. Set amid the History Center's 32 wooded acres, the **Tullie Smith House** is an 1840s plantation house that was typical in upcountry Georgia. The farmhouse and its separate kitchen and outbuildings were moved from east of Atlanta to the History Center site and set up like a working nineteenth-century farm. Visitors can watch demonstrations of blacksmithing and sheep-shearing and walk through the herb and flower gardens.

A fancier architectural example at the center is the **Swan House,** a classical mansion built in 1924 by Atlanta banker Edward Inman. Framed by a series of terraces and fountains, the house is decorated throughout with swans in the woodwork and wallpaper.

One of the most popular attractions is the **Museum of Atlanta History,** which features several exhibits depicting the origins of the city and its transformation from railroad stop to business center of the South. Don't miss the John A. Burrison Folklife Collection and the Civil War Collection. Every July, the center is the scene of a Civil War encampment, and in February a storytelling festival is held. A restaurant on the premises offers a daily lunch of Southern cuisine.

Details: Open Mon-Sat 10-5:30, Sun 12-5. $7 adults, $3 children 5-17, $5 seniors. (2-3 hours)

★★★★ FERNBANK MUSEUM OF NATURAL HISTORY
767 Clifton Rd., 404/370-0960

The largest collection of natural sciences south of the Smithsonian, this impressive museum is filled with interactive exhibits. *A Walk Through Time in Georgia* winds through 15 different galleries as it traces the development of Georgia's natural environments, complete with wildlife noises from the Okefenokee Swamp. One of the most popular features of the museum is the IMAX theater, which shows nature films on a six-story screen. A small café on the premises offers sandwiches and daily lunch specials.

Details: Open Tue-Thu and Sat 10-5, Fri 10-9, Sun 12-5. $5.50 adults, $4.50 students, children 3-18, and seniors. IMAX prices vary. (2 hours)

★★★★ HIGH MUSEUM OF ART
1280 Peachtree St., 404/733-4444
This gleaming white structure designed by architect Richard Meier is a work of art itself. Inside are five levels of exhibits, from American decorative arts and folk art to nineteenth-century American paintings and the sub-Saharan collection. Traveling exhibits such as the masterpieces of the Impressionists and the works of Norman Rockwell are scheduled on a regular basis. Youngsters who aren't interested in the grown-up exhibits can express themselves in the interactive gallery for children. The Learning to Look/Looking to Learn multimedia exhibit allows children-and adults-to explore the four basic elements of art: line, light, color, and composition, and see how these elements are applied to create paintings, photographs, and furniture. Visitors can use computers at individual kiosks to perform experiments related to art. Afterward, browse in the museum gift shop or relax in the coffee bar.
Details: *Open Tue-Thu 10-5, Fri 10-9, Sat 10-5, Sun 12-5. $6 adults, $2 children 5-17, $4 students and seniors. Special exhibits may cost extra. (2 hours)*

★★★★ SIX FLAGS OVER GEORGIA
I-20 at 8561 Six Flags Rd., 770/739-3400
If you like roller coasters, this is the place to go. The amusement park has appropriately named thrill rides such as the Mind Bender, a triple-loop roller coaster, and the Great American Scream Machine, which climbs and plunges more than 100 feet. There are other, milder rides for kids and adults, shows with Looney Tunes characters, concerts, and, of course, french fries and cotton candy.
Details: *Open daily 10 a.m.-11 p.m. June-Aug; 10 a.m.-11 p.m. weekends only March-May and Sept-Oct. $28 adults, $19 children 3-9, $14 seniors. $5 parking. (4 hours-full day)*

★★★★ STONE MOUNTAIN PARK
U.S. 78, 770/498-5690
One of the most amazing natural wonders in Georgia is Stone Mountain, a granite outcropping 16 miles east of Atlanta on Hwy. 78, soaring 825 feet. The mountain, which features carvings of Confederate heroes Robert E. Lee, Thomas "Stonewall" Jackson, and Jefferson Davis on horseback, is the focal point of a 3,200-acre park that is Georgia's number one tourist attraction. The impressive figures were done by Gutzon Borglum, of Mount Rushmore fame.

More than four million visitors come each year for a variety of events, from the Yellow Daisy Festival to the Scottish Highland Games. On summer evenings from May to September, thousands enjoy picnics on Memorial Lawn at the mountain's base to watch the popular laser show reflected off the mountainside, accompanied by music.

A new feature of the laser show is the Liquid Flame Cannon, a state-of-the-art device used to create a variety of special effects. Enormous fireballs are ignited and shot into the air from the carving's base. On the Fourth of July, a spectacular fireworks display can be seen for miles.

Regular attractions in the park include: a sky lift to the top of the mountain, a 19th-century train that circles the mountain's base, a paddle-wheel riverboat, a swimming area, hiking trails, tennis courts, a 36-hole golf course, canoe rentals, an ice rink, and batting cages.

The Wildlife Preserve and Petting Zoo offers adults and kids an opportunity to see cougars, bobcats, foxes, coyotes, and bison in a 22-acre refuge, complete with streams and waterfalls. Guests can stroll through the Naturalist's Cabin, which houses a collection of snakes from the Southeast, then visit Trader's Camp petting farm for a hands-on experience with farmyard animals. Many of the wild animals are native to Georgia and are managed by experts from ZooAtlanta.

The Antebellum Plantation is a collection of original buildings built in the late 18th and early 19th centuries. The plantation house is surrounded by authentic outbuildings moved to the park from their original sites. A tour of the complex, which includes an overseer's house, slave cabins, a smokehouse, a kitchen garden, and a cookhouse, provides a glimpse of how Georgians lived before the Civil War. Craft and cooking demonstrations also are offered, and Civil War encampments are held throughout the year.

Visiting the Antique Car and Treasure Museum is like stepping into a giant attic. The curator of the museum has spent more than half a century collecting vintage cars, jukeboxes, player pianos, dolls, toys, carousel animals, antique furniture, and Coca-Cola memorabilia.

Lodging at the park is available at the 92-room Stone Mountain Inn, 800/277-0007, and the 249-room Evergreen Conference Center, 770/879-9900, for $80 and up. Or stay at the 441-site Family Campground, 770/498-5600, complete with RV hookups and running water.

Details: Open daily 6 a.m.-midnight. $6 per car for park entrance; attractions are $4.25 adults, $3.50 seniors, $3.20 children 3-11. Alcohol is prohibited except in specified picnic areas.

★★★ **ATLANTA BOTANICAL GARDEN**
1345 Piedmont Ave., 404/876-5859
This lush 60-acre oasis in the shadow of downtown's skyscrapers is a living exhibit of flowers, plants and hardwoods. Visitors can take a soothing walk through a traditional Japanese garden, a 15-acre forest, wildflower areas, rose gardens, a Southern vegetable garden, or the Dorothy Chapman Fuqua Conservatory—a glass-enclosed world of rare and exotic plants. Guided tours are available. Special events include a Country Christmas celebration, spring and fall plant sales, and rose and bonsai shows.
Details: Open Tue-Sun 9-6. $6.50 adults, $4.75 children 6-12 and seniors. Free Thursday after 1. (1-2 hours)

★★★ **JIMMY CARTER LIBRARY AND MUSEUM**
1 Copenhill Ave., 404/331-3942
Artifacts and memorabilia from Carter's presidency and political career are housed in this museum. A 30-minute film recaps the highlights of Carter's life, including his role in the Camp David Accords that brought peace to the Middle East. A gift shop sells all the former president's books as well as White House china. A cafeteria at the center is open for lunch daily.
Details: Open Mon-Sat 9-4:45, Sun 12-4:45. $4 adults, children under 16 free, $3 seniors. (1 hour)

★★★ **KENNESAW MOUNTAIN NATIONAL BATTLEFIELD**
I-75 N., exit 116, 770/427-4686
This historic park is the site of the 1864 Battle of Kennesaw, when Confederate General James Johnson stopped the Union forces under General Sherman. Despite the Rebel victory, Sherman eventually went around Johnson's troops and captured Atlanta. Maps and a slide show detailing the battle are available at the visitors center. Civil War weapons and artifacts are displayed at a small museum. In good weather, you can walk the quarter-mile summit trail to the top of the mountain or take one of the other hiking trails through the 2,884-acre park.
Details: Open daily 8:30-5. Free. (1-2 hours)

MARGARET MITCHELL HOUSE

©2000, Kevin C. Rose,

★★★ MARGARET MITCHELL HOUSE
990 Peachtree St. at 10th St., 404/249-7012

The author called this cramped apartment "The Dump" when she lived here with her husband, John Marsh, while writing *Gone With the Wind*. Destined for the wrecking ball a few years ago, the house was saved by a group of dedicated preservationists led by Mary Rose Taylor. Twice burned by arsonists, the apartment has been restored as a museum and is furnished much as it was when the Mitchells resided here from 1926 to 1929. The typewriter she used to write the novel is on display along with a collection of movie posters from around the world. A 30-minute tour and a short film depict the author's interesting life, which tragically ended when she was struck by a car on Peachtree Street in 1949.

> **Details:** *Open daily 9-4. $6 adults, $5 students and seniors, children under 6 free. (1 hour)*

★★★ MARIETTA SQUARE

The heart of downtown Marietta is an assortment of antique shops, cafés and historic structures surrounding Glover Park with its landscaped gardens and fountain. The square is the scene of concerts, art shows, and festivals. Horse-drawn carriage rides are available on weekends at North Park Square and Church Street. Begin your tour at the **Welcome Center** in the renovated train station on Depot Street with a walking/driving tour brochure. Adjacent to the Welcome Center is the **Kennesaw House,** formerly the Fletcher House when Andrews Raiders stayed here in 1862 shortly before hijacking the Confederate locomotive, the General. General William T. Sherman also made his headquarters here during the Battle of Atlanta. Just south of the square, the **Marietta-Cobb Museum of Art** features art shows and traveling exhibits.

Details: Downtown Marietta, 15 miles north of Atlanta on U.S. 41, 770/429-1115 for Welcome Center. Open Mon-Fri 9-5, Sat 11-4, Sun 1-4. (2-3 hours). Marietta-Cobb Museum of Art, 30 Atlanta St., 770/528-1444. Open Tue-Sat 11-5. $2 adults, $1 students and seniors. (2-3 hours)

★★★ MICHAEL CARLOS MUSEUM
571 Kilgo St., 404/727-4282

When you walk into the Michael Carlos Museum on the Emory University campus, you may think you have stepped back into the time of the Pharaohs. On display are numerous Egyptian and pre-Columbian artifacts as well as Egyptian mummies. Other exhibits feature art and archaeological treasures from the Middle Ages to contemporary times.

Details: Open Mon-Thu and Sat 10-5, Fri 10-9, Sun 12-5. $3. Closed major holidays. (1-2 hours)

★★ BULLOCH HALL
180 Bulloch Ave., Roswell, 770/992-1731

The home of Theodore Roosevelt's mother, Mittie Bulloch, this 1840 Greek Revival house was built by James Stephens Bulloch, one of the town's first settlers. Roosevelt's parents were married here in 1853. Since the house is available for special occasions as well as tours, couples can get married in the same spot as the Roosevelts.

Details: Open Mon-Fri 10-2. $3 adults, $1 children 6-16, $2 seniors. (1 hour)

★★ FERNBANK SCIENCE CENTER
156 Heaton Park Dr., 404/378-4311

This small museum is best known for its 70-foot planetarium and astronomy exhibits, including an Apollo spacecraft. Constellations and planets can be viewed through the observatory's 36-inch reflecting telescope. The museum also features exhibits on gems and minerals and displays of taxidermy specimens such as rattlesnakes and other Georgia wildlife. Hikers can trek through the 65-acre Fernbank Forest, where various trees and shrubs are identified by small signs. **Details:** *Open Tue-Fri 8:30-10 p.m., Mon 8:30-5, Sat 10-5, Sun 1-5. Planetarium shows Tue-Fri 8 p.m., Wed, Fri, weekends at 3. Free admission to center. Planetarium shows are $2 adults, $1 students. (1-2 hours)*

★ **FOX THEATRE**
660 Peachtree St., 404/881-2100
Built in 1929 in a Moorish-Egyptian style for the Shriners Club, the building was bought by film mogul William Fox and turned into a movie theater. The architectural details are exquisite, from the onion domes and minarets on the exterior to the interior ceiling painted as a sky. Special lighting effects change the sky from a light blue with clouds to a dark night scene with stars. Various concerts and touring plays are held here, along with special showings of classic films. **Details:** *Guided tours Mon-Thu at 10 a.m., Sat 10 and 11:30 a.m. $5 adults, $3 students, $4 seniors. (1 hour)*

★ **STATELY OAKS PLANTATION**
100 Carriage Ln., Jonesboro, 770/473-0197
This 1839 Greek Revival mansion is probably what Margaret Mitchell had in mind for Ashley Wilkes' grand Twelve Oaks. Tours are conducted by guides wearing period costumes and speaking in sweet Southern accents. **Details:** *Open Mon-Fri 10:30-3:30. $5 adults, $2.50 children. (1 hour)*

KIDS' STUFF
Children will love the already noted **ZooAtlanta** and the storytelling at the **Wren's Nest.** But perhaps the perfect antidote for bored kids is **SciTrek,** 395 Piedmont Ave. NE, 404/522-5500. Ranked as one of the top ten science museums in the country, SciTrek has permanent exhibits on electricity, mathematics, and machines. **The Hall of Light and Perception** features a kaleidoscope, a flying mirror, and a distorted room that is really the scientific version of a carnival funhouse. For more fun, there's **Kidspace,** with a sound studio, a giant hot-air balloon, a TV theater, and a crystal cave. SciTrek is open

Tue-Sat 10-5, Sun 12-5. Admission is $7.50 adults, $6 students and seniors, $6 children 3-17. Children under 3 are admitted free.

In Midtown, children will enjoy the already mentioned **Fernbank Science Center,** the **Fernbank Museum of Natural History,** and the **Atlanta Botanical Garden,** which has added a children's garden to its other attractions. Fans of Kermit the Frog and other Jim Henson Muppets will love the **Center for Puppetry Arts,** 1404 Spring St. NW, 404/873-3391, with its collection of hundreds of puppets from around the world. Admission is $5 adults, $4 kids 2-13 and seniors.

In Marietta, north of Atlanta, **American Adventures** and **Whitewater Park,** I-75, exit 113, 770/424-9283, is one remedy for sweltering Georgia summers. Every attraction leaves participants all wet, from kiddie pools to challenging waterslides such as the Banzai Pipeline. Next door to Whitewater Park is American Adventures, an amusement park for children under 12 that offers bumper car rides, go-cart races, miniature golf, an antique carousel, and a giant arcade. Admission is $20 adults, $12 children 3-4 feet tall.

Kids definitely will want to spend a day at the already mentioned **Stone Mountain** and the amusement parks at **Six Flags.** But there are many more attractions and distractions for children in the greater Atlanta area. **The Discovery Zone,** 3701 Austell Rd., Marietta, 770/801-9993, is an indoor playground with slides and bins filled with plastic balls for jumping and tumbling. The **Montasia Family Fun Centers,** I-575 and Barrett Pkwy., Marietta, 770/422-3440, and 1099 Johnson Ferry Rd., Marietta, 770/977-1200, have fantastic miniature golf courses with looming sculptures and video game rooms. The Malibu SpeedZone, 3005 George Busbee Pkwy., Kennesaw, 770/514-8081, is a racetrack for older kids and teenagers who want to drag race miniature cars. Cars for different age groups are available, as well as super-realistic interactive video games.

Chattahoochee Nature Center, 9135 Willeo Rd., Roswell, 770/992-2055, is an outdoor educational facility where kids can take nature walks, visit wildlife being rehabilitated, and go on Night Owls overnight hikes and sleepovers from October to May. For more contact with animals, the **Yellow River Game Ranch,** 4525 Hwy. 78, Lilburn, 770/972-6643, has hundreds of birds and wildlife, from ducks to black bears. Kids can see animals in their natural habitats and are even allowed to feed them.

FITNESS AND RECREATION

With four major professional franchises and the Georgia Tech college teams, Atlanta is a haven for sports fans. The **Atlanta Braves** play home games from April to October at Turner Field, 755 Hank Aaron Dr., 404/522-7630; the **Atlanta Hawks** basketball team and the **Atlanta Thrashers** hockey team share the new Phillips Arena, 100 Techwood Dr., 404/827-3800; and the **Atlanta Falcons,** 1999 Super Bowl contenders, play their home games in the Georgia Dome, 1 Georgia Dome Dr., 404/223-8687. Tickets to individual games can be purchased at the venues or through TicketMaster, 404/249-6400 or 800/326-4000. **Turner Field** features interactive sports games as well as the **Ivan Allen Jr. Braves Museum** with Hank Aaron's record-breaking 715th home run ball and bat and other baseball memorabilia.

On the Georgia Tech campus at North Avenue and Techwood Drive, the **Yellow Jackets,** 404/894-5447, field teams in football, basketball, baseball, tennis, and other sports.

In Midtown, inline skating, hiking, and jogging are the physical activities of choice. **Piedmont Park,** Piedmont Ave. and 14th St. NE, 404/817-6744, is a 185-acre area with trails for walking, bicycling, and skating. Fields are available for softball, football, and baseball, and teams involved in pick-up games sometimes recruit bystanders who look athletic. Tennis courts and a swimming pool also are open to the public. Next door to Piedmont Park, the **Atlanta Botanical Garden,** 404/876-5859, has a scenic hiking trail through a hardwood forest. A similar trail is located at the **Fernbank Science Center,** 156 Heaton Park Dr., 404/378-4311, where a two-mile path winds through towering oaks, tulip poplars, and hickories. **Chastain Memorial Park,** 235 W. Wieuca Rd., 404/817-6744, has fields for soccer, softball, football, and baseball, a public golf course, tennis courts, swimming pool, horseback riding, a 3.5-mile jogging path, and a playground area.

The **River National Recreation Area,** 1978 Island Ford Pkwy., Dunwoody, 770/399-8070, is a walker's dream with 70 miles of scenic trails along the river. A 3.1-mile fitness trail includes exercise facilities along the way. Rafting is also a popular sport on the river, and the **Chattahoochee Outdoor Center,** 770/395-6851, rents rafts and canoes and provides pickup once you reach your destination.

Outside the I-285 perimeter, you can find miles of scenic hiking trails at the already noted Stone Mountain Park and Kennesaw Mountain National Battlefield Park. **Laurel Park,** 151 Manning Rd., Marietta, is a smaller park with tennis courts, volleyball and basketball areas, and a 1-mile paved jogging path with exercise stations beside the lake. West of Atlanta, **Sweetwater Creek State Park,** Mt. Vernon Rd., Lithia Springs, 770/389-7275, features the **Factory Ruins Trail,** a half-mile route leading to the remains of the New Manchester Manufacturing Co., a cloth mill that was burned by Sherman at the end of the Civil War.

Golfers can find public courses to fit any handicap. Acworth, a community about 30 miles north of Atlanta, offers two courses—the **Cobblestone,** 4200 Nance Rd., 770/917-5151, charges $52 weekdays, $59 weekends with a cart, and the Larry Nelson-designed **Centennial,** 5225 Woodstock Rd., 770/975-1000, offers 18 holes for $40 weekdays and $50 weekends, including a cart.

For less expensive golfing, try **Legacy Golf Links,** 1825 Windy Hill Rd., Smyrna, 770/434-6331, or **Mystery Valley,** 6094 Shadowrock Dr., Lithia Springs, 770/469-6193. Also designed by Larry Nelson, Legacy Golf Links provides a round of golf with a cart for $27 weekdays, $32 weekends. Eighteen holes at Mystery Valley are $19 with cart on weekdays, $28.50 on weekends.

FOOD
Downtown Atlanta has a small selection of moderately priced and expensive restaurants, but for the best dining choices you'll need to go to Buckhead or Midtown. For simple Southern fare, **Thelma's Kitchen,** 768 Marietta St., 404/688-5855, offers down-home cooking such as fried chicken, greens, macaroni and cheese, fried okra, sweet potatoes, and homemade cobblers and pies.

A couple of miles away in Inman Park, **Son's Place,** 100 Hurt St., 404/581/0530, serves soul food dished up on plastic compartmentalized trays like the ones you used in the school lunchroom. Greens, fried chicken and fried fish are always good. Be sure to order the flat-fried cornmeal hoecakes.

Reggie's British Pub and Restaurant, Marietta St. and Techwood, in the CNN Center, 404/525-1437, is a favorite lunch place and watering hole for many of the CNN staffers. Along with English ale or one of the 40 other varieties of beer, you can enjoy meat pies, bangers and mash, and hamburgers, all for a moderate price amid the atmosphere of an authentic Victorian pub.

Just beyond Underground Atlanta, **Lombardi's,** 94 Upper Pryor St. SE, 404/522-6568, is a moderately priced Italian restaurant that caters to the business lunch crowd. Chicken and fettuccine dishes and the fish specials with oven-roasted potatoes are delicious.

For fancier dining and a tab in the $35-$45 range, the elegant **City Grill,** 50 Hurt Plaza, is a favorite of business types on expense accounts. Specialties include meticulously prepared fish dishes, crab cakes, quail with cream gravy and shrimp and grits.

A couple of blocks north of the City Grill, you'll find **Mumbo Jumbo,** 89 Park Place NE, 404/523-0330, a funky new restaurant with a fusion cuisine that's pricey. The noise level is high because of the bare brick walls, but the food is exquisite. The gumbo and chicken salad are recommended.

GREATER ATLANTA

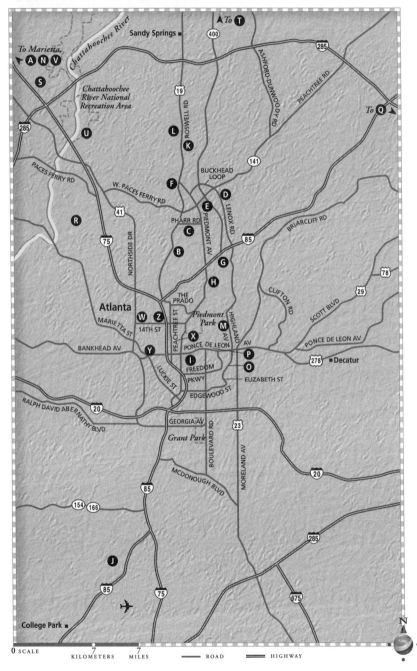

Chattahoochee River

Sandy Springs ■

To Marietta,

To Marietta

Chattahoochee River National Recreation Area

BUCKHEAD LOOP

PACES FERRY RD

W. PACES FERRY RD

PHARR RD

PIEDMONT AV

NORTHSIDE DR

ROSWELL RD

LENOX RD

ASHFORD-DUNWOODY RD

PEACHTREE RD

To T

To Q

BRIARCLIFF RD

Atlanta

THE PRADO

Piedmont Park

MARIETTA ST

14TH ST

PEACHTREE ST

BANKHEAD AV

PONCE DE LEON

HIGHLAND AV

PONCE DE LEON AV

CLIFTON RD

SCOTT BLVD

■ Decatur

FREEDOM PKWY

LUCKIE ST

ELIZABETH ST

EDGEWOOD ST

RALPH DAVID ABERNATHY BLVD

GEORGIA AV

Grant Park

BOULEVARD RD

MORELAND AV

MCDONOUGH BLVD

College Park ■

0 SCALE

KILOMETERS   MILES   — ROAD   ══ HIGHWAY

N

The Restaurant at the Ritz-Carlton Atlanta, 181 Peachtree St. NE, 404/659-0400, is another elegant downtown dining spot. Specializing in French cuisine, the restaurant offers a variety of fish and game. Reservations are recommended.

For moderately priced American fare, try **Dailey's Restaurant and Bar,** 17 International Blvd. NW, 404/681-3303, near the Hard Rock Cafe. Fish, steak, and salads are always good, but the fried ice cream for dessert is better. Slightly north of downtown, **The Pleasant Peasant,** 555 Peachtree St., 404/874-3223, features an upscale menu of rack of lamb, fish, and pork tenderloin, among other dishes. For a less expensive meal and a more casual atmosphere, **Mick's,** 557 Peachtree St., 404/875-6425, next door to the Peasant, offers meat loaf and mashed potatoes, pasta, burgers, salads, and fried green tomatoes. Other Mick's restaurants with similar menus are located in Underground Atlanta, 404/525-2825, and at Peachtree Center and International Blvd., 404/688-6425.

Diners more interested in the view than the food will want to try the **Sun Dial Restaurant and Lounge,** 210 Peachtree St., 404/589-7506, or **Nikolai's Roof,** 255 Courtland St. NE, 404/221-5362. Located on the 71st floor of the Westin Peachtree Plaza Hotel, the Sun Dial revolves to provide a view of all of Atlanta. The shrimp, prime rib, filet mignon and swordfish are expensive, so you may just want to stop at the Sun Dial for a cocktail before dining elsewhere. Nikolai's Roof atop the Atlanta Hilton falls into the same category. If price is no object, enjoy the piroshkis, the chilled flavored vodka, the French chicken or filet mignon—and the view. A five-course fixed-price dinner costs around $65.

Steak lovers may want to check out the famous **Morton's of Chicago,**

FOOD

Ⓐ 1848 House	Ⓚ Good Ol' Days	Ⓤ Ray's on the River
Ⓑ Abruzzi Ristorante	Ⓛ Horseradish Grill	Ⓥ Shillings on the Square
Ⓒ Atlanta Fish Market	Ⓜ Indigo Coastal Grill	Ⓦ Silver Skillet
Ⓒ Bone's	Ⓝ Mandarin House	Ⓧ South City Kitchen
Ⓓ Brasserie Le Coze	Ⓞ Manuel's Tavern	Ⓖ Sundown Cafe
Ⓔ Buckhead Diner	Ⓟ Mary Mac's Tea Room	Ⓣ Van Gogh's Restaurant
Ⓕ Chops	Ⓠ Matthews Cafeteria	Ⓨ The Varsity
Ⓖ Colonnade	Ⓡ Nuevo Laredo	Ⓩ Veni Vedi Vici
Ⓗ Fat Matt's Rib Shack	Ⓢ Pappadeaux Seafood	Ⓧ Vickery's
Ⓘ Flying Biscuit	Kitchen	
Ⓙ Flying Pig	Ⓣ Public House	

Note: Items with the same letter are located in the same area.

---

303 Peachtree St., 404/577-4366, for a porterhouse or prime rib. Maine lobsters are also on the menu. Reservations are recommended.

Midtown has a diverse selection of restaurants, from Southern cooking and barbecue to Southwestern and Southeast Asian. Perhaps the best place for a truly Southern culinary experience is the **Colonnade,** 1879 Cheshire Bridge Rd., 404/874-5642, an Atlanta tradition for decades. Choices include Southern fried chicken, pork loin and dressing, fried or broiled mountain trout, Cajun sea bass, fried shrimp, scallops and catfish, and a couple of dozen other entrees. A favorite dining establishment for senior citizens, gays, and locals, the Colonnade has one of the best bars in town. Bring cash, because the Colonnade doesn't accept credit cards. Prices are inexpensive to moderate.

Two other down-home restaurants popular with the locals are **Mary Mac's Tea Room,** 228 Ponce de Leon Ave. NE, 404/876-6604, and the **Silver Skillet,** 200 14th St. NW, 404/874-1388. Mary Mac's is a relic of the past. Diners are given tickets and pencils to write down their choice of meats and vegetables while the waitresses fetch baskets of hot rolls, bran muffins, and corn muffins. Potlikker—the broth from cooked, seasoned greens—is one of the specialties here. It's served in bowls with corn muffins and eaten like soup. Cinnamon rolls cost extra, but don't leave without trying them. The Silver Skillet is an old-fashioned no-frills restaurant that serves great breakfast and lunch specials such as meat loaf and pot roast for modest prices.

For a nice greasy, budget meal, drop into **The Varsity,** 61 North Ave., 404/881-1706. Billed as the world's largest drive-in, The Varsity has been serving wonderful chili dogs, hamburgers, onion rings, french fries, and frosted orange drinks since before the Depression. Other Varsities are located at 1085 Lindbergh Dr., 404/261-8843, and 6045 Dawson Blvd. NW, Norcross, 770/840-8519.

The best barbecue place in Midtown is **Fat Matt's Rib Shack,** 1811 Piedmont Rd., 404/607-1622, a cramped dwelling that lives up to the latter part of its name. Hickory-smoked ribs, chicken, and pork are served with a sweet tomato sauce, coleslaw, beans, or chips. There's usually a blues band or another musical group performing up close and personal in the small dining room.

About a mile down the street, the **Sundown Cafe,** 2165 Cheshire Bridge Rd. NE, 404/321-1118, serves Southwestern food with a touch of the South. Along with the fajitas, chile rellenos, and enchiladas with lemon cream sauce, you can get Eddie's pork and mashed potatoes with jalapeno gravy and spicy turnip greens. Menu items are moderately priced.

For Northern Italian cuisine, **Veni Vidi Vici,** 41 14th St., 404/875-8424, is an upscale restaurant with an elegant atmosphere. Specialties include roasted salmon, balsamic chicken, a variety of pastas, and appetizers such as grilled octopus. **Abruzzi Ristorante,** 2355 Peachtree Rd. NE, 404/261-8186, is equally elegant with quiet surroundings and attentive waiters. Seafood and pasta are always fresh, and the sweetbreads in wine sauce are exceptional.

In Buckhead, two of the best places are also the most crowded. **The Buckhead Diner,** 3073 Piedmont Rd. NE, 404/262-3336, looks like a diner on the outside, but inside the food is anything but ordinary. Fried calamari, veal and wild mushroom meat loaf with celery mashed potatoes, homemade potato chips with blue cheese dressing, and white chocolate banana cream pie are not the sort of dishes you would find at a 1950s diner. The restaurant does not take reservations, so be prepared for an hour or so wait at the bar. Prices are moderate to expensive.

The other Buckhead favorite is the **Atlanta Fish Market,** 265 Pharr Rd. NE, 404/262-3165, an upscale restaurant with a huge copper-and-steel fish sculpture out front. Seafood choices range from fried catfish to lobster and crab cakes. Daily fish specials can be prepared grilled or Hong Kong-style.

Steak lovers with fat wallets tend to migrate to either **Bones,** 3130 Piedmont Rd., 404/237-2663, or **Chops,** 70 W. Paces Ferry Rd., 404/262-2675, for aged beef cooked to order.

Usually a shopping mall is not the place to go to find a fine restaurant, but **Brasserie Le Coze,** 3393 Peachtree Rd., 404/266-1440, is an exception. Located in Lenox Square, this restaurant is decorated in the style of a cozy French café. Thick, medium-grilled pork chops with mustard sauce and mussels in white wine are two of the favorites.

Near Chastain Park, the **Horseradish Grill,** 4320 Powers Ferry Rd. NW, 404/255-7277, is one of the best restaurants in town. The cuisine is definitely New South, with fried chicken served on buttermilk biscuits and tomato gravy, low-country shrimp paste on grits, catfish encrusted in peanuts and cracker meal, and grilled fish and chops. Prices are moderate to high, and the atmosphere is casually elegant.

There are a number of good Mexican restaurants in the city, but **Nuevo Laredo,** 1495 Chattahoochee Ave. NW, 404/352-9009, ranks at the top of the list. Chile rellenos, barbecued brisket, and barbecued shrimp complement a menu of authentic Mexican dishes.

For dining near the Woodruff Arts center and theater district, Crescent Avenue offers a choice of thick burgers and Cuban sandwiches at moderate prices at **Vickery's,** 1106 Crescent Ave. NE, 404/881-1106, muffalettas and New Orleans food at **Front Page News,** 1104 Crescent Ave. NE, 404/897-3500, or more expensive updated Southern food such as shrimp and grits and she-crab soup at **South City Kitchen,** 1144 Crescent Ave. NE, 404/873-7358.

LOOKING FOR TARA

Fans of *Gone With the Wind* who come to Atlanta hoping to picnic on the grounds of Tara will be disappointed. Scarlett O'Hara's famous plantation home was only a product of Hollywood and Margaret Mitchell's imagination.

Actually, it was more Hollywood's than Mitchell's. The Atlanta-born author tried to convince the filmmakers to remain true to her literary version of Tara as a plain, columnless building in the middle of a working north Georgia farm. The grand houses in Charleston and Savannah had towering columns, but there were few in the area around Atlanta. Hollywood ignored Mitchell and created a movie image that visitors carry with them when they come to Atlanta.

Finding traces of *Gone With the Wind* is difficult, but not impossible. A very private person, Mitchell ordered her personal papers and manuscripts burned upon her death. She also left a will stipulating that her brother Stephens destroy her parents' home on Peachtree Street.

There are, however, a few places that remain. **The Dump,** the apartment at 999 Peachtree St. where Mitchell lived and wrote most of *Gone With the Wind* from 1925 to 1932, has been restored as the Margaret Mitchell House and Museum after two separate cases of arson (see "Sights"). Next door, a separate museum houses the doorway to Hollywood's Tara, the famous portrait of Scarlett seen in the movie, and other film memorabilia.

Other places *Gone With the Wind* fans should visit are the **Georgian Terrace,** 659 Peachtree St., and **Apartment 4** at One South Prado. The Georgian Terrace, which has been restored to its former glory as a grand hotel, was the scene of Mitchell's shocking Apache dance as a debutante at a ball in 1921. The apartment at One South Prado was the final home for Mitchell and her husband, John Marsh. They moved there from the now-demolished Russell Apartments in 1939.

A more realistic example of what Mitchell had in mind for Tara can be found at the **Tullie Smith House** at the Atlanta History

Center, 130 W. Paces Ferry Rd. The unadorned house was typical of upcountry plantation dwellings. Also check out the *Gone With the Wind* exhibit at the History Center while you're there (see "Sights").

If you can't spend the night at Tara or Twelve Oaks, the next best thing is a visit to **Inn Scarlett's Footsteps,** 40 Old Flat Shoals Rd., in Concord, 800/886-7355. Located about 45 miles south of Atlanta, the bed-and-breakfast is decked out in scads of *Gone With the Wind* memorabilia. Guests can stay in rooms named for Scarlett, Rhett, Ashley, and Melanie.

In Jonesboro, where much of the Civil War action takes place in the novel, **Stately Oaks Plantation,** 100 Carriage Lane, 770/473-0197, is an antebellum mansion/museum that portrays what life was like in the South before it was blown away by the winds of war. Also in Jonesboro, **The Road to Tara Museum & Gift Shop,** 102 N. Main St., 770/210-1017, offers an interesting collection of reproduction costumes, photographs, and movie memorabilia.

Those with morbid curiosities can visit the site of Mitchell's fatal accident (she was struck by a car in 1949 while crossing the street) at **Peachtree and 12th Streets,** not far from The Dump, or make a pilgrimage to her grave at historic **Oakland Cemetery,** 248 Oakland Ave. (see "Sights").

If you're in the mood for breakfast for lunch or dinner, **The Flying Biscuit,** 1655 McLendon Ave. NE, 404/687-8888, is a cozy place where you can sample eggs served sunny-side up on black bean cakes with turkey sausage, oatmeal pancakes with maple syrup, vegetarian or turkey burgers, and, of course, fluffy biscuits. Prices are moderate.

Virginia-Highlands is a funky neighborhood of brick bungalows, taverns, shops, and almost any kind of restaurant you want. For watering holes with good, inexpensive bar food, **Manuel's Tavern,** 602 N. Highland Ave. NE, 404/525-3447, is a local favorite. Menu items include burgers, sandwiches, hot dogs, and lunch specials with cold beer. Manuel's is the gathering place for politicians, Emory and Agnes Scott College students, journalists, and off-duty police officers. A staunch Democrat, owner Manuel Maloof has decorated the walls with all manner of political memorabilia.

For a memorable meal in the $20-and-up range, the **Indigo Coastal Grill,** 1397 N. Highland Ave. NE, 404/876-0676, serves the freshest and most artistically prepared seafood in the neighborhood. The decor is rustic and the tablecloths are brown butcher paper, but there is nothing plain about the sesame-crusted catfish or the conch fritters.

The area outside I-285—the circular highway that separates the in-town dwellers from the suburbanites—has no shortage of fast food and chain restaurants that cater to families. Finding a place for fine dining is a little more difficult, although there are a few.

Pappadeaux Seafood Kitchen, 2830 Windy Hill Rd., Marietta, is a popular Cajun seafood restaurant that's difficult to get into on weekends. Prices are higher than moderate, but the atmosphere is casual and family-friendly.

Van Gogh's Restaurant, 70 W. Crossville Rd., Roswell, 770/993-1156, has Buckhead atmosphere and expensive Buckhead prices. Fresh and delicious pasta, veal, and crab cakes are served in five separate dining rooms tastefully decorated with original art. The paintings are for sale.

Ray's on the River, 6700 Powers Ferry Rd., Marietta, 770/955-1187, is located in a picturesque setting on the Chattahoochee River. All of the fish dishes are excellent, whether you order them blackened, sautéed or fried. Sunday brunches are popular and recommended. Prices are moderate.

The 1848 House, 780 S. Cobb Dr., Marietta, 770/428-1848, is a restaurant located in an 1848 Greek Revival plantation house with 10 dining rooms. Prices can run $50 or more, but the venison, quail, and Charleston she-crab soup are worth it.

Another historic restaurant, **Public House** on Roswell Square, 605 Atlanta St., Roswell, 770/992-4646, is located in an 1854 brick warehouse that was used as a Confederate hospital. Delicious but pricey specials include fresh mountain trout and pork chops marinated in Southern Comfort.

If you're not that interested in atmosphere, there is a wide range of restaurants that serve excellent food at low to moderate prices. **Matthews Cafeteria,** 2299 Main St., Tucker, 770/491-9577, serves everything from turkey and dressing to barbecue ribs and chicken livers cafeteria style. There's also an array of side dishes, including macaroni and cheese, turnip greens, squash casserole, and deviled eggs.

Shillings on the Square, 19 N. Park Sq., Marietta, 770/428-9520, offers pub food and sandwiches downstairs and steaks and more expensive seafood upstairs in a dining room with cloth tablecloths, candles, and soft music.

For Chinese food, the **Mandarin House,** 1750 Marietta Hwy., Canton, 770/479-7621, or 1500 Pleasant Hill Rd., Duluth, 770/925-1050, is recommended by locals. Specialties include princess chicken and moo shu pork. Other good Asian restaurants can be found all along Buford Highway north of Atlanta. **Good Ol' Days,** 5841 Roswell Rd., 404/257-9183, is worth a visit just to try one of their sandwiches served in flowerpots. In good weather, you can dine on the patio and drink your favorite beverage.

Barbecue lovers have several favorites, including **The Flying Pig,** 856 Virginia Ave., Hapeville, 404/559-1000. Everything is moderately priced and cooked on-site over hickory coals.

LODGING

Compared to other large cities, Atlanta has a number of moderately priced hotels conveniently located downtown. However, because of the number of conventions held in the city, reservations need to be made well in advance.

For luxury and location, the **Ritz-Carlton Atlanta,** 131 Peachtree St. NE, 404/659-0400 or 800/241-3333, and the 73-story **Westin Peachtree Plaza,** 210 W. Peachtree St. NW, 404/659-1400 or 800/228-3000, are two of the choice hotels. The Ritz lives up to its name, with Oriental rugs, polished wood and brass, and a bay window in each of the 447 rooms and suites. The Westin Peachtree Plaza, a cylindrical hotel designed by architect John Portman, has 1,068 rooms available—all with views. Prices for these and other luxury hotels in town start at $160 per night.

Three more premium hotels in the Peachtree Center district are the 47-story **Marriott Marquis,** 265 Peachtree Center Ave., 404/521-0000 or 800/228-9290, with 1,671 rooms; the 29-story **Atlanta Hilton,** 255 Courtland St. NE, 404/659-2000, which houses the elegant restaurant, Nikolai's Roof; and the **Hyatt Regency,** 265 Peachtree St. NE, 404/577-1234 or 800/233-1234, with an impressive atrium and the revolving Polaris restaurant and bar in a futuristic blue dome overlooking the city.

The **Omni Hotel,** 100 CNN Center, 404/659-0000 or 800/843-6664, is located in the CNN Center and directly across the street from Centennial Olympic Park. The hotel has 465 luxury rooms and is close to shops and restaurants.

The seven-story **Embassy Suites Hotel,** 311 Marietta St., 404/223-2300, sits adjacent to Centennial Olympic Park and across the street from CNN Center and within a block of Phillips Arena. The rose-brick-and-precast-concrete interior complements the brick style used in Centennial Park. The hotel offers suite-only accommodations, an outdoor swimming pool, and a full-service restaurant with outdoor dining on the terrace. Rates range from $139–$265.

GREATER ATLANTA

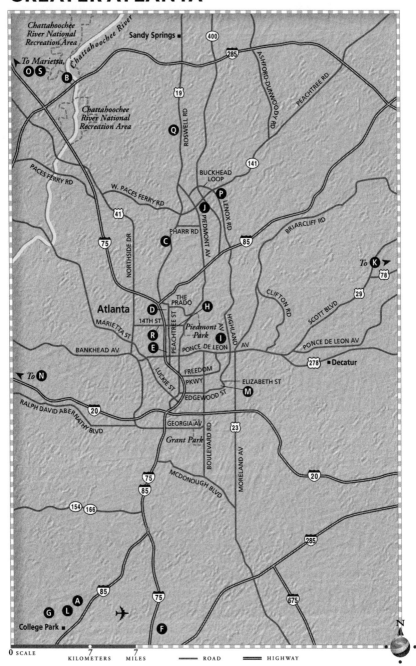

Chattahoochee
River National
Recreation Area

Chattahoochee River

To Marietta,

O **S** **B**

Chattahoochee
River National
Recreation Area

Sandy Springs

400

285

ASHFORD-DUNWOODY RD

PEACHTREE RD

19

ROSWELL RD

Q

141

PACES FERRY RD

W. PACES FERRY RD

BUCKHEAD
LOOP

P

LENOX RD

J

PIEDMONT AV

PHARR RD

C

41

NORTHSIDE DR

75

BRIARCLIFF RD

85

CLIFTON RD

To **K**

78

29

SCOTT BLVD

THE
PRADO

D

H

Atlanta

14TH ST

PEACHTREE ST

Piedmont
Park

HIGHLAND AV

MARIETTA ST

R

E

I

PONCE DE LEON AV

BANKHEAD AV

PONCE DE LEON AV

278

■ Decatur

To **N**

LUCKIE ST

FREEDOM

PKWY

ELIZABETH ST

M

EDGEWOOD ST

RALPH DAVID ABERNATHY BLVD

20

GEORGIA AV

BOULEVARD RD

23

Grant Park

MORELAND AV

75

85

MCDONOUGH BLVD

20

154 166

285

85

75

675

G **L** **A**

F

College Park ■

N

0 SCALE

7
KILOMETERS

7
MILES

ROAD

HIGHWAY

Newly renovated with 312 rooms and 24 suites, the **Wyndham Atlanta,** 160 Spring St. NW, 404/688-8600, is within walking distance of Peachtree Center and Centennial Olympic Park. Amenities include a fitness center and an outdoor pool with lush landscaping.

Near Underground Atlanta, the **Suite Hotel,** 54 Peachtree St. NE, 404/223-5555, offers 157 suites with marble baths and all the amenities of an Old World hotel for $135 and up.

More moderately priced lodging can be found at the **Days Inn Downtown,** 300 Spring St., 404/523-1144 or 800/325-2525, a 10-story building near Peachtree Center with rooms starting around $89.

The **Comfort Inn,** 101 International Blvd., 404/524-5555 or 800/535-0707, the **TraveLodge,** 311 Courtland St. NE, 404/659-4545 or 800/578-7878, and the **Quality Hotel,** 89 Luckie St. NW, 404/524-7991 or 800/228-5151, offer central locations, cable TV, and swimming pools for around $80.

There are a number of good bed-and-breakfasts in Midtown at prices ranging from $50 to $150 a night. Once a bordello, the **Woodruff Bed and Breakfast Inn,** 223 Ponce de Leon Ave., 404/875-9449, is now a respectable three-story Victorian house decorated with antiques and Oriental rugs. Conveniently located near the Fox Theatre, the inn has suites with private baths and serves a Southern breakfast of bacon, eggs, and grits.

In Inman Park, the **Sugar Magnolia,** 804 Edgewood Ave. NE, 404/222-0226, is another grand Victorian home with fireplaces, a turret, and gingerbread trim. Continental breakfasts are served. Just up the street, the Queen

LODGING

- Ⓐ Atlanta Airport Hilton
- Ⓑ Atlanta Marriott Northwest
- Ⓒ Best Western Granada Suite
- Ⓓ Colony Square Hotel
- Ⓔ Days Inn Peachtree
- Ⓕ Courtyard by Marriott Atlanta Airport North
- Ⓖ Courtyard by Marriott Atlanta Airport South
- Ⓗ Four Seasons
- Ⓘ Gaslight Inn
- Ⓙ Grand Hyatt Atlanta
- Ⓚ Hampton Inn Stone Mountain
- Ⓛ Holiday Inn Atlanta South
- Ⓜ King-Keith House Bed and Breakfast
- Ⓝ Knights Inn Six Flags
- Ⓘ Ritz-Carlton Buckhead
- Ⓞ Sixty Polk Street
- Ⓜ Sugar Magnolia
- Ⓟ Swissotel
- Ⓠ Woodruff Bed and Breakfast
- Ⓡ Wyndham Hotel Midtown

CAMPING

- Ⓝ Arrowhead Campground
- Ⓢ KOA North Atlanta Campground
- Ⓚ Stone Mountain Park Family Campground

Note: *Items with the same letter are located in the same area.*

Anne-style **King-Keith House Bed & Breakfast,** 889 Edgewood Ave. NE, 404/688-7330, offers five guest rooms with private baths. Tastefully decorated with period antiques, the house has fireplaces and 12-foot ceilings. The more expensive **Gaslight Inn,** 1001 St. Charles Ave. NE, 404/875-1001, features a walled garden, two suites with fireplaces and whirlpool tubs, and three guest rooms with fireplaces and four-poster beds.

Moderately priced motel rooms can be found at the **Days Inn Peachtree,** 683 Peachtree St. NE, 404/874-9200, near the Fox Theatre and restaurants. Other hotels in the Midtown area will cost between $100 and $200 nightly. Conveniently located near the Woodruff Arts Center and across the street from the 14th Street Playhouse, the **Colony Square Hotel,** 188 14th St., 404/892-6000, offers modern rooms and access to the Colony Square Health Club. The **Wyndham Hotel Midtown,** 125 10th St., 404/873-4800, provides large rooms, an indoor pool, a lounge, and a health club.

The Grand, 75 14th St., 404/881-9898, is an elegant and luxurious hotel with marble-tiled baths, two restaurants, an indoor pool, and a health club.

With its courtyard and Spanish red-tiled roof, the **Best Western Granada Suite Hotel,** 1302 W. Peachtree St. NW, 404/876-6100, looks as if it belongs in the Southwest. The hotel is easily accessible from I-85 and conveniently located near the Woodruff Arts Center. Rooms start at around $80.

As expected, the hotels in Buckhead are luxurious and expensive. Rooms at the **Swissotel,** 3391 Peachtree Rd. NE, 404/365-0065, start at $149. The gracious service at the **Ritz-Carlton Buckhead,** 3434 Peachtree Rd. NE, 404/365-0065, will cost you upwards of $165 a night, and rooms overlooking Japanese gardens at the **Grand Hyatt Atlanta,** 3300 Peachtree Rd., 404/365-8100, start at $215.

Outside the Perimeter, there are a number of chain motels as well as upscale hotels. If you arrive in Atlanta by plane and don't want to venture too far before settling in for the night, the **Atlanta Airport Hilton and Towers,** 1031 Virginia Ave., Hapeville, 404/767-9000, is a convenient luxury hotel. The **Courtyard by Marriott Atlanta Airport North,** 3399 International Blvd., Hapeville, 404/559-1043, and the **Courtyard by Marriott Atlanta Airport South,** 2050 Sullivan Rd., College Park, 770/997-2220, provide airport shuttles and lodging in the $80-$150 range.

Seven miles south of the airport in historic Jonesboro, the **Holiday Inn Atlanta South,** 6288 Old Dixie Hwy., 770/968-4300, offers free parking and an outdoor pool. Rates start at $65.

North of Atlanta in Cobb County, luxury accommodations for $60 and up can be found at the 400-room **Atlanta Marriott Northwest,** 200 Interstate N. Pkwy., 770/952-7900.

For romantic evenings in a Victorian setting, **Sixty Polk Street,** 60 Polk St., 770/419-1688, is a bed-and-breakfast just off the square in Marietta that offers four guest rooms with private baths for $85 and up.

Conveniently located three miles from Stone Mountain Park, the **Hampton Inn Stone Mountain,** 1737 Mountain Industrial Blvd., 770/934-0004, has 129 rooms starting at $64. And three miles from the Six Flags Over Georgia amusement park, the **Knights Inn Six Flags,** 1595 Blair Bridge Rd., 770/944-0824, provides free cable TV and a pool for $49-$79. Dozens of budget motels are also located at interstate exits.

CAMPING

Campers will have to venture farther away from the city to find a variety of campsites, but there are 431 wooded lakeside sites available at **Stone Mountain Park Family Campground,** Stone Mountain Park exit off U.S. Hwy. 78 E., 770/498-5710. Each campsite features RV hookups and more rustic sites for tent camping for around $19 a night. A $6-per-car admission is charged to enter the park.

The **Arrowhead Campground,** 7400 Six Flags Rd., exit 13 off I-20, Austelle, 770/732-1130, provides 150 tent sites and 160 RV sites for $18 and $27, respectively. There's a pool and a store and, best of all, it's about a five-minute walk to Six Flags Over Georgia.

Located near Kennesaw Mountain Battlefield, the **KOA North Atlanta Campground,** 2000 Old U.S. Hwy. 41, exit 116 off I-75, 770/427-2406, has 250 campsites and a pool. Tent sites rent for $18, RV sites for $26.

NIGHTLIFE

The music scene in Atlanta is as diverse as the population. Homegrown talent includes the Indigo Girls, Shawn Mullins, TLC, Ray Charles, and Gladys Knight, among others. Most of the action takes place in Midtown, Little Five Points, and Buckhead, but the downtown area is beginning to offer more entertainment with the influx of more city dwellers.

The hottest downtown action takes place at **The Tabernacle,** 152 Luckie St. NW, 404/659-9022, a converted Baptist church that was the site of a temporary House of Blues during the Olympic Games. Since then, it has become a venue for a number of jazz, rock, and hip-hop concerts.

The big shows, such as Ricky Martin and Elton John, are booked into the new **Phillips Arena,** 100 Techwood Dr., 404/827-3800, when the Hawks and Thrashers are not playing.

In Underground Atlanta, **Kenny's Alley** is the center of activity for the bar scene. **Fat Tuesday's,** 404/523-7404, offers a variety of frozen daiquiris and New Orleans Po'-Boy sandwiches; **Hooter's,** 404/688-0062, specializes in an array of beverages, hot wings, and Hooter's girls in tight T-shirts and short-shorts.

The famous **Hard Rock Cafe,** 215 Peachtree St. NE, 404/688-7625, rocks with piped-in music amid an environment teeming with rock-and-roll memorabilia such as one of Elton John's bejeweled outfits. A vintage Cadillac with fins hovers above the entrance.

Jocks N Jills Sports Bar, 1 CNN Center, 404/688-4225, is a popular hangout for fans heading to or returning from sporting events at Phillips Arena or the Georgia Dome. And in the Grant Park area, **Daddy D's,** 264 Memorial Dr., 404/222-0206, cooks up barbecue and blues on weekends for a multicultural crowd.

Midtown is the center of arts and theater events, but downtown does have a bit of culture. Georgia State University's **Rialto Center for the Performing Arts,** 80 Forsyth St. NW, 404/651-4727, offers a variety of plays, dance performances, and concerts, from classical music to jazz. **Actor's Express,** 887 W. Marietta St., 404/875-1606, presents classic plays as well as avant-garde productions.

Entertainment in Midtown and Buckhead runs the gamut from highbrow art to low-down blues. For a mixture of food and crime, try **Agatha's-A Taste of Mystery,** 693 Peachtree St., 404/875-1610, a dinner theater where audiences participate in solving imaginary murders. The **14th St. Playhouse,** 173 14th St., 404/872-0665, stages a variety of plays, including musicals such as *Appalachian Christmas* and *Cotton Patch Gospel*. In the same facility, **Theatre Gael,** 404/876-1138, features theatrical and musical performances with a Scottish, Irish or Welsh theme. **Theater of the Stars,** 404/252-8960, brings touring New York shows such as *Les Miserables* and *The Phantom of the Opera* to the **Fox Theatre,** 660 Peachtree St., throughout the year. Other touring productions are held at the **Atlanta Civic Center** 395 Piedmont Ave., 404/523-6275. **Jomandi Productions,** 1444 Mayson St. NE, 404/876-6346, is an African American company that has premiered many original works.

The **Atlanta Symphony Orchestra** currently performs during the fall and winter at the **Woodruff Arts Center,** 1280 Peachtree St., 404/753-5000, but plans are under way to build a new symphony hall on West Peachtree Street. Also at the Woodruff Arts Center, The **Alliance Theater Company,** 404/733-5000, stages classic and contemporary plays, including *Driving Miss Daisy,* which premiered here. The **Atlanta Ballet,** 1400 W. Peachtree St. NE, 404/873-5811, has been performing for more than seven decades. The company presents classic ballets such as *The Nutcracker* as well as recent versions of *Peter Pan*.

For more casual entertainment, Virginia-Highlands offers a taste of the blues at **Blind Willie's,** 848 N. Highland Ave., 404/873-2583, a tiny club that is usually packed with a socio-economic cross-section. Just up the street, **Limerick Junction,** 822 N. Highland Ave., 404/874-7147, features Irish music and sing-alongs.

Clubs catering to alternative lifestyles include **Backstreet,** 845 Peachtree St., 404/873-1986, a gay bar that's open 24 hours with live shows, dancing, and female impersonators. **The Otherside,** 1924 Piedmont Ave., 404/875-5238, is a lesbian bar with live music on weekends.

Masquerade, 695 North Ave., 404/577-8178, is difficult to define. Patrons who sport multiple tattoos and nose, ear, and navel rings mingle with nonpierced customers who simply want to enjoy alternative and punk rock music and dancing. The warehouse-sized building is divided into themed areas such as Heaven, Hell, and Purgatory. Live bands perform Wednesday through Sunday.

Those with a taste for martinis and music should drop in at **The Martini Club,** 140 Crescent Ave., 404/873-0794. On weekends the 1930s-style bar is packed with fashionably dressed African American men and women sipping from some of the 54 varieties of martinis and listening to jazz combos.

Over at Little Five Points, college rock bands play most nights at **The Point,** 420 Moreland Ave. NE, 404/659-3522, and rockabilly and "redneck" bands perform to packed houses at a converted bank building known as **The Star Community Bar,** 437 Moreland Ave., 404/681-9018.

In Buckhead, much of the action takes place at **Tongue & Groove,** 3055 Peachtree Rd. NE, 404/261-2325, an upscale club with big bands, swing music, and dancing. Cigar smoking and jumbo martini-sipping are encouraged. Not far away, **Otto's,** 265 E. Paces Ferry Rd. NE, 404/233-1133, is an upscale club for those who enjoy dancing to contemporary music. And nostalgia buffs will want to visit **Johnny's Hideaway,** 3377 Roswell Rd., 404/233-8026. An Atlanta fixture for years, Johnny's features big band music from the 1940s and '50s, lots of Sinatra, and suitably dim lighting for the dancing patrons—most of whom are well over 40.

Outside the Perimeter, first-rate theatrical productions are offered six times a year at the **Theatre in the Square,** 11 Whitlock Ave., Marietta, 770/422-8369. Productions such as *Always Patsy Cline* and *Smoke on the Mountain* have packed the 170-seat auditorium.

Kennesaw State University's **Stillwell Theater,** 1000 Chastain Rd., Kennesaw, 770/423-6650, produces excellent Shakespearean plays as well as English comedies such as *She Stoops to Conquer.*

And at Clayton County College & State University, **Spivey Hall,** 5900 N. Lee St., Morrow, 770/961-3683, presents excellent chamber music and other concerts. Artists have included the Preservation Hall Jazz Band and the Chamber Music Society of Lincoln Center. **Dave & Buster's,** 2215 D&B Dr., Marietta, 770/951-5554, is a giant indoor amusement park with more than 100 video games for kids and adults. A separate bar and restaurant and a mystery dinner theater are available for more grown-up fun. If you're looking for some laughs, the **Punch Line,** 280 Hilderbrand Dr. NE, 404/252-5233, books comedians on the way up as well as comics who have made it and come back for a visit. Jeff Foxworthy, Brett Butler, and Tim Allen appeared here before and after they became famous.

2
NORTHWEST MOUNTAINS

The northwest corner of Georgia is a region of diverse landscapes, Civil War battlefields, and Native American historical sites. In TAG Corner, where Tennessee, Alabama and Georgia meet, the rugged, remote Cumberland Plateau challenges hikers and backpackers. Two important Civil War battles—Chickamauga and Lookout Mountain—were fought on this plateau. General William T. Sherman visited Cumberland Plateau as he fought his way to Atlanta and the coast.

A haven for hang gliding, the region, with its network of deep limestone caves, is also a popular destination for spelunkers. Trails and trout streams beckon in the Cohutta Mountains just east of the Cumberland Plateau, and, to the south, the Western Uplands offer an opportunity for history buffs to explore a number of fascinating archaeological sites, including the Etowah Indian Mounds, and browse through the Cherokee Nation's Chieftain Museum.

Two of the most scenic drives in the state—the Lookout Mountain Parkway and the Ridge and Valley Scenic Byway—take motorists through the picturesque forests, mountains, and canyons of this largely undiscovered territory.

A PERFECT DAY IN THE NORTHWEST MOUNTAINS

Spend your early morning exploring the Etowah Indian Mounds; then visit

NORTHWEST MOUNTAINS

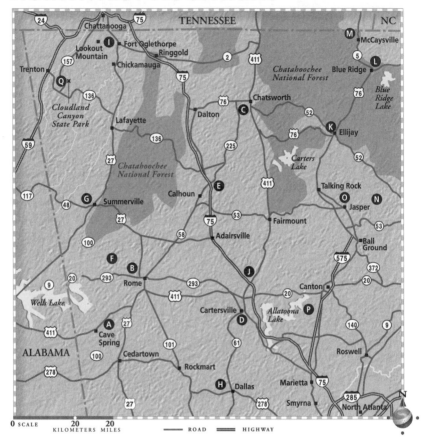

Pickett's Mill Battlefield near Cartersville to see one of the best-preserved Civil War sites in the country. Stop for a barbecue sandwich at the Hickory House in Dallas. After lunch, browse through the Chieftains Museum in Rome and tour beautiful Oak Hall and the Martha Berry Museum. Take a short drive to Summerville to see Howard Finster's Paradise Gardens, one of the most unusual outdoor collections of folk art in the world. If time permits, visit New Echota, site of the capital of the Cherokee Nation, and wander through the museum and restored buildings. End your day with a scenic drive to Chatsworth and a home-cooked chicken dinner at Edna's.

SIGHTSEEING HIGHLIGHTS

★★★★ **PARADISE GARDENS**
Hwy. 27, Summerville, 706/857-2926
Northwest Georgia doesn't have Disney World, but it has something almost as fantastic. At Paradise Gardens, three miles north of Summerville, folk artist Howard Finster has created a wonderland of sculptures—many of them angels—crafted from abandoned bicycle parts, aluminum foil, and anything else he could scavenge. Finster's art, which sells for thousands of dollars, has appeared in advertisements and on the 1985 Talking Heads album, *Little Creatures*.
> **Details:** *Open Mon-Sat 10-6. $3 adults. (1-2 hours)*

★★★ **CAVE SPRING**
3 Georgia Ave., 706/777-3382
Located on the Alabama border, Cave Spring is famous for its limestone cavern and a spring that produces millions of gallons of water a day. The water pours into a huge swimming pool built in the shape of the state of Georgia. In downtown Cave Spring, visitors can stop at a miniature stone castle in Rolater Park for tours

---

SIGHTS
- Ⓐ Cave Spring
- Ⓑ Chieftains Museum
- Ⓒ Chief Vann House
- Ⓓ Etowah Indian Mounds
- Ⓔ New Echota
- Ⓕ Oak Hill/Martha Berry Museum
- Ⓖ Paradise Gardens
- Ⓗ Pickett's Mill Battlefield
- Ⓘ Rock City
- Ⓑ Rome Area History Museum
- Ⓙ William Weinman Mineral Museum

FOOD
- Ⓚ Calico Cupboard
- Ⓖ Edna's
- Ⓛ Forge Mill Crossing
- Ⓐ Gray Horse
- Ⓗ Hickory House
- Ⓜ Michiko's
- Ⓜ Pat's Country Kitchen
- Ⓘ Rising Fawn Cafe

LODGING
- Ⓒ Cohutta Lodge and Convention Center
- Ⓓ Days Inn
- Ⓚ Elderberry Inn
- Ⓕ Fannin Inn Motel
- Ⓝ Tate House
- Ⓞ Woodbridge Inn

CAMPING
- Ⓟ Allatoona Campground and Cottage Rentals
- Ⓠ Cloudland Canyon State Park
- Ⓒ Fort Mountain State Park
- Ⓖ James H. "Sloppy" Floyd State Park
- Ⓐ John Tanner State Park
- Ⓔ KOA Kampground-Calhoun
- Ⓒ Lake Conasauga Recreation Area

Note: Items with the same letter are located in the same area.

---

of the cave, where summer temperatures rarely surpass 56 degrees. Be sure to stay and visit the town's antiques shops and stately historic homes.

Details: *Open June-Labor Day 10-5. $1.50. (2-3 hours)*

★★★ CHIEFTAINS MUSEUM
800 Riverside Pkwy., Rome, 706/291-9494
This 1794 log cabin home of the notable Cherokee leader Major Ridge houses a large collection of artifacts that tell the moving story of how the Cherokees were removed from their homeland. Located on the banks of the Oostanaula River in Rome, the museum is an anchor site on the Northwest Georgia Chieftains Trail, which includes sites such as New Echota, the Etowah Indian Mounds and Fort Mountain State Park.

Details: *Open Tue-Sat 10-4, Sun 1-4. $3 adults. (1 hour)*

★★★ ETOWAH INDIAN MOUNDS
813 Indian Mounds Rd., 770/387-3747
Located five miles southwest of Cartersville, these incredible mounds—some more than 60 feet high—provide a glimpse into what life was like for Native Americans from 900 to 1500 A.D. The well-preserved mounds were used as burial sites for the leaders of the tribe and as a worship area for the priests. An impressive interpretive museum with artifacts and other relics is located on this important archaeological site.

Details: *Open Tue-Sat 9-5, Sun 2-5:30. $4 adults, $2 children. (1-2 hours)*

★★★ OAK HILL/MARTHA BERRY MUSEUM
Hwy. 27, Rome, 800/220-5504
Built in 1847, Oak Hill is the home of Berry College founder Martha Berry. The nineteenth-century educator started a work-study program that allowed poor mountain children an opportunity to pay for their education. The antebellum plantation house is furnished with reproduction furniture handmade by Berry College students. A highlight of Oak Hill is the gardens, including the Formal Garden, Goldfish Garden, Sundial Garden, and Sunken Garden. A short walk from the house is the Martha Berry Museum, which houses the educator's memorabilia.

Details: *Open Mon-Sat 10-5, Sun 1-5. Free. (1-2 hours)*

ETOWAH INDIAN MOUNDS

Cartersville, GA

★★★ **ROCK CITY**
1400 Patten Rd., Lookout Mountain, 706/820-2531
For years, anyone driving through the South could not help but notice all the signs on the roofs of barns that read "See Rock City." Established in the 1920s just over the Tennessee state line, Rock City is an area of unusual rock formations such as Balancing Rock and Lover's Leap. A path through the park forks in two directions—one leading over a stone bride and the other over a suspension bridge that is not recommended for anyone scared of heights. On a clear day you can see seven states from an outcropping called Lover's Leap. Kids will love Fairyland Caverns and Mother Goose Village with a wax Hansel and Gretel and other characters.

Details: Open daily 8-8 between Memorial Day and Christmas; 8:30-5 the rest of the year. $8.95 adults, $4.95 children. (2 hours)

★★ **NEW ECHOTA**
1211 Chatsworth Hwy., Calhoun, 706/624-1321
The capital of the Cherokee Nation until 1838, all that remains now are several restored buildings and a museum. Among the exhibits are the printing shop where the Native American newspaper, the *Cherokee Phoenix*, was printed in English and Cherokee, and displays of

memorabilia. The Supreme Court house and Vann's Tavern are open for tours. A Cherokee Fall Festival is held every October.
Details: Open Tue-Sat 9-5, Sun 2-5:30. $4 adults, $2 children. (1-2 hours)

★★ PICKETT'S MILL BATTLEFIELD
2640 Mt. Tabor Rd., 770/443-7850
One of the best-preserved Civil War battle sites in the nation, Pickett's Mill, five miles northeast of Dallas, is where the Confederates won one of their most successful victories. A relief map shows the positions of the troops and trails, and a museum and a video interpret the battle. An annual event in May features local residents in period costumes demonstrating Civil War weapons, cooking, and other activities.
Details: Open Tue-Sat 9-5, Sun 12-5. (1-2 hours)

★★ ROME AREA HISTORY MUSEUM
303 Broad St., Rome, 706/235-8051
Take a walk through history, from Spanish explorer Hernando de Soto's visit 400 years ago to modern times. This museum in downtown Rome features exhibits about Native American culture and the area's role in the Civil War. One exhibit includes the works of author Margaret Mitchell and replicas of dresses from the movie, *Gone With the Wind*.
Details: Open Tue-Sat 10-5. Free. (1 hour)

★★ WILLIAM WEINMAN MINERAL MUSEUM
51 Mineral Museum Rd., Cartersville, 770/386-0576
This facility is recognized as one of the best mineral museums in the Southeast. Displays include minerals, gemstones, fossils, and rocks from all over the world.
Details: Open Tue-Sat 10-4:30, Sun 1-4:30. $3.50 adults, $2.50 children, $3 seniors. (1 hour)

★ CHIEF VANN HOUSE
82 Hwy. 225, Chatsworth, 706/695-2598
Built by Cherokee Chief James Vann in 1804, this brick mansion has been called the "Showplace of the Cherokee Nation." The house is decorated with beautiful hand carvings and fine antiques.
Details: Open Tue-Sat 9-5, Sun 2-5:30. $2.50 adults, $1.50 children. (1 hour)

LAKE ALLATOONA WATERSKIING

Cartersville, GA

FITNESS AND RECREATION

The varied and often rugged terrain in the Northwest Mountains challenges even the most experienced hikers, but beginners can find trails to suit their skills as well. In addition, the lakes and rivers in the area offer some of the best fishing in the state.

If you find yourself in Cave Spring on a particularly hot summer day, take a dip in the Georgia-shaped **Cave Spring Swimming Pool in Rolater Park,** Hwy. 411, 706/777-8439. The natural pool is fed with pure mountain water at the rate of several million gallons a day.

For warmer swimming, nearby **John Tanner State Park,** I-20, exit 3, 770/830-2222, has a large, sandy beach. Other activities include miniature golf, nature trails, canoe and paddleboat rentals, and bicycle rentals.

Hikers can walk among a bit of history at the **Chickamauga and Chattanooga National Military Park,** south of Fort Oglethorpe, Hwy. 27, 770/866-9241. More than 80 miles of scenic hiking trails wind through the Chickamauga Valley, where more than 35,000 died in one of the most costly battles of the Civil War. Signs along the trails describe the history of the region.

In Rising Fawn, **Cloudland Canyon State Park,** Hwy. 136, 706/657-4050, offers a pool, tennis courts, and three different trails. Backpackers can take the seven-mile **East Rim Trail** to a primitive camping area, while recre-

BLUE AND GRAY TOUR

History buffs—or anyone who saw *Gone With the Wind*—are familiar with the Civil War's impact on Atlanta. But the area north of the city was also the scene of fierce battles before General Sherman arrived.

The Blue and Gray Trail, which winds through the towns of Dalton, Dallas, Rome, Resaca, and Fort Oglethorpe, traces the path of one of the last military campaigns of the Civil War. Many battle sites can be explored along the way, and a series of reenactments are staged every year at Pickett's Mill State Historic Site, Resaca, and Chickamauga-Chattanooga National Military Park.

Begin your tour at the **Battles for Chattanooga Museum** on Lookout Mountain, 423/821-2812, where dioramas depict the 1863 Battle of Chickamauga and the fighting along Missionary Ridge and Lookout Mountain.

Established in 1895 by Union and Confederate veterans, the Chickamauga-Chattanooga National Military Park has preserved the battlefields as much as possible. It's here where Confederate troops under Generals James Longstreet and Braxton Bragg defeated Generals William Rosecrans and George Thomas and the Union army in one of the bloodiest battles of the war. More than 35,000 Union and Confederate soldiers were killed in the Battle of Chickamauga Creek. A month later, in November 1863, Union troops took over Chattanooga after the battles of Lookout Mountain and Missionary Ridge. In the spring, General Sherman resumed his march toward Atlanta and Savannah.

Maps and guides to the battle sites are available at the visitor centers at Point Park on Lookout Mountain and at Fort Oglethorpe on Hwy. 27. For a taste of what life was like back then, stay for a night at the **Gordon-Lee Mansion** in Chickamauga. The 1840s house—now a bed-and-breakfast—was used as a hospital and military headquarters during the war.

Another historic spot on the trail is the **Western & Atlantic Railroad Depot** in Ringgold, the final stop for James Andrews'

Raiders after stealing the Confederate locomotive, The General, in 1862. The Raiders were captured a short distance up the track. The daring episode was immortalized in the Disney movie, *The Great Locomotive Chase.*

At the **Old Stone Museum Church,** 706/935-5232, south of town on U.S. 41, visitors can still see the dark bloodstains on the floor where a surgeon tried to save the wounded. In Dalton, you can visit the **Confederate Cemetery and Monument** on Emory Street or the **Dug Gap Battle Park,** 2211 W. Dug Gap Battle Mountain Rd., 706/278-0217, where you can view breastworks built by the soldiers. The nearby **Crown Gardens and Archives,** 715 Chattanooga Rd., 706/278-0217, features textile exhibits, along with Cherokee and Civil War artifacts.

Resaca, south of Dalton on Hwy. 41, is the site of a major battle in the Georgia campaign in 1864. The battle is reenacted on the third weekend in May at the Confederate Cemetery, Hwy. 41, two miles north of town.

One of the final encounters (before the Battle of Atlanta) took place at Pickett's Mill on May 27, 1864, where the Confederates achieved a rare victory. The site at Mount Tabor Road off Hwy. 92, south of Acworth, is among the best-preserved Civil War battlefields.

ational hikers can choose between the **Falls Trail** that leads to two waterfalls or the five-mile **West Rim Trail** through a hardwood forest.

In the Cohutta Wilderness, hikers and backpackers can find a challenge on the 16.7-mile **Jacks River Trail** or the 78-mile **Benton MacKaye Trail** at Springer Mountain. The MacKaye Trail was named for the founder of the Appalachian Trail. Those interested in a 12-mile overnight backpacking trek can follow the appropriately named **Tearbritches Trail** to the **Conasauga River Trail** and onto the **Chestnut Lead Trail.** The Forest Service in Blue Ridge, E. Main St., 706/632-3031, provides trail maps.

One of the most unusual sights in this part of the state is the 855-foot stone wall at **Fort Mountain State Park,** Hwy. 52, 706/695-2621, near Chatsworth. Some say the wall was a religious structure built in the fifth century, but others claim it's simply a natural phenomenon. After marveling at the wall, you can follow the eight-mile **Gahuti Trail** through a wilderness area and past some primitive campsites, or take the **Old Fort Trail,** which meanders through a forest of oaks and pines. A 17-acre lake with a 400-foot waterfall features a swimming beach and boat rentals.

More swimming and boating facilities near Chatsworth are located at **Lake Conasauga Recreation Area,** 401 Old Ellijay Rd., 706/695-6736, and **Carter's Lake Marina and Resort,** 575 Marina Rd., 706/276-4891.

In Cartersville, **Lake Allatoona,** 24 Allatoona Landing, 770/974-6089, offers a full-service marina, a swimming beach, and boat rentals.

Farther north, in Blue Ridge, **Lake Blue Ridge Marina,** 335 Marina Dr., 706/632-2618, also offers swimming and boating facilities, including jet-ski rentals.

White-water rafters and canoeists can book guided trips down the Ocoee River at **Whitewater Rafting and Canoeing,** 706/632-7696 in Mc-Caysville, while the more adventurous can take a half-day or full-day trip on the Ocoee River with **Wildwater Rafting,** Hwy. 64, 800/451-9972. Other outfitters include **Southeastern Expeditions,** 800/868-7238, and **Ocoee Outdoors,** 800/533-7767.

FOOD

There is no shortage of chain restaurants at the exits along I-75, but if you're the adventurous type, sample of the local cafés on the mountain backroads.

In downtown Cave Spring, **Gray Horse,** 706/777-8327, serves three Southern-style meals a day, including a lunch buffet for reasonable rates. More country cooking can be found in Chatsworth at **Edna's,** Hwy. 411 South, 706/695-4968. Located at the foot of Fort Mountain, Edna's specializes in fried chicken and fresh vegetables. Similar fare is offered on the square in Ellijay at the **Calico Cupboard Restaurant,** 706/635-7575, and in Mc-Caysville at **Pat's Country Kitchen,** Hwy. 5, 706/492-5477. All serve heaping plates of food at inexpensive prices.

If you're near Lookout Mountain or the Rock City area, swing by Rising Fawn and stop at the **Rising Fawn Cafe,** I-59 exit 1, 706/462-2277. Located behind one of those big truck stops, this rustic restaurant serves country-fried steak, pork chops, barbecue, and chicken with vegetables and fruits fresh from the owner's garden. Prices are less than $10.

In Dallas, red sauce-style barbecue, Brunswick stew and all the trimmings are served at the **Hickory House,** 531 W. Memorial Dr. Don't try to call, because they have no phone. More barbecue and a decent country breakfast can be had in Summerville at **Armstrong's,** 216 N. Commerce St., 706/8587-9900. Prices are inexpensive.

Fancier meals are available in Blue Ridge. **Forge Mill Crossing,** Forge Mill

Rd., 706/374-5771, serves pasta, steaks and seafood, and **Michiko's,** 706/492-5093, specializes in sushi as well as other Asian dishes. Prices are moderate to expensive.

LODGING

If you're determined to stay near I-75, you'll have your pick of inexpensive motels. But for true regional flavor, nothing beats the local lodges and inns in the small towns off the beaten path.

In Chatsworth, the **Cohutta Lodge and Convention Center,** 500 Cochise Trail, 706/695-9601, offers rooms with panoramic views of the Cohutta Mountains from $49-$135. Facilities include a heated pool and tennis courts, and guests can book a llama ride through the mountains.

If you're driving on Highway 53 near Tate, look for the pink marble **Tate House,** 770/735-3122. Accommodations include luxury suites with private baths and nine log cabins with fireplaces and hot tubs. Tennis courts and riding stables also are available. Nightly rates, including breakfast, are $120.

Another fine bed-and-breakfast establishment is the **Elderberry Inn,** 75 Dalton St., 706/635-2218. Located in the picturesque apple-farming town of Ellijay, the Victorian inn rents rooms for about $60.

One reason to stay at Jasper's **Woodbridge Inn,** 411 Chambers St., 770/692-6293, is the wonderful steak and seafood served with fine wines in an elegant antebellum atmosphere. Rooms are moderately priced in the $60 range.

More standard accommodations are offered in Blue Ridge at the **Days Inn,** Hwy. 76 N., 706/632-2100, and the **Fannin Inn Motel,** Hwy. 76 S., 706/632-2005. Both offer rooms for less than $50. The Fannin Inn also has a restaurant that serves country cooking.

CAMPING

Campers have a wide selection of sites in Northwest Georgia. In Carrollton south of Cave Spring, **John Tanner State Park,** 354 Tanner's Beach Rd., 800/864-7275, has 78 campsites for $14 nightly, six efficiency units for $50 each, and a recreation area that features the largest lakefront sand beach in the state. Bicycle and boat rentals also are available.

Allatoona Campground and Cottage Rentals, 24 Allatoona Landing Rd., 770/974-3182, in Cartersville is a good place to spend a night or a week. More than 100 campsites in wooded areas or on the lake feature full hookups, dump station, cable TV, laundry, LP gas, on-site security, and a restaurant for $15-$82 per night.

CHIEFTAINS TRAIL

Long before white settlers moved in and Andrew Jackson decided to uproot an entire nation, northwest Georgia was home to a number of different Native American cultures.

The Chieftains Trail, which begins five miles southwest of Cartersville at the **Etowah Indian Mounds,** 813 Indian Mounds Rd., 770/387-3747, is a 150-mile scenic route tracing the different cultures that once flourished in the area. Archaeologists date the Etowah Indian Mounds back to 890 A.D., when the earthen structures were created as ceremonial platforms.

Museum exhibits reflect the rituals and daily village life during the Mississippian Culture period, but no one seems to know what happened to the inhabitants. By the late 17th century, the entire village was abandoned, leaving only the mysterious mounds.

Visitors to the museum can follow a footpath across a section of what was once a moat and across a ceremonial plaza. Those who are up to it can climb the steps to the top of the 63-foot mound for a panoramic view of the village site and the Etowah River. If you continue following the path, you will pass two smaller burial mounds near the river.

From the Etowah Mounds, the Chieftains Trail winds northward to **Rome and the Chieftains Museum,** 501 Riverside Pkwy., 706/291-9494. Exhibits chronicle Native American history from 500 years ago, when the village of Ulibahali stood on the banks of the Etowah and Oostanaula Rivers where they intersected to form the Coosa River. The Spanish explorer Hernando de Soto is believed to have ransacked the village during his expedition in 1540.

A frame house on the banks of the Oostanaula was the home of Cherokee chief Major Ridge, a prosperous farmer and businessman who signed the treaty of New Echota in 1835. Farther north, the Chieftains Trail loops by **New Echota,** Hwy. 225, 706/624-1321, near Calhoun. Established in 1825 as the capital of the Cherokee Nation, New Echota was once a thriving community. Today, only the courthouse, a printing shop, some restored buildings, and several homes that belonged to Cherokee leaders remain. A 1.5-mile trail winds through the village past the building where the bilingual Cherokee newspaper, *The Phoenix,* was published, then continues on to the banks of New Town Creek.

A few miles away in Chatsworth is the **Chief Vann House,** 82 Hwy. 225, 706/695-2598, an impressive brick mansion called the "Showplace of the Cherokee Nation." Built in 1804 by wealthy Cherokee chief James Vann, the house is decorated with hand carvings and fine antiques. Vann owned several inns along the Federal Road (present-day Hwy. 53) and was murdered at one of his taverns in 1809.

More information about Native American heritage sites in Georgia is available by writing to Chieftain's Trail, 300 S. Wall St., Calhoun, GA 30701.

Located in the foothills of the mountains near Calhoun, the **KOA Kampground-Calhoun,** 2523 Redbud Rd., 706/629-3490, provides full service campsites for $17-$31 per night.

In Rising Fawn, **Cloudland Canyon State Park,** 122 Cloudland Canyon Park Rd., 800/864-7275, two- and three-bedroom cabins rent for $65 and up. Each of the 75 campsites includes water and electric hookups for $15. And, in Summerville, 25 campsites with hookups are available for $14 nightly at **James H. "Sloppy" Floyd State Park,** Hwy. 27, 706/857-0826. The park features water sports and fishing on two lakes nestled in the Chattahoochee Forest.

Near Chatsworth, **Lake Conasauga Recreation Area,** 401 Old Ellijay Rd., 706/695-6736, offers hiking, swimming and picnicking along with a 35-site campground with restrooms and water for $5 a night. By the way, this area is one of the best habitats for songbirds in the state. More good camping can be found five miles east of Chatsworth at **Fort Mountain State Park,** 181 Fort Mountain Park Rd., 706/695-2621. The 15 cottages rent for $65 and up, and 70 campsites with water and electric hookups are located on the shores of the lake. Nightly rentals are $16 and daily parking is $2 per car.

3
NORTHEAST MOUNTAINS

A little more than an hour's drive from Atlanta, the Appalachian Mountains of Northeast Georgia are a wonderland of majestic peaks, clear bubbling streams, and green, unspoiled valleys. Thousands of visitors every year enjoy white-water rafting on the Chattooga River where *Deliverance* was filmed, hiking along the Appalachian Trail, or simply browsing through the antiques shops and country stores in Clarkesville, Cleveland, and other picturesque mountain towns.

From Dahlonega, the site of the nation's first gold rush, to Helen and its Bavarian village facade, the Northeast Mountains invite travelers to explore the backroads for man-made and natural wonders. Along the way, roadside stands beckon visitors to stop for a taste of crisp mountain apples, salty boiled peanuts, or freshly bottled sorghum syrup.

The Cherokees called this the "enchanted land" hundreds of years ago, before many of their people were sent to Oklahoma on The Trail of Tears. It still is an enchanted land.

A PERFECT DAY IN THE NORTHEAST MOUNTAINS

Begin with a stroll around the town square in Dahlonega to check out the crafts and antiques shops. Look over the novelties at the General Store and have a cup of coffee for a nickel. Visit the Gold Museum and then try your luck at panning some of the yellow nuggets at Crisson Gold Mine. After lunch at the Wagon Wheel, drive to nearby Cleveland to witness the "birth" of one of Xavier Roberts' Cabbage Patch dolls at BabyLand General Hospital. Spend the afternoon browsing through the Bavarian-style shops in Helen. Dine on mountain trout at the Unicoi Lodge Restaurant and take an after-dinner walk on one of Unicoi Park's scenic trails.

SIGHTSEEING HIGHLIGHTS

★★★★ DAHLONEGA

Twenty years before the California gold rush, Benjamin Parks literally stumbled over a sizable lump of the precious metal and Dahlonega became the first mining boomtown. Today, most of the gold in this picturesque mountain town 55 miles north of Atlanta comes from the pockets of tourists. Gold panning equipment, gold coins, and mining tools from the town's past are displayed in the **Dahlonega Gold Museum,** 706/864-6962, on the town square. A 20-minute film explains the history of the gold rush and the area's Appalachian heritage. For more of a hands-on tour, drop in at the **Consolidated Gold Mine,** 185 Consolidated Rd., 706/864-8473. Visitors are taken 125 feet below ground into mine shafts and then brought above ground to watch experienced prospectors separate the gold flecks in sluice boxes. Amateurs can try their hands at panning just across the road at the **Crisson Gold Mine,** Hwy. 19, 706/864-7998. Prices range from $1 a pan to $8 for a five-gallon bucket of ore. Both mines are open daily.

One of the major festivals in Dahlonega is the annual **Gold Rush Days** in October with crafts demonstrations, dancing, greased pig contests and other fun and games.

Details: Take Ga. 400 from Atlanta to Hwy. 60. Dahlonega Gold Museum is on the town square, 706/864-6962. Open Mon-Sat 9-5, Sun 10-5. $4 adults, $2 children. (2-3 hours)

★★★★ HELEN
85 miles north of Atlanta
Until 1969, Helen was just another sleepy mountain town on the banks of the Chattahoochee River. That's when some of the local businessmen decided to transform Helen into a Bavarian village.

NORTHEAST MOUNTAINS

Alpine Helen now attracts hundreds of thousands of visitors to its rows of Tyrolean-style shops that look as if they have been lifted out of the Alps. Other attractions besides the shops on Main Street are the **Museum of the Hills,** with exhibits documenting the town's evolution from frontier days to the Alpine era, and the **Doll and Toy Museum,** 706/878-3493, which has a collection of more than 2,000 dolls. Would-be prospectors can take an underground tour at the **Gold Mines of Helen,** 706/878-3052, on Hwy. 75 south of town. Nearby on Hwy. 75 is the **Nora Mill Granary,** where an old water-powered gristmill grinds cornmeal, grits, and flour for sale in the store.

Another interesting sight is the **Sautee-Nacoochee Indian Mound,** Hwys. 75 and 17, 706/878-2181, the resting place of two young lovers from warring tribes. Historians estimate that the grave was built in 10,000 B.C.

North of Helen on Georgia 365, visitors can hike up a half-mile trail to see the spectacular twin waterfalls of **Anna Ruby Falls.** A museum at the **Anna Ruby Falls Visitor Center,** 706/754-6221,

SIGHTS

- Ⓐ Babyland General Hospital
- Ⓑ Clarkesville
- Ⓒ Dahlonega
- Ⓓ Foxfire Museum
- Ⓔ Helen
- Ⓕ Tallulah Gorge

FOOD

- Ⓖ Blair House
- Ⓗ Dillard House
- Ⓘ Green Shutters
- Ⓔ Hofbrauhaus Inn
- Ⓙ LaPrade's
- Ⓔ Mountain Valley Kitchen
- Ⓖ North Georgia Restaurant
- Ⓒ Renee's Cafe and Wine Bar

FOOD (continued)

- Ⓒ Smith House
- Ⓑ Taylor's Trolley
- Ⓔ Unicoi Lodge Restaurant
- Ⓒ Wagon Wheel

LODGING

- Ⓞ A Small Motel and Cabin
- Ⓚ Amicalola Falls Lodge
- Ⓑ Chattahoochee Riverfront Motel
- Ⓗ Dillard House Motel
- Ⓒ Econolodge
- Ⓛ Fieldstone Inn
- Ⓑ Glen-Ella Springs Inn
- Ⓔ Helendorf River Inn
- Ⓘ Old Clayton Inn
- Ⓒ Smith House
- Ⓔ Unicoi Lodge

LODGING (continued)

- Ⓒ Worley Homestead
- Ⓓ York House Bed and Breakfast Inn

CAMPING

- Ⓜ Bald Mountain Campground and Resort
- Ⓝ Black Rock Mountain State Park
- Ⓜ Brasstown Village Resort
- Ⓒ Dockery Lake Recreation Area
- Ⓛ Hiawassee Campground
- Ⓞ Moccasin Creek State Park

Note: Items with the same letter are located in the same area.

ALPINE HELEN'S OKTOBERFEST

features a gift shop and a display where kids can touch the fur of different kinds of animals.

The biggest annual event in Helen is **Oktoberfest,** a two-month festival in September and October that features German food, music, and lots of beer.

Details: *Take I-85 to I-985 north to Hwy. 384. Turn left; go 20 miles to Hwy. 75. Turn right and go three miles to Helen. Museum of the Hills, 8590 Main St., 706/878-3140. Open daily 10-6. $4 adults, $3 students, $2 children, $3.50 seniors. (2-4 hours)*

★★★★ FOXFIRE MUSEUM
2837 Hwy. 441, 706/746-5828

In Mountain City north of Clayton, bits and pieces of Appalachian heritage are preserved as exhibits in a log cabin built by local students involved in the Foxfire project. Former Rabun County schoolteacher Eliot Wigginton initiated Foxfire in the 1960s as a way for students to collect oral histories and learn Appalachian skills such as basket-weaving and hog-butchering from the older residents of the area. The interviews and articles were compiled in a series of Foxfire magazines and books. Guided tours are available through a Foxfire village constructed of authentic log cabins and furniture.

Details: Open Mon-Sat 9-4:30. $7.50 adults, $3 children. (1-2 hours)

★★★ CLARKESVILLE

One of the first resort towns in Northeast Georgia, Clarkesville was the place where coastal Georgians came to escape the heat and mosquitoes of summer. The town is now a favorite shopping stop for travelers on their way to Helen or the mountains of Rabun County. The historic town square features antique shops, boutiques, craft stores, and an interesting bookstore. The **Habersham Bank Hospitality Center** on the square provides refreshments and information on area attractions.

One of the most popular destinations is the **Mark of the Potter,** 706/947-3440, 10 miles north of town on Hwy. 97 on the Soque River. The former gristmill has been converted into a shop filled with the works of local potters. Children can stand on the porch overlooking the river and drop food pellets to the enormous trout swimming below.

Details: From Helen, take Hwy. 75 north to Hwy. 356. Turn right and go to Hwy. 197. Turn right and follow that into town. Habersham Bank Hospitality Center, on the Square, 706/754-5259. Open Mon-Wed 9-4, Tue-Fri 9-6, Sat 9-12. (2-4 hours)

★★★ TALLULAH GORGE
Hwy. 441, Tallulah Falls, 706/754-7979

If looking over the rim of this 1,000-foot gorge makes you dizzy, imagine crossing it on a tightrope. That's what circus patriarch Karl Wallenda did in 1970 to the amazement of hundreds of spectators. The spectacular two-mile gorge is carved through quartzite rock by the Tallulah River, which cascades 700 feet to the canyon floor in a series of three waterfalls. The Tallulah Gorge State Park has an interpretive center with exhibits and a film, and the Tallullah Gallery across the road from the gorge features paintings, pottery, and weavings by local artists.

Details: Park is open 8-dark. (1-2 hours)

★★ BABYLAND GENERAL HOSPITAL
19 Underwood St., Cleveland, 706/865-2171

The obsession over Xavier Roberts' Cabbage Patch dolls is just a memory in the toy business, but the pinched-face dolls are still being born with regularity at BabyLand General Hospital in Cleveland. Thousands of visitors gather in the hospital for "live" births of preemies, and anxious little girls wait for the adoption papers to be filled out for their new Cabbage Patch babies. The hospital also does restoration on vintage dolls who have suffered wear and tear at the hands of their owners.

Details: *Open Mon-Fri 8:30-5:30, Sat 9-5, Sun 10-5. Free. (1 hour)*

FITNESS AND RECREATION

Even if you don't want to hike the **Appalachian Trail** the entire 2,144 miles to Maine, you can walk 78 miles and still stay in Georgia. The beginning of the trail is on **Springer Mountain,** about eight miles from **Amicalola Falls State Park,** 18 miles west of Dahlonega on Hwy. 52, via an approach trail. For a shorter hike, the **Lake Winfield Scott** area off Hwy. 180 has a 5.3 - mile loop that connects with the Appalachian Trail. Or at **Unicoi Gap,** Hwys. 17 and 75, you can take a 10.4-mile hike to Tray Mountain for an incredible view.

In **Vogel State Park,** south of Blairsville on Hwy. 19, a network of trails includes a four-mile loop for average hikers and a more strenuous 12.7-mile stretch.

North of Blairsville, **Lake Nottely** offers fishing and rafting opportunities. Inner tubes can be rented at the **Nottely River Campground,** Hwy. 19, 706/745-6711. A shuttle will pick you up downriver.

For more adventurous water sports, the **Chattooga River** in Rabun County is one of the most popular spots for white-water canoeing, rafting, and kayaking. Section One above the Highway 28 bridge is calmer and is perfect for swimming or floating on inner tubes. Section Two is suitable for beginners and Section Three is a 12-mile stretch of several Class III and Class IV rapids. Only experienced rafters venture onto Section Four with its hazardous rapids. All of the white-water scenes in the movie *Deliverance* were filmed on the Chattooga.

Guided white-water adventures can be booked through **Nantahala Outdoor Center,** 800/232-7238; **Wild Water Ltd.,** 800/451-9972; or **Southeastern Expeditions,** 800/868-7238. Most of the trips take up to six hours. In addition to white-water rafting, the outfitters offer packages that include biking or horseback riding and accommodations at local motels.

Hikers and backpackers who don't want to get wet can follow the **Chattooga River Trail** on a scenic 20-mile trek beginning at the Highway 76 bridge. The trail is clearly marked.

Out-of-state fishing licenses and trout stamps are available for those who want to try their luck in some of the streams, but make sure to drop by **Andy's Trout Farm,** Betty's Creek Rd., 706/746-2550, in Dillard. Fishing equipment is provided and catches are guaranteed. Just be prepared to pay for each fish. For skiers, **Sky Valley,** 706/746-5301, east of Dillard on Hwy. 246, is the only resort in North Georgia. Man-made snow is blown on the slopes when the weather doesn't cooperate. In addition, the resort features an 18-hole golf course, tennis courts, a swimming pool, and chalet rentals.

FOOD

Finding a place to eat in the Northeast Mountains is no problem. Dozens of restaurants offer everything from Southern fried chicken to German strudel. In Dahlonega, the **Smith House,** 84 S. Chestatee St., 706/864-2348, is legendary for its enormous family-style meals. Be prepared to eat heartily. Prices are in the $12-$15 range.

For a lighter meal, **Renee's Cafe and Wine Bar,** 135 N. Chestatee St., 706/864-6829, serves grilled fish and pasta with a good selection of wines at moderate prices. About a mile out of town on Hwy. 19, the **Wagon Wheel,** 706/864-6677, draws a mostly local crowd for cafeteria-style lunches and dinners of fried catfish, Southern vegetables, and fried chicken. Prices are very reasonable.

In Blairsville, a good place to get an inexpensive breakfast of biscuits and country ham is the **North Georgia Restaurant** on the square, 706/745-5888. Fancier fare such as fish and shrimp can be found for moderate to expensive prices at the **Blair House,** 706/745-3399, five miles north of town on Hwy. 19.

Helen has an eclectic mix of restaurants, from the down-home **Mountain Valley Kitchen,** Chattahoochee St., 706/878-2508, to the **Hofbrauhaus Inn** Main St., 706/878-2248, where you can dine on stroganoff and schnitzel at moderate prices. For probably the best meal in town, your best bet is the **Unicoi Lodge Restaurant** north of town at Unicoi State Park, 706/878-2201. The restaurant serves three meals a day and specializes in mountain trout. Prices are in the $10-$20 range.

If you're hungry when you pass through Clarkesville, **Taylor's Trolley** on the square, 706/754-5566, offers sandwiches, burgers, shakes, and daily specials. Or, if you're really hungry, take a drive up Highway 197 to **LaPrade's,** 706/947-3313, a rustic mountain resort with a restaurant that serves family-style meals of fried chicken, country steak, hot biscuits, and fresh vegetables at moderate prices.

Visitors to Clayton will want to be sure and stop at **Green Shutters** on S. Main St., 706/782-3342, for a reasonably priced family-style meal of fried chicken, seasoned vegetables, and homemade cinnamon rolls. Those with bigger appetites should wait until they get to the **Dillard House** off Hwy. 441, 706/746-5348. This famous restaurant offers a spectacular view of valleys and mountains and serves all-you-can-eat family-style meals with fresh vegetables from the Dillard House garden. Fried chicken and country ham are almost always on the menu with another meat and eight or nine different vegetables and a dessert. Prices are $12-$15.

LODGING

The best thing about most of the hotels and lodges in Northeast Georgia is the view. In Dawsonville, the **Amicalola Falls Lodge,** 418 Amicalola Falls Lodge Rd., 800/864-7275, offers 57 rooms with a spectacular view of the Blue Ridge. Most of the rooms have porches and rent for around $80. For slightly higher rates, you can rent one of the 14 fully equipped cottages with fireplaces. Guests can dine at the Lodge Restaurant, which features a delicious buffet for breakfast, lunch and dinner.

Another lodge with a great lake and mountain view is Hiawassee's **Fieldstone Inn,** 3499 Hwy. 76, 706/896-2262. The wood-and-stone building offers a fine restaurant, 66 guest rooms overlooking Lake Chatuge, tennis courts, and a swimming pool for $80 and up.

In addition to serving fine meals, Dahlonega's **Smith House,** 84 S. Chestatee St., 706/864-2348, provides 16 moderately priced rooms in a Victorian setting. The **Worley Homestead,** 410 W. Main St., 706/864-7002, is a quaint bed-and-breakfast with eight guest rooms in an 1845 house just off the square. Rates are $65-$85.

For more economical lodging in Dahlonega, the **Econolodge,** Hwy. 19, 706/864-6191, offers modern rooms and a pool a half mile from downtown for $39-$90.

In Helen, the **Unicoi Lodge,** Hwy. 356, 800/864-7275, offers rooms and cottages from $49-$69 in a beautiful wooded setting in Unicoi State Park. Downtown Helen has a number of good motels, including the **Chattahoochee Riverfront Motel,** 8949 N. Main St., 706/878-2184, with rooms starting at $40, and the **Helendorf River Inn,** 33 Munichstrasse, 706/878-2271, with rates ranging from $24-$160, depending on the season. Both overlook the river and are convenient to the downtown shopping district. For a secluded stay in the mountains, Clarkesville's **Glen-Ella Springs Inn,** Bear Gap Rd. off Hwy. 441, 800/552-3479, is ideal for a romantic getaway. The

100-year-old inn offers 16 guest rooms with rocking chair porches and a tin roof for $100 and up. Tastefully prepared dinners are served in the dining room, and guests are invited to take walks around the wooded grounds or relax by the fireplace in the cozy lobby.

A number of moderately priced motels welcome visitors entering Clayton, including the **Old Clayton Inn,** Main St., 706/782-7722, with rooms for $49 and up, and **A Small Motel and Cabin,** Hwy. 76, 706/782-6488, with rates starting at $38. Farther north up Hwy. 441 in Mountain City, the **York House Bed and Breakfast Inn,** York House Rd., 706/746-2068, offers antiques-filled rooms with fireplaces in an 1896 house for $69 and up.

Adjoining the Dillard House restaurant in Dillard, the **Dillard House Motel,** Hwy. 441, 706/746-5348, rents rooms in a picturesque setting for $55 and up. Attractive features include tennis courts, riding stables, and a convenient location near the restaurant.

CAMPING

There is no shortage of campsites in North Georgia, and most are near lakes or streams. In Dahlonega, the **Dockery Lake Recreation Area,** Hwy. 60, provides campsites beside a three-acre trout lake for $6. In Hiawassee, the **Bald Mountain Campground and Resort,** 3540 Fodder Creek Rd., 706/896-2274, is set beside a rushing stream and a spring-fed swimming pool. Rates are $15-$20 and activities include miniature golf, paddleboats, and a playground. The **Brasstown Village Resort,** 1000 State Rte. 180, 706/896-1641, is an upscale resort nestled on 48 acres in the Chatthoochee National Forest with waterfalls and trout streams. Thirteen cabins rent for $74 to $160. Thirty-five RV sites with full hookups also are available. The **Hiawassee Campground,** 2068 W. Hwy. 76, 706/896-1216, has 42 full hookups for RVs, large motorhomes, or tents. The campground is located near the site of the annual Georgia Mountain Fair in August.

On Lake Burton, **Moccasin Creek State Park,** Hwy. 197, 706/947-3194, offers 54 campsites with hookups for around $15. And, in Rabun County, **Black Rock Mountain State Park,** off Hwy. 441, 800/864-7252, is the highest state park in Georgia. Ten cottages with fireplaces and 64 campsites are located in secluded woods near a 17-acre lake. Campsites rent for $16 and cottages for $60 and up.

NIGHTLIFE

As you might expect, most of the nightlife in the mountains takes place among the forest creatures unless there's a festival going on. In September and October, Helen's Oktoberfest features daily and nightly activities and **Unicoi State Park,** Hwy. 56, 706/878-2201, near Helen features a **Spring Bluegrass Concert and Dance** the third week in March and an **Appalachian Music Festival** in July.

The Reach of Song, a play performed every summer at Young Harris College, Hwy. 76, in Hiawassee, draws visitors from as far away as Atlanta. The play tells the story of the Appalachian people to the accompaniment of banjo and fiddle music. Call 800/262-7664 for reservations.

Scenic Route: North Georgia Mountains

One of the prettiest routes in the mountains is along Hwy. 76 from Dalton to Clayton. **Dalton**, the carpet capital of the world, is easily accessible from Atlanta via I-75. If you're interested, tours of some of the carpet mills are available.

From Dalton, head across the foothills of the Cohutta Mountains 11 miles to **Chatsworth**, an isolated town that is the gateway to hiking trails in the Cohutta Wilderness. A Forest Service Office, 401 Old Ellijay Rd., 706/695-6736, offers maps to the area.

Detour a couple of miles over to the **Chief Vann House**, Hwy. 52, 706/695-2598, to see a restored brick mansion that was built in 1804 for Chief James Vann of the Cherokee Nation. Stay on Hwy. 52 for five miles to the **Cohutta Lodge and Restaurant**, 706/695-9601. Stay long enough to take a four-hour llama ride through the mountains or have lunch in the lodge with a panoramic view of the Cohuttas.

Continue on Hwy. 52 for 18 miles to **Ellijay**, an apple-growing town with antique shops and quaint stores. From there, follow the Hwy. 76 scenic route along the Ellijay River north for 15 miles to **Blue Ridge**. The gateway to the Blue Ridge Mountains, the town features 13-mile train rides on the Blue Ridge Scenic Railway, 706/532-9833, in the heart of downtown. Stop at the Blue Ridge Lake recreation area for swimming, fishing, hiking, or boating.

Continue east of Hwy. 76 through some glorious mountain scenery for 21 miles to **Blairsville** and **Lake Nottely** on Hwy. 19. If it's summer, rent tubes at the Nottely River Campground, 706/746-6711, and cool off.

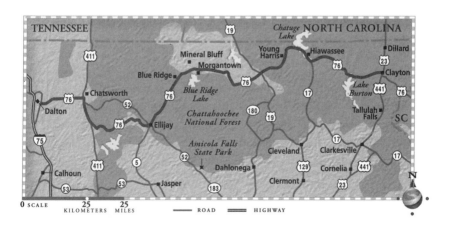

Nine miles east of Blairsville is **Young Harris**, a scenic mountain town that is the home of Young Harris College and former governor Zell Miller. From there, it's five miles to **Hiawassee**, scene of the Georgia Mountain Fair every August. The lakeside Fieldstone Inn and Restaurant, Hwy. 76, 706/545-3408, is a good place to spend the night or just stop and enjoy steak and seafood.

Continue east on Hwy. 76 through more beautiful scenery for 21 miles to **Clayton** in Rabun County. The largest town in the county, Clayton has a number of interesting stores and antiques shops. It also is near the Bartram Trail and the Chattooga River. White-water excursions can be booked at Southeastern Expeditions, 800/868-7238. Accommodations are available at the Old Clayton Inn, Main St., 706/782-5485, for about $50, and delicious country meals of fried chicken are served at Green Shutters, S. Main St., 706/782-3342. The trip from Dalton to Clayton takes about three hours without stops.

4
GAINESVILLE AND LAKE LANIER AREA

Nestled in the foothills of the Blue Ridge on the shores of Lake Lanier, Gainesville is an outdoor lover's dream. More than 25 golf courses, miles of hiking trails, and dozens of recreational areas on Lake Lanier provide opportunities for a multitude of activities.

Gainesville itself, the largest city in North Georgia and the Poultry Capital of the World, is a picture-postcard town that has retained much of its charm despite creeping industrial development. Shady and attractive streets of Victorian and antebellum homes lead to a downtown square that is still commercially vibrant.

Gainesville's main attraction, of course, is Lake Lanier with its beaches, marinas, and resort complex. Named for Georgia poet Sidney Lanier, the 38,000-acre lake was built in 1957 when the Army Corps of Engineers constructed Buford Dam on the Chattahoochee River. When the area was flooded, however, the engineers were surprised to find several parcels of land had remained above water. Making the best of the situation, they developed them as the Lake Lanier Islands resort.

In addition to the numerous outdoor activities available, Gainesville also offers attractions for art and history buffs. The Quinlan Arts Center has exhibited works by Andrew Wyeth and other great American artists, and the Georgia Mountain Museum provides a fascinating introduction to the Appalachian heritage.

GAINESVILLE/LAKE LANIER

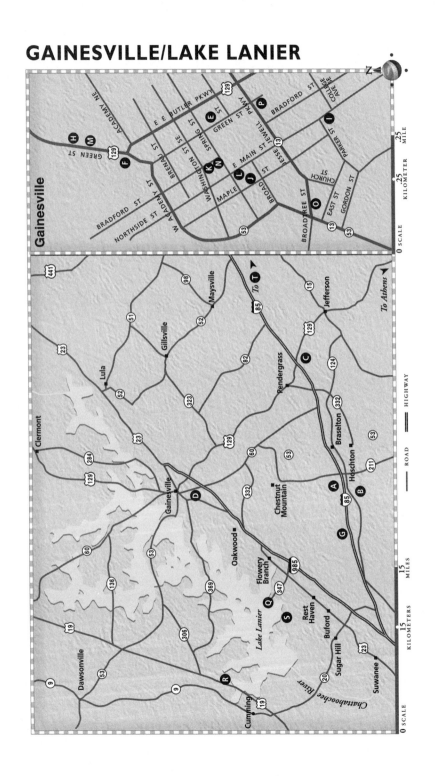

A PERFECT DAY IN THE GAINESVILLE AND LAKE LANIER AREA

Start your day with muffins and coffee at Penny University. Stroll by the Big Chicken statue a block off the downtown square on your way to the Georgia Mountains Museum. Browse through the exhibits at the Quinlan Art Center and grab a salad or sandwich at the Two Dog Cafe and Bakery before heading for Lake Lanier. Spend the afternoon swimming, sunbathing, or playing in the water park. Dine at one of the fine restaurants at the Renaissance Pine Isle Resort and end your evening with a houseboat ride as the sun sets over the lake.

ORIENTATION

Gainesville is located about 60 miles north of Atlanta. Take I-85 north to I-985 to exit 6. An Amtrak rail route also runs through Gainesville with a stop on Main St. about a mile from downtown. Schedules are available by calling 800/872-7245. A Greyhound bus station is located on Myrtle St. at Hwy. 129. Call 800/231-2222 for schedules. The downtown area, developed around the courthouse square, is ideal for walking.

SIGHTS

- **A** Chateau Elan Winery
- **B** Chestnut Mountain Winery
- **C** Crawford W. Long Museum
- **D** Elachee Nature Center
- **E** Georgia Mountains Museum
- **F** Green Street Historic District
- **G** Mayfield Dairy Farms
- **H** Quinlan Arts Center

FOOD

- **I** Big Bear Cafe

FOOD (continued)

- **A** Chateau Elan
- **J** Luna's
- **K** The Monkey Barrel
- **L** Penny University
- **M** Rudolph's
- **N** Two Dog Cafe and Bakery

LODGING

- **A** Chateau Elan Hotel
- **A** Days Inn-Chateau Elan
- **O** Days Inn-Gainesville
- **F** Dunlap House Bed & Breakfast
- **P** Hampton Inn-Gainesville

LODGING (continued)

- **Q** Lake Lanier Islands Hilton
- **Q** Renaissance Pine Isle Resort

CAMPING

- **R** Bald Ridge Creek Park Campground
- **Q** Lake Lanier Islands
- **R** Sawnee Park Campground
- **R** Shady Grove Park Campground
- **S** Shoal Creek Campground
- **T** Victoria Bryant State Park

Note: Items with the same letter are located in the same area.

SIGHTSEEING HIGHLIGHTS

★★★★ **GEORGIA MOUNTAINS MUSEUM**
311 Green St., 770/536-0889
Designated as a Smithsonian Museum, this facility features a number of exhibits on local history, including memorabilia from artist Ed Dodd, creator of the Mark Trail comic strip. Other attractions include a section on black history, a collection of crafts and books by North Georgians, a Cabbage Patch Kids display, and an exhibit devoted to Confederate General James Longstreet.
Details: Call for tour hours. $2 adults, $1 children. (1-2 hours)

★★★★ **QUINLAN ARTS CENTER**
514 Green St., 770/536-2575
This small gallery scored something of a coup when it landed an exhibit of the works of the Wyeth family. The center offers films, lectures and classes and displays the work of member artists in the historic Redwine House next door.
Details: Open Mon-Fri 9-5, Sat 10-4, Sun 1-4. (1-2 hours)

★★★ **ELACHEE NATURE CENTER**
Old Atlanta Hwy., 770/535-1976
A natural history museum with live animal exhibits and a native plant garden is the centerpiece of this 1,200-acre woodland preserve. Other features include hiking trails, botanical gardens, wildlife exhibits, a picnic site, and a gift shop.
Details: Open Mon-Sat 10-5. (1-2 hours)

★★★ **GREEN STREET HISTORIC DISTRICT**
Just north of downtown, this half-mile section of Gainesville features several nineteenth- and twentieth-century Victorian and Neoclassical residences that have been included on the National Register of Historic Places.
Details: Tour information available at Visitors Bureau, 830 Green St., 770/536-5209. (1 hour)

★★★ **CRAWFORD W. LONG MUSEUM**
28 College St., Jefferson, 706-367-5307
A few miles east of Gainesville, this small but interesting museum pays tribute to the medical contributions of Dr. Crawford W. Long, the

physician who discovered and developed modern anesthesia. Other exhibits focus on the history of Jackson County and include a typical nineteenth-century general store and an 1840s doctor's office.
Details: Open Tue-Sat 10-4. Free. (1 hour)

★★★ **CHATEAU ELAN WINERY**
I-85 north from Atlanta, exit 48, 800/233-9463
Built as a reproduction of an eighteenth-century French chateau, Chateau Elan is the centerpiece of a resort that includes acres of vineyards, a winery, restaurants, a hotel, shops, golf courses, a health spa, and an Irish pub. (The pub may seem out of place in a French winery, but the owner of Chateau Elan, Donald Panoz, is Irish.) Located near Braselton, the chateau is decorated with murals of French landscapes and features a gift shop, restaurant, and wine-tasting area. Tours of the vineyards and winery are conducted daily.
Details: Open daily. (2 hours)

★★ **CHESTNUT MOUNTAIN WINERY**
I-85 north from Atlanta, exit 48, 770/867-6914
This smaller, less elaborate version of Chateau Elan is also located near Braselton, the little town that movie star Kim Basinger bought. Set in 30 wooded acres, the winery offers free tastings and a tour of the wine cellar.
Details: Open Tue-Sat 10-6, Sun 12:30-5. (1 hour)

★ **MAYFIELD DAIRY FARMS**
1160 Broadway, Braselton, 706/654-9180
Got milk? If you don't, this is the place to go. Kids will enjoy a close-up and personal look at the dairy herd and a tour of the milk processing plant. Best of all, there's a gift shop with an ice cream bar.
Details: Open Mon-Sat 9-5, Sun 1-5. Last tour begins at 4. (1 hour)

FITNESS AND RECREATION
With its 540 miles of shorelines, 10 marinas, and 20 beaches, **Lake Lanier** is one of the most popular water playgrounds in North Georgia. Information for all of the public facilities is available at the **Resource Manager's Office,** Buford Dam Rd., 770/945-9531.
If you don't have your own boat, don't worry. **Thrill Sports,** 770/614-

1602, located about a mile east of the Resource Manager's Office, rents boats and ski equipment.

For family fun, **Lake Lanier Islands,** 6950 Holiday Rd., 770/932-7200, on the southeastern end of the lake offers an elaborate water park, sandy beaches, swimming pools, and paddleboat and canoe rentals. Swimming areas are open on weekends in May and daily from June until Labor Day. Admission is $19.95 adults, $12.95 children.

Golfers can test their skills on the resort's two 18-hole courses at **Emerald Pointe Golf Club,** 770/945-8787, and **Pinelsle Golf Course,** 770/945-8921. More golf is available in Braselton at the 63-hole **Chateau Elan Golf Club,** 6060 Golf Club Dr., 770/271-6050. Tennis courts and an equestrian center are also open to the public at Chateau Elan.

Racing fans can catch some action on Saturdays from March through October at **Lanier National Speedway** in Braselton, One Raceway Dr., 770/967-8600, where NASCAR drivers compete on a 3/8-mile asphalt track. Tom Cruise and Paul Newman have occasionally been spotted behind the wheels of their racecars at **Road Atlanta,** 5300 Winder Hwy., 770/967-6143, a premier 2.52-mile circuit for sports cars and motorcycles. Open daily 9-5 and on weekends during race events.

FOOD

Most of the best restaurants in the Gainesville area are located in the hotels. An exception is **Rudolph's,** 700 Green St., 770/534-2226, an upscale restaurant in an English Tudor mansion. Specialties include Georgia mountain trout, steaks, and prime rib. Other fine dining at moderate to expensive prices in Gainesville can be found at **Luna's,** 200 Main St., in the art deco Hunt Tower Building.

For more reasonably priced dining, **The Big Bear Cafe,** 895 Main St., near the Amtrak station, serves breakfast, meat-and-three meals, and burgers. A great place to get fresh-baked breads, soup, and sandwiches is the **Two Dog Cafe and Bakery,** 109 Bradford St. A favorite is the portabello mushroom and roasted pepper sandwich.

And **The Monkey Barrel,** 115 Washington St., serves everything from pizza and pasta to sandwiches and microbrews.

Also in Gainesville, **Penny University,** Main St., 770/287-3664, offers pastries, muffins, and gourmet coffee for breakfast and sandwiches for lunch and dinner.

Chateau Elan in Braselton, I-85, exit 48, 800/233-9463, offers a variety of dining experiences, from its café with French country dishes and selection of local wines to its Irish pub with traditional items such as fish and chips, lamb stew, and shepherd's pie. Meals are moderately priced to expensive, depending on your choice of wines.

LODGING

If it's a romantic occasion and you don't mind splurging on $200-plus rooms, **Chateau Elan Hotel** near Braselton, 100 Rue Charlemagne, 800/233-9463, is an elegant place to spend the night. Otherwise, the **Days Inn-Chateau Elan,** 2069 Hwy. 211, 770/867-8100, is conveniently located near the resort for rates starting at $69.

In Gainesville's historic district, the **Dunlap House Bed & Breakfast,** 635 Green St., 770/536-0200, features 10 rooms nicely decorated with period furniture. Each room has a private bath, and a full breakfast is served. Rates are $95-$105.

For other accommodations, the **Days Inn-Gainesville,** 809 Jesse Jewell Pkwy., 770/534-0303, with rates at $55 and up, and the **Hampton Inn-Gainesville,** 450 Jesse Jewell Pkwy., 770/503-0300, with rates around $40, are conveniently located near downtown.

In the Lake Lanier area, the **Lake Lanier Islands Hilton,** 7000 Holiday Rd., 770/945-8787, provides 216 rooms with resort amenities for $160 and up. Similar prices and accommodations are available at **Renaissance Pine Isle Resort,** 9000 Holiday Rd., 770/932-7200. Rates vary by season.

CAMPING

Campers can rent lakeside sites in the **Lake Lanier Islands** area for tents or RVs, 770/932-7270, bunk in one of 30 cabins, or spend the night on a houseboat. Camping sites range from $15.50 and up, depending on location. For cabin rentals, 770/831-9400, a one-bedroom with room for four people rents for $200. Or, if you prefer, you can rent a houseboat that sleeps 10 for $349 a night. For houseboat reservations, call 770/932-7255.

Near the dam on Lake Lanier, **Shoal Creek Campground,** 6300 Shadburn Ferry Rd., 770/945-9541, offers campsites and hookups for $10-$18 from April to September.

North of Gainesville, **Victoria Bryant State Park,** Hwy. 27 two miles north of Franklin Springs, 706/245-6270, provides 25 campground sites with hookups for $14 a night. The 406-acre park also offers hiking trails and a swimming pool.

And, in Cumming, campsites and hookups for less than $20 are available at

Bald Ridge Creek Park Campground, 4100 Bald Ridge Rd., 770/889-1591; **Sawnee Park Campground,** 3200 Buford Dam Rd., 770/887-0592; and **Shady Grove Park Campground,** 7800 Shadburn Ferry Rd., 770/945-9531. Bald Ridge is open year-round; Sawnee and Shady Grove are open from April through Labor Day.

NIGHTLIFE

Lake Lanier Islands, 6950 Holiday Rd., 770/932-7200, features several musical events, including a **Beach Music Blast** on Memorial Day weekend, a special concert with fireworks on the Fourth of July, and a series of free concerts on Fridays during the summer.

    Chateau Elan, exit 48 off I-85, 800/233-9463, also sponsors a number of outdoor summer concerts, and top-notch country music stars appear regularly from May through November at Cumming's **Lanierland Music Park,** 6115 Jot'em Down Rd., 770/887-7464.

    For a true Southern experience, however, the **Lantern Inn** in Cumming, Hwy. 369, 770/887-3080, provides the best show east of Las Vegas. Club owner Mike Jones performs as an Elvis impersonator in addition to cooking catfish and fried chicken in the kitchen. Jones works the crowd, singing and handing out polyester scarves, while his father, Harold, operates the karaoke machine. A country buffet is served before the shows every Friday and Saturday night.

5
ATHENS

Known as "the Classic City," Athens is home to the University of Georgia and the cradle for popular bands such as R.E.M., the B-52s, and others.

Unlike Atlanta, Athens managed to escape the wrath of General Sherman. The result is a number of charming historic cottages and some grand antebellum homes that would make Scarlett O'Hara envious.

Located about 65 miles east of Atlanta, Athens is definitely a college town. When classes are in session, 30,000 students double the size of the city. During Georgia Bulldogs home football games, the town turns into one big parking lot and party.

There's more to life in Athens than sports and music, of course, and visitors interested in strolling along shady, picturesque streets and touring classic antebellum homes will find much to do. And for those not attuned to the alternative music scene, the city and university offer a cultural variety of theater, classical music, and art. A number of authors reside in Athens, and the nationally acclaimed *Georgia Review* and University of Georgia Press have made the town something of a literary oasis in the state.

Whatever your interest, Athens and the neighboring towns of Watkinsville and Washington are wonderful places to see the results of the merging of the Old South and the New South.

ATHENS

Downtown Athens

NORTH AV

STRONG ST

FOUNDRY ST

BROAD ST

BUS 78

THOMAS ST

BROAD ST

15

JACKSON ST

Q

COLLEGE ST AV

B

CLAYTON ST

COLLEGE ST

K

DOUGHERTY ST

HANCOCK ST

WASHINGTON ST

O

LUMPKIN ST

BUS 78

R

HULL ST

BROAD ST

PRINCE ST

15A

10

Y

BOGART RD

BUS 78

10

.25 MILE

.25 KILOMETER

0 SCALE

72

Z

29

8

J

NEW HULL RD

DANIELSVILLE RD

COMMERCE RD

441

15

A

U

441

15

LOOP

10

129

PRINCE AV

L

JEFFERSON RD

LOOP

10

15A

129

HAWTHORNE

ATHENS PERIMETER

BUS 78

P

EPPS BRIDGE PKWY

10 LOOP

316

29 78

78

316

29

8

78

OLYMPIC DR

CHEROKEE RD

10 LOOP

8 29

NORTH AV

N THOMAS ST

LEXINGTON RD

EAST CAMPUS

15

Downtown

E

T V

S W M

B

CARLTON

LUMPKIN ST

MLLEDGE

N

BROAD ST

BAXTER ST

KING AV

ALPS RD

WESTLAKE ST

TIMOTHY RD

S LUMPKIN ST

ATHENS PERIMETER

15

10 8

LOOP

78

G

78

10

University of Georgia

29

15

C

F

78

441

15A

SOUTH MILLEDGE RD

D

15

441

123

X

H

GAINES SCHOOL RD

COLLEGE STATION RD

BARNETT SHOALS RD

WHITEHALL RD

I

N

0 SCALE   2 KILOMETERS MILES

2

━━━ ROAD   ━━━ HIGHWAY

A PERFECT DAY IN ATHENS

Begin your tour of Athens downtown at the statue of Athena in front of the Classic Center on Thomas Street. Drop in at The Steeple on Oconee Street, the site of R.E.M.'s musical debut, and rest a moment at the University Arch, a landmark on College Street and entrance to the campus. Stroll along the shaded walkways between the historic buildings of the Old College and visit University Chapel.

Take a reading break at the Main Library or stop for a lunch of burgers, fries, and a milkshake at The Grill on College Avenue. After lunch, spend the afternoon at the Georgia Museum of Art on the campus and finish the day with a Cajun dinner at Harry Bissett's. Cap off your evening with drinks and music at the 40 Watt Club.

ORIENTATION

Athens is located about 60 miles east of Atlanta via I-85 to Hwy. 316. Another route is Hwy. 78 east from Atlanta. Walking is the best way to get around the downtown area and the University of Georgia campus. College Avenue is the main drag with side streets crossing east and west. Bus tours are available at Classic City Tours, 280 E. Dougherty St., 706/353-1820.

SIGHTS

- **Ⓐ** ENSAT Center
- **Ⓑ** Founders Memorial Garden
- **Ⓒ** Georgia Museum of Art
- **Ⓓ** State Botanical Garden
- **Ⓔ** Taylor-Grady House
- **Ⓕ** University of Georgia Campus
- **Ⓖ** Washington
- **Ⓗ** Watkinsville

FOOD

- **Ⓖ** Another Thyme
- **Ⓗ** Aunt Gail's Bake Shop
- **Ⓘ** Charlie Williams' Pinecrest Lodge

FOOD (continued)

- **Ⓙ** Fresh Air Barbecue
- **Ⓚ** The Grill
- **Ⓛ** The Grit
- **Ⓜ** Henry Bisset's New Orleans Cafe
- **Ⓝ** Hot Thomas Barbecue & Peach Orchard
- **Ⓝ** Jittery Joe's
- **Ⓞ** Last Resort Grill
- **Ⓟ** Pinecrest to Go
- **Ⓠ** Weaver D's Fine Foods
- **Ⓡ** Wilson's Soul Food Inc.
- **Ⓢ** The Varsity

LODGING

- **Ⓗ** Ashford Manor Bed and Breakfast

LODGING (continued)

- **Ⓣ** Best Western Colonial Inn
- **Ⓤ** Bulldog Inn
- **Ⓗ** Hawks Nest Hostel
- **Ⓝ** Holiday Inn
- **Ⓥ** Magnolia Terrace
- **Ⓖ** Maynard Manor
- **Ⓦ** TraveLodge

CAMPING

- **Ⓧ** Alexander H. Stephens State Historic Park
- **Ⓨ** Fort Yargo State Park
- **Ⓩ** Watson Mill Bridge State Park

Note: Items with the same letter are located in the same area.

SIGHTSEEING HIGHLIGHTS

★★★ UNIVERSITY OF GEORGIA CAMPUS
College Ave.

Founded in 1785, the University of Georgia is the country's oldest chartered state university. Located in the heart of Athens, the 40,000-acre campus begins at **The University Arch,** an iron structure that was erected in 1857. According to tradition, no freshmen were allowed to pass under it. Beyond the arch is the **Old College,** a collection of historic buildings set amid stately hardwoods. Be sure to visit the **University Chapel,** an excellent example of neo-classic architecture, and stop at the Main Library, where book lovers are invited to come in and browse.

Details: Guided tours and maps available at the University of Georgia Visitors Center, Four Towers Bldg., College Station Rd., 770/542-0842. (2 hours)

★★★ GEORGIA MUSEUM OF ART
90 Carlton St., 706/542-4602

Exhibits in this new facility feature more than 7,000 paintings and sculptures from nineteenth- and twentieth-century artists. In addition, lectures are scheduled on a regular basis and art films are shown weekly. Souvenirs and works by local artists are for sale at the museum's gift shop, and a small café offers a scenic view of the campus.

Details: Open Tue-Sat 10-5, Sun 1-5. Free. Admission to film screenings, $3. (2 hours)

★★★ STATE BOTANICAL GARDEN
2450 S. Milledge Ave., 706/542-1244

This lush 313-acre garden bordering the Middle Oconee River is a wonderland of greenery. Five miles of nature trails wind through gardens of roses and rhododendrons and wooded areas where you might catch a glimpse of deer, squirrels and other wildlife. A visitors center, café, and gift shop are located in the three-story Conservatory.

Details: Conservatory is open Mon-Sat 9-4:30, Sun 11:30-4:30. Gardens are open daily 9-sunset. Free. (2-3 hours)

★★ FOUNDERS MEMORIAL GARDEN
325 S. Lumpkin St., 706/542-3631

Formal gardens with camelias and native plants afford visitors a quiet place to walk and relax. The **Athens Garden Club,** located in an 1857 Greek Revival house next door, also opens their garden museum for tours.

Details: Gardens are always open; Garden Club museum is open Mon-Fri 9-4. $1. (1 hour)

★★ ENSAT CENTER
Sandy Creek Park on Hwy. 441, 706/613-3615

This ecologically correct facility devoted to environmental technology is an engineering marvel. All of the materials in the 11,400-square-foot energy-efficient building are recycled. Educational exhibits demonstrate the use of wetlands and urban environments. The highlight is a 2,000-gallon aquarium with a beaver lodge.

Details: Open Tue-Sat 8:30-5:30. Free. (1-2 hours)

★★ TAYLOR-GRADY HOUSE
634 Prince Ave., 706/549-8688

This impressive 1840s Greek Revival mansion was the home of Henry Grady, editor of *The Atlanta Constitution* in the late nineteenth century. Built by General Robert Taylor, the house was bought by Grady's father, Major William S. Grady, in 1863. Grady became famous for his "New South" speech at the International Cotton States Exposition in 1895. The large house is furnished with priceless nineteenth-century antiques.

Details: Open Mon-Fri 10-5. $3 adults. (1 hour)

ATHENS VICINITY SIGHTSEEING HIGHLIGHTS

★★★ WASHINGTON
Forty miles east of Athens on Hwy. 78

This town of 4,800 is steeped in history. The first town chartered in honor of the first president, Washington is best known in Georgia for its annual antebellum home tours and the **Robert Toombs House State Historic Site.** The white-columned mansion and grounds are open to visitors who want to view exhibits and displays about the successful Civil War-era lawyer, legislator and planter known as "the Unreconstructed Rebel." Toombs was secretary of the Confederacy for five months, then resigned to serve as a brigadier general in the Army of Northern Virginia.

The town of Washington is a compact area of interesting new and old shops where you can buy modern crafted jewelry or an 1875 pine and copper bathtub. **The Plunder Room,** an antiques and collectibles shop, is housed in the oldest brick store in the county.

The **Washington Historical Museum** boasts an eclectic collection of Native American and Civil War artifacts.

Five miles west of town, the **Callaway Plantation** offers tours of the brick plantation house and several historic outbuildings. Demonstrations of farming skills and crafts are held periodically.

Details: Welcome center, 104 E. Liberty St., 706/678-2013. Toombs House, 216 E. Robert Toombs Ave., 706/678-2226. Open Tue-Sat 9-5, Sun 2-5:30. $2 adults. Washington Historical Museum, 308 E. Robert Toombs Ave., 706/678-7660. Open Tue-Sat 10-5, Sun 2-5. $2 adults, $1 children. (4 hours-full day)

★★ **WATKINSVILLE**
Eight miles south of Athens on Hwy. 441
This small town south of Athens has become an arts and crafts haven. Several antiques shops and art galleries line the streets with unusual folk art creations. Information about the shops that sell works by local artists is available at the **Oconee Cultural Arts Foundation,** School St., 706/769-4565. The **Eagle Tavern,** once a nineteenth-century stagecoach stop, has been converted into a crafts shop and welcome center. Nine miles south of Watkinsville on Carson Graves Rd., the **Happy Valley Pottery** is the headquarters for potters and other craftsmen. And five miles south of town on Elder Mill Rd. off Hwy. 15, you'll find **Elder Mill Covered Bridge,** one of the few such structures still standing.

Details: Eagle Tavern welcome center, Main St., 706/769-5197. Open Mon-Sat 10-5, Sun 2-5. (2-4 hours)

FITNESS AND RECREATION
In addition to the hiking trails at the State Botanical Garden in Athens, the **Sandy Creek Park and Nature Center,** Hwy. 441, 706/613-3631, offers lake swimming, canoeing, fishing, and hiking. For canoeing and rafting, the **Broad River Outpost,** 706/795-3243, conducts excursions down the Broad River north of Athens.

Golfers and tennis players are allowed to use the facilities at the **University of Georgia Golf Course,** 706/369-5739, or the indoor courts at the **University Tennis Center,** 706/542-4584.

West of Athens on Hwy. 81, **Fort Yargo State Park,** 706/867-3489, features a 260-acre lake for swimming, boating, and fishing; four tennis courts; hiking trails; and a miniature golf course. Paddleboats and canoes can be rented as well. Included in the park is the **Wil-A-Way Recreation Area,** a barrier-free facility designed for visitors with disabilities.

Sports fans can enjoy a variety of collegiate contests at the University of Georgia. The nationally ranked Bulldogs have four to five home football games each season at **Sanford Stadium;** the men's and women's basketball and gymnastics teams compete at the 11,000-seat **Stegeman Coliseum;** and the UGA tennis teams host national matches at the **University Tennis Center.** Tickets to university athletic events can be bought on weekdays only at the **Butts-Mehre Heritage Hall,** Pinecrest Dr. and Rutherford St., 706/542-9036.

FOOD

As in most college towns, there is no shortage of eating establishments in Athens and the surrounding area. Most of the restaurants are geared toward students who want plenty of food for very little money. Athens' **Charlie Williams Pinecrest Lodge,** off Whitehall Rd., 706/353-2606, meets one of these criteria. Prices are in the $15-$20 range, but the rustic buffet-style restaurant allows you to eat all you want of fried chicken, fried quail, fried catfish, crab legs, Brunswick stew, barbecue, and all the trimmings. There's also a **Pinecrest to Go,** 2020 Timothy Rd., 706/549-6552, which offers the same menu for dine-in or take-out.

Another favorite of students and the band R.E.M. is **Weaver D's Fine Foods,** 247 E. Washington St., 706/543-4770, a soul food cafeteria whose "Automatic for the People" slogan became the title of the musical group's 1992 album. For more authentic Southern food, get all the chitlins (hog intestines), pork chops, turnip greens and sweet potato pie you want for a few dollars at **Wilson's Soul Food Inc.,** 350 N. Hull St., 706/353-7288.

Pasta, salmon enchiladas, and other California cuisine are available at the **Last Resort Grill,** 174 W. Clayton St., 706/549-0810, and burgers and diner food are served at **The Grill,** 171 College Ave., 706/543-4770, a popular student hangout. Vegetarians can get a tofu dog or a vegetarian burger.

Harry Bissett's New Orleans Cafe & Oyster Bar, 279 E. Broad St., 706/353-7065, is a great place for a fancier-than-usual dinner. The cuisine is

Cajun style and includes specialties such as blackened fish, crawfish cakes, and oysters on the half shell. Beef, veal, duck and burgers are also on the menu, along with an extensive wine list.

A few blocks from campus, **The Varsity,** 1000 W. Broad St., 706/548-6325, serves fried onion rings, french fries, chili dogs, and a specialty known as "frosted orange" drinks. The counter help has its own vocabulary, so you need to learn that a "naked dog" is a hot dog without chili and a "walk through the garden" is a burger with lettuce and tomato.

The Grit, 199 Prince Ave., 706/543-6592, is a vegetarian restaurant that was started by Michel Stipe of R.E.M. The menu has expanded to include Southern cooking as well as pasta and hearty soups. Try the traditional home-style veggie plate of macaroni and cheese, creamed corn, greens, and cucumber salad.

For a caffeine fix, **Jittery Joe's,** 1210 S. Milledge Ave., 706/208-1979, is the place for strong black coffee or fancy espressos and cappuccinos. Students gather here to study, snack on pastries, and chat.

If you're looking for barbecue, drop in at the **Fresh Air Barbecue,** 1110 Hull Rd., 706/546-6060, and 5170 Atlanta Hwy., **Bogart,** 770/725-5227, for chopped pork, ribs, chicken, and Brunswick stew served with baked beans, slaw, and slices of white bread. Another good choice is **Hot Thomas Barbecue & Peach Orchard,** 3753 Hwy. 15, Watkinsville, 706/6550, which sells pork barbecue, coleslaw, and peaches in season (usually from mid-June through July). If Hot Thomas is closed, stop by **Aunt Gail's Bake Shoppe & Restaurant,** 18 Barnett Shoals Rd., Watkinsville, 706/769-7398, for delicious baked goods and country-style meals with meat loaf, chicken, and an assortment of vegetables.

In Washington, the best place to eat is **Another Thyme,** 5 E. Public Square, 706/678-1672, located in an 1895 yellow brick building. Lunches include chicken salad sandwiches, BLTs, barbecue, and homemade peach ice cream. Dinners are a little fancier with marinated shrimp and fresh salmon, but prices are still less than $15.

LODGING

With the exception of a few bed-and-breakfasts, most of the accommodations in the Athens area stress function over fanciness.

The **Bulldog Inn,** Hwy. 441 N., 706/543-3611, is just a mile from downtown and reasonably priced at $35. The closest motel to the campus is the **Holiday Inn,** 197 E. Broad St., 706/548-3860, with an indoor pool, airport shuttle from Atlanta, and rooms that start at $84. Vacancies are rare here, so make reservations well in advance.

A half-mile from campus, the **TraveLodge,** 898 W. Broad St., 706/549-5400, provides singles for $40, doubles for $48, and the **Best Western Colonial Inn,** 170 N. Milledge Ave., 706/546-7959, charges $59 for singles and doubles.

For those who desire a bed-and-breakfast atmosphere, the **Magnolia Terrace,** 277 Hill St., 706/548-3860, provides comfortable rooms in a historic 1912 house near The Grit restaurant at moderate prices. In Watkinsville, the **Ashford Manor Bed and Breakfast Inn,** 5 Harden Hill Rd., 706/769-2633, has seven rooms with private baths in a two-story Victorian house for $95 and up. A hot breakfast is served each morning and cocktails are brought to you at poolside.

For travelers on a tight budget, the best choice is **Hawks Nest Hostel,** 1760 McRee Mill Rd., Watkinsville, 706/769-0563, a very tiny cabin for $10 a night. The cabin has a bed and running water, but the bathroom is located in the owners' house next door.

Visitors to Washington can choose from several chain motels along the way or splurge and stay at **Maynard's Manor,** 219 E. Robert Toombs Ave., 706/678-4303, an 1820 antebellum mansion with six rooms with private baths. Complimentary wine and hors d'oeuvres are served in the afternoon on the front porch, and breakfast includes strawberry crepes and fresh fruit. Smoke-free rooms are $85-$215, and no children under 12 are allowed.

CAMPING

Camp in luxury or rough it at **Fort Yargo State Park,** Hwy. 81 west of Athens near Winder, 706/867-3489. The park, which features a 260-acre lake and beach, rents three two-bedroom cottages with appliances for around $50 a night. Or you can pitch your tent or park your camper at one of the 47 campsites for $12-$14 per night. Parking fee is $2. Call 800/864-7275 for reservations.

Watson Mill Bridge State Park, Hwy. 22 east of Athens, 800/864-7275, provides 21 campsites for $12-$14 nightly with a $2-per-car parking fee.

At the **Alexander H. Stephens State Historic Park,** Crawfordville, 706/456-2602, you can spend the night at a 36-site campground and tour a historic home and museum. Gaslight tours of the 1875 house, Liberty Hall, are conducted regularly, and Civil War buffs can view the Confederate artifacts in a museum next door. The campground, located in a picturesque wooded setting behind the house, offers RV hookups for $14. The park includes a fishing lake, boat rentals, a pool, and hiking trails. Call 800/864-7275 for reservations.

NIGHTLIFE

Athens is primarily a sports and music town, but due to the influence of the university, a certain amount of nightlife exists. The **UGA Drama Department,** 706/542-7375, presents a variety of productions at the University Theater or in association with **Thalian Blackfriars** and **Commedia dell'Arte.** The Blackfriars perform everything from experimental theater to Shakespeare, while the Commedia focuses on Italian comedies from the Renaissance era. The **Fine Arts Theater,** Baldwin St., 706/542-2838, is the venue for the University Theater's larger productions, and the **Performing Arts Center,** River Rd., 706/542-4400, is the setting for a variety of nationally known artists to perform at either the 360-seat **Ramsey Concert Hall** or the 1,100 seat **Hugh Hodgson Concert Hall.**

Once a black vaudeville theater, the restored 1910 **Morton Theater,** 195 W. Washington St., 706/613-3770, is now a venue for performing arts. And the **Classic Center,** 300 N. Thomas St., 706/357-4444, brings touring Broadway shows such as *Holiday on Ice* to Athens during the fall and spring seasons.

For alternative music, the **40 Watt Club,** 285 W. Washington St., 706/549-7871, is famous as the showcase for some of the best and worst bands. **Boneshakers,** 433 E. Hancock Ave., 706/543-1555, features the only drag queen revue in the area, but the clientele is a mixture of gays and straights who like good dance music. Local DJs make regular appearances on Retro Disco Wednesdays or House Party Hell Fridays.

The **Uptown Lounge,** 120 E. Washington St., 706/613-7817, is a great place to smoke cigars, watch games on the big-screen TV, and enjoy your favorite beverage. The lounge features Swing Mondays and holiday-themed nights.

The **High Hat Music Club,** 321 E. Clayton St., 706/549-5508, is a favorite of students who want to catch the latest local band or one of the already successful musical groups who happen to drop by. Don't be surprised if you run into a member of R.E.M. here.

And, for something completely different, there's the **Georgia Theatre,** 215 Lumpkin St., 706/549-9918, an old-fashioned movie house that offers a full bar, cheap films, and concerts featuring local and national bands.

6
AUGUSTA

Once a year during Masters Week, television cameras zoom in on the lush greens and colorful azaleas of Augusta National Golf Course. Of course, that's only part of the picture. The oldest and largest city in this region of the state, Augusta is a sometimes-uneasy blend of the historic and the contemporary. Families that have tried to maintain Old South traditions are continually challenged by an influx of newcomers more interested in economic progress than genealogy.

Located 160 miles east of Atlanta, Augusta was founded as a trading post in 1736 by General James Oglethorpe and served as the state capital from 1785 to 1895. Because of its access to the river, Augusta rapidly grew to become the second largest inland cotton market in the world.

Unlike Atlanta, Augusta survived the Civil War with most of its historic buildings intact. After the war, the town became a thriving resort area for wealthy northerners in search of a milder winter climate and entertainment at the polo matches and horse races across the river in Aiken, South Carolina.

Today, Augusta is a quiet town of stately homes and boasts a revitalized downtown with art and antiques shops and restaurants. Riverwalk, a redeveloped section along a levee on the Savannah River, has become a cultural attraction with its art galleries and boutiques. And less than a half hour away, visitors can enjoy a variety of outdoor recreation on Lake Thurmond, the largest man-made lake east of the Mississippi.

GREATER AUGUSTA

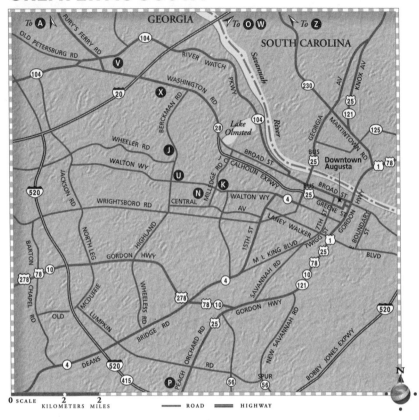

A PERFECT DAY IN AUGUSTA

Begin on Riverwalk and note the high-water marks on the levee entrance. Stroll along the brick esplanade, watch the boats along the river, or enjoy the refreshing spray from the fountain on a hot summer day. Browse through the Shoppes of Port Royal and stop at the historic Cotton Exchange building to look at the exhibits detailing the history of cotton trading. After lunch at the King George Pub, tour the Morris Museum of Art to view some of the finest examples of Southern landscape paintings. Finish the afternoon with a visit to National Science Center's Fort Discovery with more than 250 interactive exhibits. Watch the sunset from one of the benches on the esplanade; then have dinner at Luigi's, one of Augusta's finest Italian restaurants.

DOWNTOWN AUGUSTA

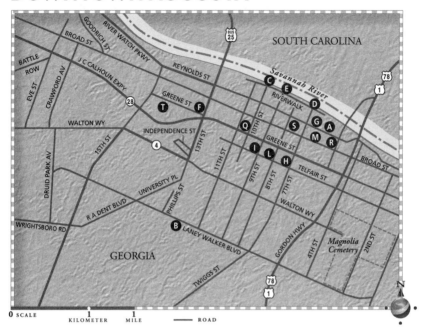

SIGHTS

- Ⓐ Augusta-Richmond County Museum
- Ⓑ Laney-Walker Historic District
- Ⓒ Morris Museum of Art
- Ⓓ National Science Center's Fort Discovery
- Ⓔ Riverwalk
- Ⓕ Sacred Heart Cultural Center
- Ⓖ St. Paul's Episcopal Church
- Ⓗ Woodrow Wilson Boyhood Home

FOOD

- Ⓘ Boll Weevil Cafe
- Ⓙ Calvert's
- Ⓚ Duke Restaurant
- Ⓔ King George Pub
- Ⓛ La Maison
- Ⓜ Luigi's
- Ⓝ Magnolia Tea Room
- Ⓞ Old McDonald Fish Camp
- Ⓟ Sconyer's Barbecue
- Ⓠ White Elephant
- Ⓡ Word of Mouth Cafe

LODGING

- Ⓢ Augusta Budget Inn
- Ⓣ Azalea Inn
- Ⓤ Partridge Inn
- Ⓒ Radisson Riverfront Hotel
- Ⓥ Radisson Suites
- Ⓦ Rosemary Hall
- Ⓧ West Bank Inn

CAMPING

- Ⓨ Bobby Brown State Park
- Ⓩ Elijah Clark Memorial State Park
- ⓐ Mistletoe State Park

Note: Items with the same letter are located in the same area.

ORIENTATION

Located about 160 miles from Atlanta off I-20 E. at exit 65, Augusta is designed around a downtown area with a wide central plaza and a commercial district that is in the midst of revitalization. The city's main attraction is Riverwalk, a newly developed promenade in the city's historic district along the canal.

USAir and **Delta** have flights into **Bush Field Airport,** and **Greyhound** bus service is available as well. Call 800/231-2222 for schedules. Get local bus service schedules at the Greene St. terminal, 706/722-6411. Both Riverwalk and downtown are suitable for walking.

SIGHTSEEING HIGHLIGHTS

★★★★ RIVERWALK
8th and Reynolds Sts.

This scenic plaza along the Savannah River was created in the late 1980s from a section of town that was the center of the cotton trade in the nineteenth century. A brick esplanade, benches, and a spraying fountain make this area a popular place for walks, concerts, and picnics. The entrance to Riverwalk is through a break in a levee built to protect the town from flooding. The Shoppes of Port Royal offer a variety of retail stores, boutiques, and restaurants, and other streets leading into Riverwalk are crowded with antiques shops and art galleries. Water sport competitions such as the Augusta Invitational Rowing Regatta and Formula One boat races are held in spring and summer. The 1886 **Cotton Exchange** doubles as a visitors center and a museum with exhibits about the history of the cotton trade. Original items from the era include tools for picking and planting cotton and a 45-foot wooden blackboard with cotton prices from the early 1900s written in chalk. Listed on the National Register of Historic Places, the Cotton Exchange is an exquisite example of Queen Anne and Second French Empire architecture. The interior is made of heart pine whose natural beauty was recovered from beneath multiple layers of paint.

Riverwalk has become the site for several festivals and holiday events, including Sunrise Easter services, St. Patrick's Day celebrations, Oktoberfest, and the Junior League's Festival of Trees in late November.

Details: Take I-20 east and exit at River Watch Pkwy. Cotton Exchange Visitor Center is at 32 Eighth St., 706/724-4067. Open Mon-Sat 9-5, Sun 1-5. Free. (2-3 hours)

★★★ MORRIS MUSEUM OF ART
One 10th St., 706/724-7501

Many paintings by American artists are featured here, but the museum specialty is Southern art. More than 2,500 works from 1790 to the present include Southern landscapes, antebellum portraits and Civil War art. A small separate gallery contains an interesting collection of contemporary folk art. The museum hosts touring exhibitions and features a museum shop. A recent exhibit was "On the Road With Thomas Hart Benton: Images of a Changing America."
Details: *Open Tue-Sat 10-5:30, Sun 12:30-5:30. $3 adults, $2 students and seniors. (2 hours)*

★★★ NATIONAL SCIENCE CENTER'S FORT DISCOVERY
One Seventh St., 706/821-0200

Consider this one giant playground for kids and adults. The 128,000-square-foot facility features more than 250 interactive exhibits where visitors can watch an indoor lightning display, participate in virtual sky-diving, ride a high-wire bicycle, or do many other high-tech activities. A gift shop and interactive theater are also on the premises.
Details: *Open Mon-Sat 10-6, Sun 12-6. $8 adults, $6 children and seniors, $3 additional for theater. (2-3 hours)*

★★ AUGUSTA-RICHMOND COUNTY MUSEUM
360 Reynolds St., 706/722-8454

Opened in 1996, this museum is filled with interesting exhibits tracing the rich history of the Augusta area, from the Archaic period through the early twentieth century. Permanent and traveling displays include a restored 1914 locomotive and a graphic overview of Augusta's medical history. (The Medical College of Georgia was the first medical school established in the state and served as a hospital for wounded Confederate veterans during the Civil War.)
Details: *Open Tue-Sat 10-5, Sun 2-5, closed Mondays. $4 adults, $2 children, $3 seniors. (1-2 hours)*

★★ LANEY-WALKER HISTORIC DISTRICT
Laney-Walker Blvd.

This section of town is named for Lucy Laney, a former slave who became an influential educator and civic leader. She founded an African American school in 1883 and instituted nurses' training classes that educated thousands of black children. The school is now

Lucy Laney High School, and Laney's restored home is the **Lucy Craft Laney Museum of Black History.** The house, which is open for tours by appointment, is used as a conference center.

A more contemporary feature of the Laney-Walker district is **James Brown Boulevard,** a street named for the famous Godfather of Soul—"the hardest-working man in show business." The singer, who got his start shining shoes in his hometown, now owns a local radio station, WAAW 94.7 FM, and is depicted in a large mural on 10th St.

Details: *Lucy Craft Laney Museum, 1116 Phillips St., 706/724-3576. Tours by appointment. (1-2 hours)*

★★ SACRED HEART CULTURAL CENTER
1301 Greene St., 706/826-4700

Originally a Catholic church, this turn-of-the-century Romanesque Revival structure features more than 15 patterns of brickwork, intricate stained-glass windows, and an exquisitely carved marble interior. The Augusta opera, symphony, ballet, and theater companies perform here now. Works by local artists are for sale in the gift shop. Just down the street in the 500 block is the **Signers' Monument.** George Walton and Lyman Hall, two of the three Georgia signers of the Declaration of Independence, are buried beneath this 50-foot obelisk in front of the Municipal Building.

Details: *Open Mon-Fri 9-5. Free. (1 hour)*

★★ ST. PAUL'S EPISCOPAL CHURCH
605 Reynolds St., 706/724-2485

Located just past the Shoppes of Port Royal at Riverwalk, this historic church was built in 1918 after a disastrous fire in 1916 destroyed much of downtown. This is actually the fourth building on the site. The first church was built in 1750 as part of Fort Augusta. The current church still has the original 1751 baptismal font that was brought over from England.

Details: *Tours by appointment Mon-Fri 9-5, Sat 10-12. Worship services every Sunday. (1 hour)*

★ WOODROW WILSON BOYHOOD HOME
418 7th St., 706/724-0436

President Woodrow Wilson spent his childhood in this house from 1860 to 1870 while his father served as pastor of the First Presbyterian Church. As an eight-year-old boy at the end of the Civil War,

THE COTTON EXCHANGE

Wilson witnessed the turmoil when Union troops imposed martial law and marched the captured Confederate President Jefferson Davis through the streets in manacles.

Details: *Tours by appointment.*

FITNESS AND RECREATION

If you're not tired after walking around Riverwalk, head to the **Savannah Rapids Park,** 706/868-3349, northwest of town on Evans-To-Lock Rd. in Martinez, where there's an eight-mile trail for hiking or biking. The pavilion offers a spectacular view of the rapids and the Augusta Canal. The river is also open for rafting and canoeing.

The **Augusta Canal,** 706/823-0440, built in 1845 as a source of water power to attract manufacturing plants to the South, was used to transport thousands of bales of cotton on barges. Now the canal has been designated as a heritage area and is a popular spot for biking, walking, and boating. Plans for a canal museum and improved trails are in the works.

For those interested in renting equipment or taking an organized canoe or boat trip, **American Wilderness Outfitters Ltd.,** 706/738-8500, at 2328 Washington Rd., will handle everything from the launch to the pickup.

Twenty miles northwest of Augusta on Washington Rd., **Clarks**

Hill/Thurmond Lake, 706/722-3770, provides a vast recreation area for fishing, boating, camping, and outdoor sports. With 1,200 miles of shoreline, this is the largest man-made lake east of the Mississippi. A welcome center with exhibits and maps is located at Strom Thurmond Dam.

For more water recreation and a choice of two short hiking trails, try **Mistletoe State Park,** 706/541-0321, on Hwy. 150. Located about 12 miles north of exit 60 on I-20 with a 1,920-acre shoreline, the park offers five miles of hiking trails, a beach for swimming, and camping facilities. Two of the most popular hiking paths are the **Turkey Trot Trail** and the **Cliatt Creek Trail.**

Most golfers would kill to play a round at the Augusta National Golf Course, and that's almost what you have to do since membership is limited and exclusive. Tickets to the Masters during the first week in April are also hard to get (and very expensive), but visitors usually can buy tickets to the practice rounds at the Augusta National office. There are other courses open to the public, however. The **Forest Hills Golf Club,** 706/733-0001, at 1500 Comfort Rd., and the **Augusta Golf Course,** 706/796-5058, at 2023 Highland Ave., offer 18 holes with moderate greens fees.

FOOD

Augusta has a surprising number of good restaurants for a city its size. The influx of northern visitors, a growing Asian population, and the proximity of Fort Gordon have resulted in a diverse dining atmosphere, with everything from barbecue joints to continental restaurants.

La Maison, 404 Telfair St., 706/722-4805, is an elegant dining establishment that was voted best in the city by Augusta magazine. Specialties include hot pecan wood-smoked salmon in a potato crust for $20, and a game sampler platter of pheasant sausage, quail, venison, and buffalo for around $30.

For more fine dining, **Calvert's,** 475 Highland Ave., 706/738-4514, offers an exceptional selection of beef, veal and seafood dishes served in an ambiance of candlelight and dark wood paneling. Two of the house favorites are the Calvert Bagger, a New York strip steak stuffed with lemon-pepper crabmeat and Calvert's seafood crepes with shrimp, scallops, and crab in a lobster sauce. Prices are in the $15-$30 range.

Luigi's, 590 Broad St., 706/722-4056, has been an Augusta tradition for decades. The family-owned restaurant serves traditional pasta and veal dishes at moderate prices in a casual, friendly atmosphere. The baked chicken with olive oil and lemon is especially delicious. This is a favorite stop of professional golfers during the Masters.

Down-home cooking abounds in Augusta, but one of the best places for simple, inexpensive Southern cuisine is **Duke Restaurant,** 1920 Walton Way, 706/736-6879. Plate lunches change daily and include a choice of one meat and three vegetables. The chicken and dumplings, country fried steak, and roast chicken and dressing are recommended.

Those who want a taste of England can find it at the **Magnolia Tea Room,** 2107 Kings Way, 706/733-8815. Every afternoon, a classic English tea is served with currant scones, an assortment of open-faced sandwiches, a choice of lemon curd, Devonshire cream, and fresh fruit. For heartier meals, the restaurant offers sandwiches, shrimp kabobs, quiche, and a flaky delicacy known as an Olde English Chicken Puff. Prices are moderate.

Other English specialties can be found along with traditional American food and beverages for reasonable prices at the **King George Pub,** 2 8th St. in Riverwalk, 706/724-4755. James Brown sightings in the pub on Sundays are not unusual. The **Boll Weevil,** 10 9th St., 706/722-7772, is a good choice for coffee and dessert after dinner, or for a break from shopping at Riverwalk.

Over on Broad Street, described as the widest main street in the world, the upscale **Word of Mouth Cafe,** 724 Broad St., 706/722-3477, serves superb steak and seafood dinners with a good wine selection for moderate to expensive prices. A few blocks up the street, the **White Elephant,** 1135 Broad St., 706/722-8614, specializes in trendy ethnic dishes for less than $20.

For some of the best hickory-smoked pork and ribs in town, most of the locals go to **Sconyer's Barbecue,** 2250 Sconyers Way, 706/790-5411. Rated one of the top barbecue restaurants in the country, Sconyer's serves its cooked-to-perfection meat with a tangy sauce. The easiest way to get there is to take exit 6 on I-520 to Peach Orchard Rd., then turn left on Sconyers Way.

Seafood lovers who want fish and plenty of it will want to drive across the river to **Old McDonald Fish Camp,** 355 Currytown Rd., 803/279-3305, in North Augusta. This sprawling, rustic restaurant serves all-you-can-eat fried catfish, frog legs, scallops, hush puppies and grits on Thursday, Friday, and Saturday nights for less than $15. Restless kids can wander around outside on the covered bridge over a moat or feed the collection of animals that includes a pot-bellied pig, peacocks, ducks, chicken, geese, and Texas longhorn cattle.

LODGING

Conveniently located across from the Morris Museum, the **Radisson Riverfront Hotel,** 2 10th St., 800/333-3333, offers a nice bed-and-breakfast package for $124 double.

Radisson Suites, 3038 Washington Rd., 706/868-1800, provides a full breakfast and an outside pool for about the same price.

Another elegant place to stay is the **Partridge Inn,** 2110 Walton Way, 706/737-2428, a 100-year-old restored Italianate landmark in the historic Summerville district. The 155 rooms are furnished in a modern style and rent for $110 and up.

For a cozier setting, the **Azalea Inn,** 312 Greene St., 706/724-3454, offers 21 bed-and-breakfast rooms in a residential area near downtown for $85 and up.

The best buy in the downtown area is the **Augusta Budget Inn,** 441 Broad St., 706/722-0212, with 60 rooms in the $50 range, a free continental breakfast, and an outdoor pool.

A couple of miles down Washington Rd., rooms start at $30 at the **West Bank Inn,** a small, 47-room independent motel with basic accommodations and a free continental breakfast.

Just across the Savannah River in North Augusta, **Rosemary Hall,** 804 Carolina Ave., 800/531-5578, offers eight smoke-free rooms with private baths and breakfast for $75 and up.

For other inexpensive lodging, there are a number of chain motels such as Masters Economy Inn, Shoney's Inn, and Days Inn along Washington Road and Gordon Highway, or at any of the exits off of I-20.

If you're planning to go to Augusta during Masters Week, be sure to make reservations. Not only are most hotels booked months in advance, but rates are often doubled.

CAMPING

About 35 miles north of Augusta, **Elijah Clark Memorial State Park,** Hwy. 378, Lincolnton, 706/359-3458, is a scenic area on Clarks Hill Lake. (On the South Carolina side of the Savannah River, the reservoir is known as Thurmond Lake.) The park is named after Revolutionary War hero Elijah Clark, who defeated the British at Kettle Creek in neighboring Wilkes County. A replica of Clark's log cabin has been erected in the park as a museum. The cabin and grounds are the site for a Fall Pioneer Rendezvous the second week of each October with musket shooting and pioneer cooking and crafts demonstrations. An annual bluegrass festival with the locally renowned gospel group, the Lewis Family, is held the first week in May.

There are 20 two-bedroom lakefront cottages available for $55 and up, and 165 campsites that rent for $14. Parking fees are $2 per car.

Both cottages and campsites are available at **Mistletoe State Park,** Hwy. 150, 706/541-0321, a scenic area with a swimming beach, boating facilities and hiking trails. Each of the 107 campsites rent for $14, including hookups, or you can spend the night more comfortably in one of the 10 fully equipped two-bedroom cottages for $55 and up. **Bobby Brown State Park,** Hwy. 72 between Middleton and Chenault, 706/213-2046, sits on the site of Petersburg, a town that flourished during the 1790s before fading away. The 665-acre park offers hiking, boating, and swimming as well as 61 campsites with hookups for $14. Parking fees are $2 per car. To reserve campsites, call 800/864-7275.

NIGHTLIFE

Performances by the Augusta Ballet, Augusta Symphony, Augusta Opera, the Augusta Players, and other cultural groups are scheduled regularly throughout the year at the **Sacred Heart Cultural Center,** 1301 Greene St., 706/826-4700, the **Augusta-Richmond County Civic Center Auditorium,** 601 Seventh St., 706/722-3521, the Jessye Norman Amphitheater, Ninth St., 706/821-2804, and other venues around town. Information about tickets and concerts is available at the Greater Augusta Arts Council, 706/826-4702.

Touring theatrical productions and concerts also are scheduled at the Civic Center and **William B. Bell Memorial Auditorium,** 712 Telfair St., 706/724-2400.

For live entertainment, the **Soul Bar,** 984 Broad St., is the place where young professionals hang out. The **Cotton Patch,** 816 Cotton Ln. on Riverwalk, 706/724-4511, is also a popular spot.

GEORGIA HEARTLAND

This section of the state east and south of Atlanta is mainly an area of rural farmland, stands of forests, and interesting little towns situated away from the busy interstate highways. Some of Georgia's most beautiful homes can be found in Madison and Milledgeville, and dozens of historic markers signify the price this part of the state paid during the Civil War.

Three of Georgia's most famous writers, Alice Walker and Joel Chandler Harris of Eatonton and Flannery O'Connor of Milledgeville, grew up in the heartland and left their literary marks. An Uncle Remus Museum and a statue of Br'er Rabbit in Eatonton commemorates Harris' contribution to folklore.

Those interested in outdoor recreation will find multiple opportunities for fishing, boating, hiking, swimming, and golf at the half dozen or so state parks in the area.

And, for pure driving pleasure, five themed trails, including the Peach Blossom Trail and the Antebellum Trail, loop through the heartland to show off the natural beauty and other attractions.

A PERFECT DAY IN THE GEORGIA HEARTLAND

Begin your day with a light breakfast at The Yesterday Cafe in Rutledge; then tour the little village's antiques shops. Head to Madison for a walking tour of the downtown historic district and the Morgan County African-American Museum. After a late lunch at Ye Olde Colonial Restaurant, drive to nearby Eatonton and visit the Uncle Remus Museum. Continue your drive to Milledgeville and a tour of the Old State Capitol and the Flannery O'Connor Room. Have a cold beverage and a pizza at The Brick and end your day with a night of dancing at Cowboy Bill's.

SIGHTSEEING HIGHLIGHTS

★★★★ MADISON
50 miles east of Atlanta off I-20

This historic town has the kinds of white-columned mansions that Hollywood had in mind when it filmed *Gone With the Wind*. The town retains much of the flavor of a nineteenth-century village with brick sidewalks around a square of quaint shops shaded with magnolias and oaks. Historic buildings near downtown include the 1804 **Rogers House,** W. Jefferson St., a Piedmont Plain-style townhouse typical of a middle-class residence before the Civil War, and **Heritage** Hall, 277 S. Main St., 706/342-9627, a restored 1833 mansion. **Rose Cottage,** W. Jefferson St., built by a laundress who was a former slave, has a lovely garden that connects to the Rogers House. Walking-tour maps are available at the **Madison-Morgan County Chamber of Commerce Welcome Center,** 115 E. Jefferson St., 706/342-4454.

More examples of African American life in Middle Georgia can be found at the **Morgan County African-American Museum,** 156 Academy St., 706/342-9197, which houses an interesting art collection and an exhibit of musical instruments.

For an overview of the town's history, visit the **Madison-Morgan Cultural Center** at 434 S. Main St. The 1895 Romanesque Revival mansion now houses an art gallery, classrooms, a theater, and a museum. A series of exhibits trace Madison's roots from the early 1800s, when the economy was based on cotton farming. *Details: Madison-Morgan Cultural Center, 706/342-4743. Open Tue-Sat 10-4:30, Sun 2-5. $3 adults. (4-6 hours)*

★★★★ MILLEDGEVILLE

This Antebellum Trail city was the capital of Georgia from 1804 to 1868. Now it's a small college town with many fine homes, interest-

HEARTLAND

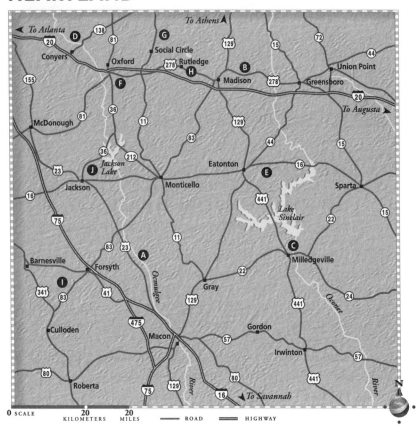

◄ To Atlanta
To Athens ▲
To Augusta ►
To Savannah

Conyers
Oxford
Social Circle
Rutledge
Madison
Greensboro
Union Point
McDonough
Eatonton
Jackson Lake
Jackson
Monticello
Lake Sinclair
Sparta
Barnesville
Forsyth
Gray
Milledgeville
Culloden
Macon
Gordon
Irwinton
Roberta

Ocmulgee
Oconee
River

0 SCALE   20 KILOMETERS   20 MILES   ——— ROAD   ═══ HIGHWAY

N

ing shops, and a trolley tour that takes visitors through the historic district. The 1807 **Old State Capitol** building, 201 E. Green St., 912/445-2700, is now a part of Georgia Military College. The building is considered to be a prime example of Gothic architecture. Another historic building from Milledgeville's days as the state capital is the 1838 **Governor's Mansion,** 120 S. Clark St., 912/453-4545. Now used as the administration building for Georgia College, the mansion is open for tours daily.

One of the more enlightening places is the **Museum and Archives of Georgia Education,** 131 S. Clark St., 912/453-4391, with exhibits tracing the history of education in Georgia.

Fans of author Flannery O'Connor can view memorabilia and copies of *Wise Blood* and her other books at the **Flannery O'Connor Room** of the Ina D. Russell Library, 912/445-2700, on the Georgia College campus.

Details: *Milledgeville Convention and Visitors Bureau, 200 W. Hancock St., 912/452-4687 or 800/653-1804. Open Mon-Fri 9-5, Sat 10-4. (4 hours)*

★★★ JULIETTE
60 miles south of Atlanta

If this little community looks familiar, you may have seen it in the movie *Fried Green Tomatoes,* which was filmed here. The town, the site of the world's largest water-powered gristmill, was basically a ghost town until the Hollywood crew arrived. The gristmill was in ruins and other industry had closed. Since its revival, Juliette has become a popular tourist stop with more than a dozen antiques and gift shops and, of course, the restaurant known as the Whistle Stop Cafe.

A few miles outside of town, the **Jarrell Plantation** features a working nineteenth-century farm with 20 outbuildings and a collection of antique tools and artifacts. Monthly demonstrations include sheep-shearing, quilting, and syrup-making.

Details: *Take exit 61 off I-75. Jarrell Plantation, Jarrell Plantation Rd., 912/986-5172. Open Tue-Sat 9-5, Sun 2-5:30. $4 adults, $2 children.*

SIGHTS
- Ⓐ Juliette
- Ⓑ Madison
- Ⓒ Milledgeville
- Ⓓ Monastery of Our Lady of the Holy Spirit
- Ⓔ Uncle Remus Museum
- Ⓕ Geri Wayne Emu & Petting Ranch (Covington)

FOOD
- Ⓖ Blue Willow Inn Restaurant
- Ⓒ The Brick

FOOD (continued)
- Ⓗ Cowboy's Feed Lot
- Ⓘ Farm House Restaurant
- Ⓐ Whistle Stop Cafe
- Ⓑ Ye Olde Colonial Restaurant
- Ⓗ The Yesterday Cafe

LODGING
- Ⓑ Brady Inn
- Ⓓ Burnett Place
- Ⓔ Crockett House Bed and Breakfast
- Ⓑ Hampton Inn

LODGING (continued)
- Ⓑ Holiday Inn Express
- Ⓒ Jameson Inn
- Ⓒ Mara's Tara
- Ⓔ Rosewood Bed and Breakfast

CAMPING
- Ⓗ Hard Labor Creek State Park
- Ⓘ High Falls State Park
- Ⓒ Lake Sinclair Recreation Area
- Ⓑ Talisman CamPark

Note: Items with the same letter are located in the same area.

OLD CAPITAL GATES

★★ **MONASTERY OF OUR LADY OF HOLY SPIRIT**
Hwy. 212, 770/483-8705
For a peaceful break, stop and enjoy the tranquil setting, eight miles southwest of Conyers. Tours of the grounds, church, and bonsai greenhouse are offered, and visitors can picnic by a duck pond. A gift shop sells religious ornaments, books, and bread baked by the monks.
Details: Gift shop open Mon-Sat 10-4:30. (1-2 hours)

★★ **UNCLE REMUS MUSEUM**
Hwy. 441, Eatonton, 706/485-6856
To commemorate native son and Uncle Remus creator Joel Chandler Harris, Eatonton has erected a Br'er Rabbit statue on the courthouse square and built a museum from two slave cabins similar to the one Uncle Remus occupied. The museum houses carvings of Harris' critters and other memorabilia.
Details: Open Mon-Sat 10-5, Sun 2-5. (1 hour)

★ **GERI WAYNE EMU & PETTING RANCH**
12818 Alcovy Rd., Covington, 770/786-0755
This animal farm is a worthwhile stop if you have children or if you

like to spend time with six-foot-tall birds. Other animals include pot-bellied pigs, baby calves, goats, sheep, rabbits, and chickens. **Details:** *Call for tour times. $5. (1 hour)*

FITNESS AND RECREATION

One of the legacies of the 1996 Olympics in Conyers is the **Georgia International Horse Park,** 1996 Centennial Olympic Pkwy., 770/860/4190. The facility has an Arnold Palmer-designed golf course, a 165-acre nature center, biking trails, and arenas for equestrian events.

In Rutledge, **Hard Labor Creek State Park,** Fairplay Rd., 800/864-7275, has a challenging 18-hole golf course, horse trails, hiking trails, bike trails, and boat rentals for two lakes.

On Lake Oconee east of Madison, **Parks Ferry Recreation Area,** Parks Ferry Rd., 706/485-8704, also offers a swimming beach and a fishing lake.

And, in Monticello, the **Charlie Elliott Wildlife Center,** 2425 Marben Farm Rd., 770/784-3059, is a 6,000-acre wildlife wonderland with 29 ponds and areas for hiking, fishing, birdwatching, and hunting.

FOOD

You won't find a lot of white-tablecloth dining establishments in the Georgia Heartland, but there are plenty of places that serve good Southern cooking. One of these, Social Circle's **Blue Willow Inn Restaurant,** 294 N. Cherokee Rd., 770/464-2161, offers a delicious all-you-can-eat Southern buffet in an elegant 1907 Greek Revival mansion. Reservations are suggested, but if you like, you can put your name on the list at the door and browse through the gift shop while you wait. Prices are around $12-$15.

In Madison, more Southern food is served at **Ye Olde Colonial Restaurant,** 108 E. Washington St., 706/342-2211. Popular with locals and tourists alike, this restaurant in an old bank building features a cafeteria-style menu of fried chicken, roast beef, country-fried steak, and vegetables from area farmers. Prices are moderate.

After hitting all of the antiques shops in tiny Rutledge, most folks stop in for lunch or dinner at **The Yesterday Cafe,** 120 Fairplay St., 706/557-9337. Housed in a converted pharmacy, the restaurant offers daily specials such as meat loaf and mashed redskin potatoes. Dinner is fancier—and a little pricier—with prime rib, herbed catfish, and fried seafood. The buttermilk pie is recommended for dessert. Or, if you're really in the mood for red meat, drive a few more miles to **Cowboy's Feed Lot,** 7201 Hwy. 278,

706/557-9552, for huge T-bone steaks or barbecued ribs at reasonable prices. The restaurant also features a dance hall and country-and-western bands most nights.

A must-stop restaurant is Juliette's **Whistle Stop Cafe,** I-75 exit 61, 912/994-3670, where you can get fried green tomatoes as an appetizer or as a side dish for traditional meat-and-three lunches or dinners for less than $10. Breakfast is also served.

In Forsyth, a small town off exit 62 on I-75, **The Farm House Restaurant,** 22 W. Main St., 912/994-2165, has earned a reputation among travelers heading to and from Florida as the place to get authentic Southern food. Specialties include homemade biscuits, ham pot pie, and sweet potato pie, and breakfasts of country ham and grits. Prices are reasonable for the amount of food you get.

For something other than Southern-fried specialties in Milledgeville, try **The Brick,** 136 W. Hancock St., 912/452-0089. Menu items include vegetarian pizzas, sandwiches, and salads at inexpensive prices.

LODGING

The most convenient accommodations in Madison are at the **Brady Inn,** 250 N. Second St., 706/342-4400, and the **Burnett Place,** 317 Old Post Rd., 706/342-4034. Both are within walking distance of the historic square, and both offer rooms with private baths for around $90.

In Eatonton, the **Crockett House Bed and Breakfast,** 671 Madison Rd., 706/485-2248, and the **Rosewood Bed and Breakfast,** 301 N. Madison Ave., 706/485-9009, provide rooms decorated with period furniture in the $65-$95 range.

Not far from downtown Milledgeville, **Mara's Tara,** 200 W. Hancock St., 912/452-4687, offers rooms with private baths in a historic 1825 mansion for around $65.

If you want less ambiance, you have a choice of chain motels along Hwy. 441, I-20, or I-75. In Milledgeville, the **Jameson Inn,** 2251 N. Columbia St., 912/453-8471, has no-frills rooms for $39 and up, and in Madison, the **Holiday Inn Express,** 2080 Eatonton Rd., 706/342-3433, and the **Hampton Inn,** 2012 Eatonton Rd., 706/342-9003, offer basic accommodations beginning at $45.

CAMPING

Several state parks in the area provide clean campsites with outdoor recre-

THE GREENING OF THE SOUTH

There's a story behind that ubiquitous green vine growing everywhere in Georgia and the South, wrapping its tendrils around trees and swallowing up junk cars, abandoned houses, and slow-moving cows. Kudzu was imported into this country in the 19th century from Japan as a means of controlling erosion in farmed-out cotton lands. When times were desperate for farmers during the Great Depression, the federal government paid them $8 an acre to plant kudzu.

It controlled erosion, all right, but it soon spread like some alien invader. The government eventually banned the vine from its list of acceptable ground covers.

Now Southerners have learned to live with it, and actually love it. The topiary landscapes that kudzu creates along the back roads are far more interesting than many billboards. And some enterprising entrepreneurs have profited from baskets, necklaces, and even jelly made from kudzu.

ation facilities. In Rutledge, **Hard Labor Creek State Park,** Fairplay Rd., I-20 exit 49, 800/864-7275, features a 49-site campground for $16 with hookups and fully equipped two-bedroom cottages for $65 and up. For camping near Madison, the Talisman Campark, Hwy. 441, 706/342-1799, has 67 sites for tents and RVs. Tent sites are $12 and RV sites are $16 and up. Amenities include a pool and nature trails.

In the vicinity of Milledgeville, **Lake Sinclair Recreation Area,** Hwy. 212, 912/452-4687, offers campsites and hookups for $7 a night. There's a hiking trail as well as a swimming beach.

And, in Jackson, campsites with water and electricity rent for $14 a night at **High Falls State Park,** 76 High Falls Park Rd., 800/864-7275. The nearby lake features a scenic waterfall and facilities for swimming, hiking, fishing, and picnicking.

NIGHTLIFE

Most of the residents in this area usually head for Athens, Macon, or Atlanta for nightlife, but there are a few attractions. In Madison, the **Madison-Morgan Cultural Center,** 434 S. Main St., 706/342-4743, offers plays and concerts periodically and hosts traveling productions. In the college town of Milledgeville, students and others go to **Cowboy Bill's,** Hwy. 441, 912/453-9902, for dancing and country-rock music. More sedate cultural performances are scheduled by the **Allied Arts, Inc.,** 201 N. Wayne St., 912/452-3930.

8
MACON

Resting comfortably in the heart of the Georgia Heartland, Macon is what some folks think Atlanta would have been if it had not become a Sunbelt boom town. With a population just over 100,000, Macon combines small-town charm with many of the attractions of a big city.

Long before Macon was founded as a town in 1823, Native Americans enjoyed a flourishing civilization on the Ocmulgee River. The European explorer Hernando de Soto is said to have erected the first cross on the river.

Spared largely from damage in the Civil War, Macon boasts a number of fine Greek Revival mansions. Each year the city hosts the Cherry Blossom festival, when more than 270,000 cherry trees burst into bloom. And each evening, hundreds of thousands of lights go on for Lights on Macon, an illuminating tour designed to spotlight some of the city's 5,500 historic landmarks.

Most of all, Macon is a music town. The cradle of the Allman Brothers, Little Richard, Otis Redding, and Capricorn Records, Macon is now home of the Georgia Music Hall of Fame. In this impressive new building, Georgia artists such as Ray Charles, Brenda Lee, and R.E.M. are honored along with dozens more. The latest addition to Macon's music scene is Sweet Georgia Jam, a 10-day September celebration with concerts in a variety of historic venues.

MACON

SHURLING AV

EMERY HWY

COLISEUM DR

2ND ST

Central
City
Park

Ocmulgee River

To M Q S T U

RIVERSIDE DR

WALNUT ST

GEORGIA AV

FORSYTH AV

COTTON AV

OGLETHORPE ST

1ST ST

BROADWAY

POPLAR ST

5TH ST

7TH ST

ASH ST

EDGEWOOD AV

2ND ST

HOUSTON AV

PLANT ST

COLLEGE ST

WALNUT ST

PIERCE AV

PIO NONO AV

MONTPELIER AV

MERCER UNIVERSITY DR

ANTHONY RD

EISENHOWER PKWY

MERCER UNIVERSITY DR

NAPIER AV

VINEVILLE AV

PARK ST

FORSYTH RD

To L

SCALE

0   1
KILOMETER

0   1
MILE

ROAD   HIGHWAY

A PERFECT DAY IN MACON

Begin with a hearty breakfast at the H & H Restaurant, then head for the Georgia Music Hall of Fame for a morning of musical entertainment and education. After soup and salad at Cherry Corner, spend the rest of the afternoon at the Museum of Arts and Sciences and the Tubman African American Museum. Dine on barbecue at Fincher's or enjoy some fine Italian food and wine at Nathalia's. Take a romantic Lights on Macon nighttime tour of the historic district.

ORIENTATION

Located about 85 miles south of Atlanta on I-75, Macon was designed in the early 1800s with wide avenues and space for many gardens and parks. The core of the city is developed around a beautifully restored historic district along Georgia Avenue, where dozens of white-columned mansions line shady streets.

The new Georgia Music Hall of Fame, the Georgia Sports Hall of Fame, and the Douglass Theater are all located in the area just off of Martin Luther King Jr. Boulevard near the Macon-Bibb County Convention and Visitors Bureau. To the north, the African American section of town is bordered by Vineville, Neal, College, and Rogers Streets.

Macon is ideal for walking, but although the **Macon-Bibb County Transit Authority's** bus system is good, using your own car or renting one is advis-

SIGHTS

- Ⓐ Cannonball House
- Ⓑ Georgia Music Hall of Fame
- Ⓒ Georgia Sports Hall of Fame
- Ⓓ Hay House
- Ⓔ Historic Intown
- Ⓕ Museum of Arts and Sciences
- Ⓖ Ocmulgee National Monument
- Ⓗ Rose Hill Cemetery
- Ⓘ Sidney Lanier Cottage
- Ⓙ Tubman African American Museum

FOOD

- Ⓚ Cherry Corner
- Ⓛ Fincher's
- Ⓜ Fresh-Air
- Ⓝ Good-to-Go
- Ⓞ H & H Restaurant
- Ⓟ Len Berg's
- Ⓠ Nathalia's

LODGING

- Ⓡ 1842 Inn
- Ⓢ Best Western Riverside
- Ⓣ Comfort Inn
- Ⓤ Courtyard Marriott-Macon
- Ⓥ Crowne Plaza

Note: Items with the same letter are located in the same area.

able for extensive excursions. Two-hour bus tours of the city are offered at **Sidney's Tours,** 200 Cherry St., 917/743-3401.

The city is served by **Atlantic Southeast Airlines** at the **Lewis B. Wilson Airport** 10 miles south of town, and shuttle service to and from Atlanta's Hartsfield International Airport is available from **Groome Transportation,** 912/471-1616. Statewide bus service is provided by **Greyhound,** 65 Spring St., 912/743-5411.

SIGHTSEEING HIGHLIGHTS

★★★★ **GEORGIA MUSIC HALL OF FAME**
200 Martin Luther King Jr. Blvd., 912/750-8555
Opened in 1996, this 43,000-square-foot facility was designed to honor the state's musical heritage, from gospel to rock. Inside, a fictional village known as Tune Town features a 1950s soda fountain, a blues club, a country music cafe, and jazz in the streets. Visual and musical exhibits document the lives and careers of artists from "Ma" Rainey and Johnny Mercer to Otis Redding and R.E.M. Other exhibits include clothes and album covers from the 1950s and a vintage record store. On the second floor, the Zell Miller Center for Georgia Music provides hundreds of books, videotapes, sheet music and manuscripts for the serious scholar. And, in the gift shop, you can buy recordings from more than 115 Georgia artists.
Details: Open Mon-Sat 9-5, Sun 1-5. $7.50 adults, $5.50 students and seniors, $3.50 children. (2-4 hours)

★★★★ **GEORGIA SPORTS HALL OF FAME**
301 Cherry St., 912/752-1585
This new building, which opened in 1999, resembles a turn-of-the-century ballpark with a green roof and red brick exterior. Inside the 14,000-square-foot hall, exhibits honor the nearly 300 members, from golf great Bobby Jones to baseball heroes Hank Aaron and Ty Cobb. Also inside is a 205-seat theater based on the design of Ponce de Leon Park where the old Atlanta Crackers baseball team played. There are interactive exhibits such as a NASCAR simulator, and an extensive gift shop. A must for any sports fan.
Details: Open Mon-Sat 9-5, Sun 1-5. $6 adults, $5 students and seniors, $3.50 children. (2-4 hours)

GEORGIA MUSIC HALL OF FAME

Macon-Bibb County CVB

★★★★ MUSEUM OF ARTS AND SCIENCES
4182 Forsyth Rd., 912/477-3232

You will find everything from art objects and zoological specimens to a planetarium and an inventor's laboratory in this fascinating museum. The unusual Discovery House features interactive exhibits, a 40-million-year-old whale fossil named Ziggy, a Velcro wall, a treehouse overlooking live animals, and a backyard exhibit with a group of mini-habitats. A fantastic art gallery encourages visitors to hear, smell and touch the art as well as look at it. Daily planetarium shows and other events are included in the price of admission.

Details: Open Mon-Thu 9-5, Fri 9-9, Sat 9-5, Sun 1-5. $5 adults, $3 students, $2 children under 12, $4 seniors. Free Mon 9-5, Fri 5-9. (2-4 hours)

★★★★ TUBMAN AFRICAN AMERICAN MUSEUM
340 Walnut St., 912/743-8544

Georgia's largest African American museum, the Tubman attracts more than 60,000 visitors a year. The museum is named in honor of Harriet Tubman, but it celebrates the cultural and historic contributions of other African Americans. Visitors can explore 14 different exhibit areas, including the Local History Gallery, the Inventors

Gallery, the Folk Art Gallery, and the Mural Gallery, which presents a visual history of black culture. The Soul on Rice exhibit, which explains the African influence on American cuisine, is particularly interesting. Other galleries showcase African art, jewelry, and textiles; entertainers; and military leaders.

Details: *Open Mon-Sat 9-5, Sun 2-5. $3 adults. (1-2 hours)*

★★★ HAY HOUSE
934 Georgia Ave., 912/742-8155

Macon's most famous home is this Renaissance Revival mansion built in the late 1850s. Recognized on the A&E television series *America's Castles* as "The Palace of the South," this 18,000-square-foot house was built by William B. Johnson, a railroad magnate and Treasurer of the Confederacy. The ornate house took four years to build and, when completed, featured indoor bathrooms, hot and cold running water, an elaborate heating and cooling system, and an elevator. Three of the seven levels are open for tours.

Details: *Open Mon-Sat 10-4:30, Sun 1-4:30. $6 adults, $2 students, $1 children, $5 seniors. (2 hours)*

★★★ OCMULGEE NATIONAL MONUMENT
1207 Emery Hwy., 912/752-8257

Ocmulgee is a memorial to the civilization that existed here from 900 A.D. to 1100 A.D. Known as Mississippians, they were farmers who built huge earthen temples the size of football fields. Visitors can tour the remnants of these worship sites, including the Great Temple Mound, which rises 45 feet and extends from a base that is 270 by 300 feet. A visitors center houses a major archaeological museum with exhibits describing the human habitation of the area. Walking trails connect most of the sites. Spring and fall are the best seasons for walking tours.

Details: *Open daily 9-5. Free. (2-3 hours)*

★★ CANNONBALL HOUSE
856 Mulberry St., 912/745-5982

Since Macon has little physical damage to show from the Civil War, the town's historians are particularly proud of the Cannonball House. Located two doors down from the Hay House, this 1853 Greek Revival mansion was struck by a Union cannonball meant for the more elegant residence. The cannonball itself is prominently displayed.

HAY HOUSE

Two of the rooms are re-creations of the original meeting rooms of the first two secret societies for women in the world—Phi Mu and Alpha Delta. A small two-story brick building out back that was once servants' quarters now houses the Confederate Museum and an exhibit of Civil War memorabilia.

Details: *Open Tue-Fri 10-1 and 2-4, Sat-Sun 1:30-4:30. $4 adults, $1 students, 50¢ children. (1 hour)*

★★ HISTORIC INTOWN

Macon's residential district features some of the most magnificent historic houses in the state. In addition to the **Hay House** and the **Cannonball House,** this neighborhood along Georgia Avenue and College Street includes the impressive **Neel Reid Garden Center,** 730 College St., and a number of other architectural treasures. Visitors can sign up for a professional tour or obtain maps for a self-guided tour at the **Macon Convention & Visitors Bureau.** The nightly **Lights on Macon** tour is recommended. That's when 30 architectural gems are beautifully illuminated with lighting created by the designer of Disney's Electric Light Parades.

Details: *Macon Convention & Visitors Bureau, 200 Cherry St., 912/743-3401. (2-3 hours)*

★★ SIDNEY LANIER COTTAGE
935 High St., 912/743-3851

This is the birthplace of Georgia's most famous poet, Sidney Clopton Lanier, author of *The Marshes of Glynn* and *Song of the Chattahoochee*. Lanier fought in the Civil War, was captured as a blockade runner, and developed consumption while in a Union prison. He spent the rest of his life as a lecturer at Johns Hopkins University and playing flute in Baltimore's Peabody Symphony Orchestra. The cottage where he was born is decorated with period furniture and is headquarters for the Middle Georgia Historical Society.

Details: Open Mon-Fri 9-1 and 2-4, Sat 9:30-12:30. $3 adults. (1 hour)

★ ROSE HILL CEMETERY
1091 Riverside Dr., 912-751-9119

It may seem macabre to some, but many people enjoy touring old cemeteries, especially picturesque ones. Rose Hill is an outstanding example of a nineteenth-century cemetery with terraced hills sloping down to the river. More than 600 Civil War soldiers are buried in Confederate Square, but the most notable gravesites belong to two of the Allman Brothers band members. Duane Allman, who was killed in a motorcycle accident in 1971, and Berry Oakley, who was also killed in a motorcycle accident a year later, are buried side by side in graves outlined in the shape of electric guitars. The graves are usually decorated with gifts from mourning fans. Maps are available at the cemetery office.

Details: Open daily. (1 hour)

FITNESS AND RECREATION

Sports fans who enjoy the relaxing atmosphere of a minor league baseball game can watch the Atlanta farm team **Macon Braves** play at the Luther Williams Stadium, 912/745-8943, in Central City Park during the season from April to August. The field is located on Coliseum Dr. at the intersection of I-16 and I-75.

Ice hockey fans can see the **Macon Whoopee** team compete in the Central Hockey League at the Macon Coliseum, 200 Coliseum Dr., 912/741-1000. The season runs from September until mid-April.

For those who like participatory sports, Central City Park south of downtown provides ball fields and recreation facilities. West of town, the **Tobesofkee Recreation Area,** 6600 Mosley Dixon Rd., 912/474-8770, offers swimming, boating, and fishing in a 1,750-acre lake.

Golfers can tee off at **Bowden Golf Course,** 3111 Millerfield Rd., 912/742-1610, for $10. And tennis players can use any of the city's 36 lighted courts at **North Ingle Place** or **Tattnall Square Park,** Oglethorpe and College Sts., 912/741-9196.

FOOD

You expect to find soul food in a town that has as much soul as Macon, and the best place to get it is at Mama Louise Hudson's **H & H Restaurant,** 807 Forsyth St., 912/742-9810. In addition to traditional Southern breakfasts, the H & H serves blue-plate specials with a meat and two vegetables for about $5. This was a favorite dining spot for the Allman Brothers, as you can tell by the numerous photographs and mementos on the wall.

Another local favorite is **Len Berg's,** Old Post Office Alley, 912/742-9255, with old wooden booths and no ferns. Daily specials at reasonable prices include baked chicken with cornbread dressing, fried chicken, and wonderful homemade pimiento cheese sandwiches.

Barbecue can be found in abundance, too, at the **Fresh-Air,** 3076 Riverside Dr., 912/477-7229, or **Fincher's,** 3947 Houston Ave., 912/788-1900, known as the only barbecue restaurant to have its smoked pork shot into space. Astronaut Sonny Carter, who frequented Fincher's when he was stationed at nearby Warner Robins Air Force Base, smuggled some of the barbecue aboard the space shuttle. Prices are inexpensive.

If you're on the go and want takeout, **Good to Go,** Spring and Walnut, 912/743-4663, offers real dinners of meat and vegetables for busy travelers at reasonable prices.

For Italian food, **Cherry Corner,** 502 Cherry St., 912/741-0086, serves great sandwiches and salads. And, for upscale dining, **Nathalia's,** 2720 Riverside Dr., 912/741-1380, offers classic Italian dishes such as grilled veal chops and pasta without heavy red sauce. The restaurant has a good wine list, too.

LODGING

To spend the night in historic style, the best place is the **1842 Inn,** 353 College St., 912/741-1842. With an atmosphere straight from *Gone With the Wind,* this Greek Revival mansion features 21 rooms with English antiques, tapestries, and fireplaces for $115-$185.

For downtown convenience, the **Crowne Plaza,** 108 First St., 912/746-1461, provides first-class accommodations starting at $89.

The **Best Western Riverside Inn,** 2400 Riverside Dr., 912/743-6311, offers rooms starting at $44 with all the amenities as well as a lounge and Southern-style restaurant.

Other accommodations are available at reasonable prices at the **Comfort Inn,** 2690 Riverside Dr., 912/746-8855, which features a pool and cocktail lounge for $54 and up, or the **Courtyard by Marriott-Macon,** 3990 Sheraton Dr., 912/477-8899, with rates starting at $59. Rooms have been renovated and facilities include an outdoor pool, indoor whirlpool spa, and exercise rooms.

For a wide choice of chain motels, just get off at any exit on I-75 leading into town.

NIGHTLIFE

Macon has several interesting venues for concerts, theatrical performances, and local entertainment. One of the most historic is the **Douglass Theatre,** 355 Martin Luther King Jr. Blvd., 912/742-2000, a 1920s African American movie and vaudeville hall that was a showcase for great performers such as Duke Ellington and Cab Calloway. In the 1960s, Otis Redding and others made their debuts here. The theater stood silent for 20 years until it was reopened as a state-of-the-art film and performance venue in 1996. Visitors can see live musical and theatrical performances in addition to 3-D IMAX films.

The **Macon Centreplex Coliseum,** 200 Coliseum Dr., 912/751-9152, books some outstanding traveling shows as well as the circus, and the 1884 **Grand Opera House,** 651 Mulberry St., 912/752-5460, presents Broadway shows and other events in an elegantly restored theater.

For nightly live entertainment, wander down to Cherry Street and listen to everything from folk music at the **Coffee Connection,** 517 Cherry St., 912/745-0070, to Southern rock at **The Rookery,** 543 Cherry St., 912/746-8658. Disco dancing and billiards attract a young audience at **Elizabeth Reed Music Hall,** 557 Cherry St., 912/741-9792.

Blues lovers can listen to down-and-dirty tunes at **Riverfront Bluez,** 550 Riverside Dr., 912/741-9970, while bluegrass fans usually travel 30 miles to Toomsboro and the **Swampland Opera House,** Hwy. 57 and Hwy. 12, 912/628-5314.

Also, special festivals during the year, such as the **Sweet Georgia Jam** in September, feature a variety of concerts from jazz to blues. And, during the 10-day **Cherry Blossom Festival** in late March, downtown becomes one big party with parades, cultural arts performances, and street music.

9
MAGNOLIA MIDLANDS

This south-central region of Georgia is known as the Magnolia Midlands for more than the obvious reason. Yes, the fertile farmland is dotted with magnolia trees, but Southerners know that the word conjures up images of sleepy summer days when people were not too busy to sit on the front porch and share stories and glasses of iced tea. Sweetened tea, of course.

Magnolia Midlands is a beautiful land of lakes and rivers, cotton fields stretching to the horizon, pine forests thick with deer and other game, historic small towns with inviting shops and restaurants, and, of course, sweet Vidalia onions.

Four state parks and several campgrounds are located in this region, as well as a number of challenging golf courses. I-16 will take you through the heart of Magnolia Midlands, but adventurous travelers will want to explore some of the quiet backroads that are barely on the map. Just be prepared for hot, humid weather in the summer and highways that seem to go on forever without a town—or gas station—in sight.

Otherwise, this part of the state offers visitors an opportunity to step back in time and enjoy the best of the rural South, from Dublin, where the town turns out a huge St. Patrick's Day celebration, to Jesup and the scenic Altamaha River.

MAGNOLIA MIDLANDS

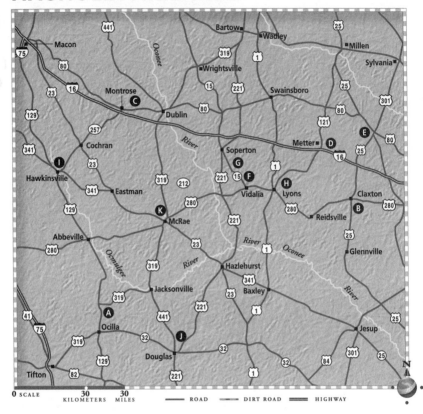

SIGHTS

- Ⓐ Blue & Gray Museum
- Ⓑ Claxton
- Ⓒ Dublin
- Ⓓ Guido Gardens
- Ⓔ Statesboro
- Ⓕ Vidalia

FOOD

- Ⓔ Beaver House Restaurant
- Ⓒ Ma Hawkins Cafe
- Ⓕ Sweat's in Vidalia
- Ⓖ Sweat's Turf N Surf
- Ⓔ Vandy's Barbecue

LODGING

- Ⓔ Comfort Inn
- Ⓒ Days Inn-Dublin
- Ⓕ Days Inn-Vidalia
- Ⓐ Dominy-Massee House
- Ⓗ Robert Toombs House
- Ⓔ Statesboro Inn & Restaurant
- Ⓘ Trotter's Inn

CAMPING

- Ⓙ General Coffee State Park
- Ⓚ Pete Phillips Lodge

Note: Items with the same letter are located in the same area.

WILDLIFE VIEWING AREA

Cartersville CVB

A PERFECT DAY IN THE MAGNOLIA MIDLANDS

Start your day in Dublin with a country breakfast at Ma Hawkins Cafe and a tour of the Dublin-Lauren County Museum. Detour to the Fish Trap Cut and a look at the ancient mounds and tribal fishing hole. Stop at Chappell's Mill and buy a bag of stone-ground cornmeal and head to Metter for a quiet time in Guido Gardens. Take the short drive to Vidalia and browse through the porcelain collection at the Altama Museum of Art and History or take a tour of the local onion farms. After a barbecue lunch at Sweat's, drive to Statesboro and spend the afternoon walking through the Georgia Southern Museum, Lamar Q. Ball Jr. Raptor Center, and the Georgia Southern Botanical Garden. End your day with a fine meal at the Statesboro Inn & Restaurant. Afterward, relax on the wraparound porch.

SIGHTSEEING HIGHLIGHTS

★★★★ **STATESBORO**
Hwy. 301 north of I-16, 60 miles west of Savannah
Home of Georgia Southern University, Statesboro has a charming

downtown that features one of the most beautiful courthouses in the state and the restored historic Jaekel Hotel, where Blues legend Blind Willie McTell once performed. Period street lights and interesting stores add to the charm.

Points of interest on the university campus include the **Georgia Southern Botanical Garden** with 10 acres of rare and native plants, and the **Lamar Q. Ball Jr. Raptor Center,** 912/681-0831, where eagles, hawks, owls, and kestrels thrive in a four-acre woodland. Visitors can watch demonstrations by falconer Steve Hein. Also on campus at the **Georgia Southern Museum,** Hwy. 301, 912/681-5444, you can view the 26-foot skeleton of a Mosasaur, a sea serpent from the Mesozoic era, and other eclectic exhibits. Several hands-on displays will appeal to children.

Details: Visitor Center, 204 S. Main St., 912/484-1869. (2-4 hours)

★★★ **DUBLIN**
45 miles east of Macon off I-16
If Norman Rockwell were going to paint a portrait of a small Southern town, he might choose Dublin. Here is where Main Street still exists with dime stores, soda fountains, and quaint shops. To see what the town was like when it was founded by the Irish in 1812, drop in at the **Dublin-Lauren County Museum** for historical exhibits, a collection of native artifacts, and maps for a walking tour of the town. Two interesting sights just outside of Dublin are **Chappell's Mill,** Hwy. 441, 912/272-5128, an 1811 gristmill that is still in operation, and **Fish Trap Cut,** Hwy. 19, a large scooped-out area on the Oconee River that archaeologists speculate is a 2,000-year-old fishing hole Native Americans used. If you like festivities, the best time to visit Dublin is during the week of St. Patrick's Day.

Details: Dublin-Lauren County Museum, 311 Academy Ave., 912/272-9242. Open Tue-Fri 1-4:30 and by appointment. (2-3 hours)

★★★ **VIDALIA**
This small farming town east of Dublin is known for its sweet Vidalia onions, a delicacy that can be eaten without bringing tears to your eyes. The 10-day Vidalia Onion Festival, with musical events and crafts exhibits, celebrates the first harvest of the onions in late April. For tours of local onion and tobacco farms and processing plants, check with the **Vidalia Welcome Center,** 2805 First St., 912/538-8687. Also of interest is the **Altama Museum of Art and History** with

a collection of more than 260 pieces of English Staffordshire porcelain in 210 different patterns. Other exhibits include paintings by South-eastern artists, Southern wood carvings, and antique Audubon prints. *Details: Take the Vidalia exit off I-16. The town is 16 miles south. Altama Museum of Art and History, 611 Jackson St., 912/537-1911. (2-3 hours)*

★★ CLAXTON
South of Statesboro on Hwy. 301

If you're one of those people who truly likes fruitcake, visit the **Claxton Bakery,** 203 W. Main St., 912/739-3441, or the **Georgia Fruit Cake Co.,** 5 S. Duval St., 912/739-2683, for some free samples. Known as the Fruitcake Capital of the World, Claxton ships six million pounds of the holiday dessert every year. While you're in town, drop by **Wilbanks Apiaries,** Hwy. 280 W., 912/739-3441, for a tour of a major beekeeping operation, and buy some fresh honey. Also, if you're afraid of snakes, don't go to Claxton the second weekend in March. That's when the annual **Rattlesnake Roundup** is held.

Details: 1-2 hours

★ BLUE & GRAY MUSEUM
Old Depot, Johnston St., Fitzgerald, 912/423-5375

This small museum features collections of Civil War memorabilia from both sides. Interpretive displays trace the town's beginnings in 1895 as an area where Union veterans could be resettled. Streets on the west side of the town are named for Confederate generals and those on the east side are named for Union generals.

Details: Open April 1-Oct. 1 Mon-Fri 2-5. Free. (1 hour)

★ GUIDO GARDENS
600 N. Lewis St., Metter, 912/685-2222

These three-acre gardens offer a quiet break in a busy day. Located next to "The Sower" studios of syndicated radio evangelist Michael Guido, the gardens feature waterfalls, fountains, gazebos, inspiring music, and a beautiful prayer chapel.

Details: Open daily. Studio tours Mon-Fri 8-12 and 1-5. (1-2 hours)

FITNESS AND RECREATION

There is an abundance of golf courses in Magnolia Midlands, including an 18-

hole course at **Lake Ocmulgee State Park,** Hwy. 319 and Hwy. 441, 912/868-2832, two miles north of McRae. The park also offers boat rentals and a scenic hiking trail ideal for birdwatching.

In Reidsville, the **Gordonia-Altmaha State Park,** Hwy. 280, 912/557-7744, has a nine-hole golf course and facilities for fishing, swimming, and tennis.

Metter's **Outdoor Nature Trail,** 431 W. Vertia St., provides a sheltered area for picnicking and a quiet paved trail for walking, running, or biking.

More water sports are available at **Paulk Park,** Perry House Rd., 912/423-9357, in Fitzgerald. The park features a large lake with a boat ramp, camping facilities, and athletic fields.

And the **Evans County Public Fishing Area,** Hwy. 280 E., 912/685-6424, in Claxton offers lake fishing, boat ramps, and fishing piers.

FOOD

In Dublin, **Ma Hawkins Cafe,** 124 W. Jackson St., 912/272-0941, serves country-fried steak, chicken, and other Southern meals three times a day at very reasonable prices.

Local barbecue lovers can be found at **Sweat's Surf N Turf,** Hwy. 29, Soperton, 912/529-3637, a nondescript concrete block restaurant that's short on ambiance and long on tangy sauce. You can get the same fine barbecue at the Vidalia branch of **Sweat's,** 215 N.W. Main St., 912/537-3934. Prices are inexpensive to moderate.

The college town of Statesboro offers all-you-can-eat family-style meals of fried chicken, fried okra, and an assortment of vegetables at the **Beaver House Restaurant,** 121 S. Main St., 912/764-2821. If you're hungry for barbecue in Statesboro, **Vandy's Barbecue,** 22 W. Vine St., 912/764-2444, is the place to go. Prices are all moderate.

LODGING

In Lyons, a small farming community five miles east of Vidalia, the **Robert Toombs Inn,** 101 S. State St., 912/526-4489, rents elegantly furnished rooms for moderate prices. Enjoy the flavor of a Victorian house at the **Statesboro Inn & Restaurant,** 106 S. Main St., 912/489-8628. Rates start at $75.

The **Dominy-Massee House,** 516 W. Central Ave., 912/423-3123, in Fitzgerald rents comfortable rooms with private baths for $75 and up.

A number of moderately priced motels and inns are located along I-16 and in several of the small towns. Some of the best choices are the **Days Inn-Dublin,** 2111 Hwy. 441 S., 912/275-7637, with rates starting at $42; **Trotter's Inn,**

111 N. Warren St., 912/783-2914, in Hawkinsville, for $38 and up; the **Comfort Inn,** 316 S. Main St., 912/489-2626, in Statesboro, for $38; and the **Days Inn-Vidalia,** 1503 Lyons Hwy., 912/537-9251, where rates start at $34.

CAMPING

Located near Douglas, the **General Coffee State Park,** Hwy. 32, 912/384-7082, rents 250 campsites for $14 with hookups. Facilities include hiking trails and a swimming pool.

Cottages and campsites are available at **Pete Phillips Lodge** in **Little Ocmulgee State Park,** 912/868-2832, near McRae. Rooms overlooking the golf course rent for $50 and up, and fully equipped cottages rent for $55 and up. Campsites with water and electric hookups go for $14 a night. The park has extensive recreational facilities, including a golf course, boat rentals, and tennis courts.

10
SAVANNAH

Like Garrison Keillor's fictional Lake Wobegon, Savannah appears to be a town that time forgot. Surrounded in the suburbs by industry and shopping malls, downtown Savannah retains all of the charm of an eighteenth-century colonial village.

Consistently ranked as one of the top 10 cities to visit in the United States, Savannah's shady streets lined with moss-draped oaks are perfect for quiet strolls. More than 1,000 historic eighteenth- and nineteenth-century houses in a variety of architectural styles, from English Regency and Italianate to Victorian, have been restored in a downtown area once threatened by the wrecking ball.

The city was founded in 1733 by General James Oglethorpe, who meticulously designed Savannah on a grid system dotted with public squares. Savannah was captured in the Civil War, but General Sherman was so enthralled by the city's beauty that he refused to burn the elegant homes. Instead, he presented Savannah to President Abraham Lincoln as a Christmas gift.

Nearly a century and a half later, Savannah has managed to preserve its charm and beauty in the face of booming commercialization along the coast. The cobblestone Riverfront Plaza, once an area of old warehouses, has been restored as a nine-block shopping and dining district with quaint shops and fine restaurants.

In the last few years, Savannah has been the subject of an invasion of a different sort. Thousands of visitors, fascinated by *Midnight in the Garden of Good and Evil,* John Berendt's best-selling book about a local murder case, have flocked to the city. Avid fans can even take special *Midnight* tours to some of the houses mentioned in the book.

A few miles outside of town, Tybee Island (formerly known as Savannah Beach) provides more contemporary distractions such as swimming, sunbathing, miniature golf, and an old-fashioned amusement park.

A PERFECT DAY IN SAVANNAH

Begin with a visit to the Savannah History Museum. Explore the exhibits and stay for an 18-minute audiovisual presentation that explains the history of the city. Stop in at the Massie Heritage Interpretation Center at Abercorn and Gordon Streets for exhibits and information on the architectural and cultural history of Savannah. Take a stroll along the cobblestone streets of Riverfront Plaza and browse in the galleries and shops. After lunch at the Shrimp Factory, relax on a harbor cruise. Spend the afternoon at the City Market Arts Center and peruse the galleries along Bull Street. Dine early at Elizabeth on 37th or one of the other fine restaurants and end your evening with a horse-and-carriage tour.

ORIENTATION

With its grid layout designed around 21 parklike squares, Savannah is truly a town made for walking. The 2.5-square-mile historic district is divided into sections with River Street on the south, Martin Luther King Jr. Boulevard on the west, and East Broad on the east. Gaston Street marks the northern boundary. If you don't like walking, trolleys, buses, horse-drawn carriages, and bicycles are available. For bus tours, contact **Gray Line,** 912/234-8687, and for a slower pace, call **Carriage Tours of Savannah,** 912/236-6756. **Chatham Area Transit,** 912/233-5767, also operates bus service in the historic district.

Located about 250 miles southeast of Atlanta, Savannah is accessible by car via I-16, by **Amtrak** 800/872-7245, by **Greyhound-Trailways** bus service, 912/233-7723, or by air. Seven airlines, including Delta and Continental, fly into **Savannah International Airport,** 912/964-0514, off I-95 about 16 miles from downtown. Several car rental agencies are located here and taxi service is also available.

SIGHTSEEING HIGHLIGHTS

★★★★ RIVER STREET

This nine-block stretch along the river was once a series of empty

GREATER SAVANNAH

ATLANTIC OCEAN

Tybee Island

Little Tybee Island

Wassaw Sound

Wilmington Island

Wilmington River

Wilmington

Skidaway Island

Skidaway Island State Park

McWHORTER DR

DIAMOND CAUSEWAY

Tybee Island National Wildlife Refuge

Savannah River

SOUTH CAROLINA

SAVANNAH BRIDGE

ISLANDS EXPWY

PRESIDENT ST

JOHNNY MERCER DR

367

80

80

80

26

Tybee Island

E
G
I
F
B

80

Savannah

Forsyth Park

Historic District

BONAVENTURE

SKIDAWAY RD

TRUMAN PKWY

VICTORY DR

Savannah

A
D
C

GASTON
BROAD ST
DRAYTON
WHITAKER
BULL ST
BAY ST
ML KING JR DR

17

16

17

80

516

OGEECHEE

To 95
To H

DE RENNE AV

WATERS AV

ABERCORN ST

MONTGOMERY CROSS RD

204

SPUR
204

WHITEFIELD AV

FERGUSON AV

J

204

516

204

To 95

ROAD   HIGHWAY

0 SCALE   4
KILOMETERS   MILES
                    4

cotton warehouses. Restored as a shopping district in the 1960s, River Street now offers an assortment of pubs, restaurants, art galleries, hotels and shops. Visitors can stroll along the cobblestone streets and watch ships and tugboats as they cruise by. On weekends and during festivals, the streets are packed with revelers and live bands. At the far end of the street is the "waving girl" statue, a sculpture designed by the artist who created the Iwo Jima monument in Washington. Florence Martus was the girl who waved to passing ships every day for 50 years. Some say she was awaiting the return of a sailor she loved, but Martus insisted she did it out of boredom.

Details: *River St. runs parallel to Bay St. and Factors Walk just off the main square in downtown Savannah. Savannah Visitors Center, 301 Martin Luther King Jr. Blvd., 912/944-0460, has more information. (2-4 hours)*

★★★★ SHIPS OF THE SEA MUSEUM
503 E. River St. and 504 E. Bay St., 912/232-1511

Even landlubbers will find something to admire in this unique exhibit. The museum is located in the 1819 Scarbrough House, an elegant mansion built by William Scarbrough. The merchant prince was one of the chief investors in the *Savannah,* the first steamship to cross the Atlantic. A model of that ship is featured here, along with four floors of maritime antiques and memorabilia. The intricate ship models range in size from a few inches to eight feet. One of the most popular is a replica of the *Titanic.*

Details: *Open daily 10-5. $3 adults, $1.50 children. (1-2 hours)*

★★★ TELFAIR ACADEMY OF ARTS AND SCIENCES
121 Barnard St., 912/232-1177

SIGHTS
Ⓐ Bonaventure Cemetery

FOOD
Ⓑ Chimney Creek Crab Shack
Ⓒ Elizabeth on 37th
Ⓓ Johnny Harris
Ⓔ Oar House

LODGING
Ⓕ Hunter House Bed and Breakfast
Ⓔ Ocean Plaza Beach Resort
Ⓖ Presidents' Quarters

CAMPING
Ⓗ Bellaire Woods Campground
Ⓘ River's End Campground and RV Park
Ⓙ Skidaway Island State Park

Note: Items with the same letter are located in the same area.

Built in 1818 by the notable architect William Jay, the Telfair Mansion is the oldest public art museum in the South. A former residence for the royal governor, the mansion has an impressive collection of European paintings, silver, decorative arts, and furniture from the eighteenth and nineteenth centuries.

Details: Open Mon 12-5, Tue-Sat 10-5, Sun 2-5. $5 adults, $1 children. Free on Sundays. (1-2 hours)

★★★ **DAVENPORT HOUSE MUSEUM**
324 E. State St., 912/236-8097
One of the first houses to be restored in the area, this 1820 mansion is a splendid example of the Federal style of architecture. The proposed demolition of this house in 1955 sparked the organization of the Historic Savannah Foundation. Built by master builder Isaiah Davenport and furnished with period antiques, the house represents what life was like for a middle-class businessman in the 1820s.

Details: Open daily 10-4. $5 adults. (1 hour)

★★★ **JULIETTE GORDON LOW BIRTHPLACE**
142 Bull St., 912/233-4501
This 1821 Regency-style house is the home of the founder of the Girl Scouts of America and the First National Historic Landmark in Savannah. Furnishings and memorabilia focus on the life of the Gordon family in the late nineteenth century. More information and exhibits are located in a museum at the **Andrew Low House,** 329 Abercorn St., 912/233-6854, where Low resided after she married.

Details: Open Mon-Tue, Thu-Sat 10-4, Sun 12:30-4:30. $5 adults, $4 children. Girl Scouts receive a discount. (1 hour)

★★ **CITY MARKET**
West St. Julian between Barnard and Montgomery
This renovated four-block section in the heart of Savannah's historic district was designed to capture the atmosphere of the city's old marketplace. It does that and more. On any day you can find artists working in their lofts or displaying their paintings on the street. The market also features dozens of restaurants, jazz clubs, and interesting shops selling crafts and gifts.

Details: 1-2 hours

★★ OWENS-THOMAS HOUSE
124 Abercorn St., 912/233-9743
Designed by English architect William Jay in 1819, this house is a beautiful example of Regency architecture. Features include a museum shop, slave quarters, a carriage house, and a regional art gallery. *Details: Open Mon 12-5, Tue-Sat 10-5, Sun 2-5. Closed in September. $7 adults, $2-$4 children. (1 hour)*

★★ RALPH MARK GILBERT CIVIL RIGHTS MUSEUM
460 Martin Luther King Jr. Blvd., 912/231-8900
Named after the late pastor of the First African Baptist Church, this museum features a variety of exhibits commemorating African American contributions to civil rights in Savannah. A film and other displays show how blacks in Savannah achieved equality through a 15-month boycott of local businesses. *Details: Open Mon-Sat 9-5, Sun 1-5. $4 adults, $2 students. (1-2 hours)*

★★ SAVANNAH HISTORY MUSEUM
301 Martin Luther King Jr. Blvd., 912/238-1779
Located in the Visitor Center, the museum is on the site of the 1779 Siege of Savannah during the Revolutionary War. Exhibits, artifacts, and a short film depict the city's history. Other items of note are an 1890 locomotive and the park bench from the movie *Forrest Gump.* Information about organized tours is available at the Visitor Center, and **Carriage Tours of Savannah,** 912/236-6756, can be booked here. *Details: Open Mon-Fri 8:30-5, Sat-Sun 9-5. Free. (1 hour)*

★ BONAVENTURE CEMETERY
After Jack Leigh's photograph of the statue of a girl in this cemetery appeared on the cover of John Berendt's book, *Midnight in the Garden of Good and Evil,* the family had to remove the statue because throngs of curious people were trampling the graves. Even without the statue, however, Bonaventure Cemetery is a fascinating place. Set amid moss-draped oaks and dogwoods, the cemetery is filled with unusual statuary and tombstones marking the resting places of some of Savannah's most prominent citizens. The famous poet Conrad Aiken and *Moon River* composer Johnny Mercer are buried here. *Details: Take Hwy. 80 east out of Savannah and turn left on Mechanics Ave., left onto Bonaventure Rd., then right at the stop sign. (1-2 hours)*

'ROUND MIDNIGHT

New York writer John Berendt has become the most famous Yankee visitor to Savannah since General Sherman paid his respects at the end of the Civil War. (Sherman was so taken by the beauty of the coastal city that he presented Savannah to President Lincoln as a Christmas present.) Savannah's charm likewise captivated Berendt when he first visited. But he was even more intrigued with the city's wonderful assortment of eccentric characters, many of whom were present during the sensational murder trial of antiques dealer Jim Williams. These same characters later found their way into Berendt's best-selling book about the case, *Midnight in the Garden of Good and Evil*.

Instead of embarrassing Savannah, the book sparked a tourism boom that shows no signs of abating. Some tour companies added special *Midnight* tours that point out locations familiar to those who read the book or saw the Clint Eastwood-directed movie.

One of the main tour attractions, the **Mercer House,** 429 Bull St., is a private residence not open to the public. That doesn't stop visitors from stopping to stare at the Italianate mansion where Williams shot and killed 21-year-old Danny Hansford.

Nearby is the **Hamilton-Turner House,** 330 Abercorn St., a Gothic-style mansion that was the home of Joe Odom, the charming con man glorified in *Midnight*. The house is now a bed-and-breakfast.

The **Mary Marshall Row townhouses** on Oglethorpe Avenue also play a role in the book. Savannah resident Lee Adler, a neighbor and nemesis of Williams, spearheaded a move to save the buildings from demolition in the 1960s and instead restore them to their original charm. Aside from their architectural value, the buildings also have historical significance. Pulitzer Prize-winning poet Conrad Aiken was born in one of the townhouses, moved away when his father killed Aiken's mother and himself, and later returned to spend the last years of his life in the house next door.

One of the two most famous figures associated with the book is no longer in place at **Bonaventure Cemetery** just off Victory Drive. The owners of the "bird girl" statue photographed for the cover of *Midnight in the Garden of Good and Evil* removed it because of the throngs of visitors tromping through the cemetery. You can still see the graves of songwriter Johnny Mercer and Williams' victim, Danny Hansford (see "Sights").

The other famous real-life character is **Lady Chablis,** an African-American transvestite who performs at Club One Jefferson. Fittingly, Lady Chablis' shows begin around midnight. And **Emma Kelly,** the "Lady of 6,000 Songs" featured in Berendt's book, performs regularly at Hannah's East (see "Nightlife").

★ **FLANNERY O'CONNOR HOME**
207 E. Charlton St., 912/233-6014
Readings and other literary events are held in this small cottage where one of Georgia's most famous writers was born. O'Connor, who spent most of her life in Milledgeville, captured the Gothic South in *Wise Blood* and *Everything That Rises Must Converge.*
Details: Open Fri-Sun 1-4. $2. (1 hour)

★ **KING TISDELL COTTAGE**
514 E. Huntingdon St., 912/234-8000
The 1896 Victorian-style house offers exhibits on slave history, African art and the Sea Island culture. It served as an African American residence during the 1890s.
Details: Tours by appointment. $3 adults. (1 hour)

★ **MASSIE HERITAGE INTERPRETATION**
207 E. Gordon St., 912/651-7022
Here is where visitors can get a real overview of Savannah. Exhibits include a scale model of the city, architectural displays, and a hands-on classroom where schoolchildren can learn what life was like in Colonial times.
Details: Open Mon-Fri 9-4:30. Free, but $1.50 donation is suggested. (1 hour)

FITNESS AND RECREATION

With its numerous parks and flat, shady streets, Savannah is ideal for walkers and joggers. Bike rentals are available, too, at **Savannah Bicycle Rentals** in the City Market, 912/232-7900. Rentals are $8 an hour or $30 all day.

Golfers can play a few rounds at the 27-hole **Bacon Park Golf Course** on Shorty Cooper Dr., 912/354-2625, or at the 18-hole **Henderson Golf Course** on Hwy. 204, 912/920-4653. **Bacon Park** offers a lighted driving range as well as tennis courts and ball fields. Tennis courts are also open to the public at **Daffin Park,** 1500 E. Victory Dr., 912/351-3851, and **Forsyth Park,** Gaston and Drayton Sts., 912/351-3852.

Farther afield, fishermen can buy a one-day freshwater license for $3.50 or a nonresident license for the season for $24. No license is required for saltwater fishing. Fifteen miles from Savannah on Tybee Island, the **Chimney Creek Fishing Camp,** 48 Estill Hammock Rd., 912/786-9857, provides freshwater and saltwater charters and all the bait and tackle you'll need.

About 20 miles from downtown, **Skidaway Island Park** on the Diamond Causeway, 912/598-2300, offers boat rentals, swimming, and a scenic one-mile hiking trail that winds through the marshlands.

For beach fun, **Tybee Island** at the end of Hwy. 80 is a sort of Coney Island of the South. Those who don't want to sunbathe or swim in the Atlantic Ocean can spend the day riding the Ferris wheel or other rides at **Tybee Island Amusement Park,** 16th St. and Butler, 912/786-8806.

Serious canoeists and kayakers can find plenty of places to paddle in the inlets around Tybee Island and Little Tybee Island, but beginners may want to book a guided trip with **Sea Kayak Georgia,** 912/786-8732.

FOOD

Savannah offers a multitude of culinary options, from boarding house restaurants to nationally recognized dining establishments. This is the land of collard greens and Hoppin' John, oyster roasts and low-country boils. Hoppin' John is a traditional New Year's dish made with rice and cowpeas. The rice is cooked separately and the cowpeas (or black-eyed peas, if you prefer) are cooked with hamhocks or smoked hog jowls. The low-country boil combines sausages, onions, new potatoes, corn on the cob, and shrimp in one big pot.

One of the landmark eating places in Savannah is **Mrs. Wilkes' Dining Room,** 107 W. Jones St., 912/236-9816, an old boarding house where diners are seated at big oilcloth-covered tables with complete strangers. Great platters of fried chicken, biscuits, chicken and dumplings, and vegetables are placed on the table and everyone eats family style. Prices are less than $15.

The Lady & Sons, 311 W. Congress St., 912/233-2600, serves fried chicken, squash casserole, hoecakes, and other Southern food in a less frantic environment than at Mrs. Wilkes for moderate prices.

Other popular low-country establishments are **Nita's,** 140 Abercorn St., 912/238-8233, a tiny storefront café where you can get a heaping plate of vegetables and cornbread for around $5, and **Clary's Cafe,** 404 Abercorn St., 912/233-0402, which serves daily specials and sandwiches along with milk-shakes and root beer floats at inexpensive prices.

The most acclaimed restaurant in town is **Elizabeth on 37th,** 105 E. 37th St., 912/236-5547. Owner and chef Elizabeth Terry serves gourmet dishes with freshly caught seafood in a historic house. Touted as one of the best restaurants in the country by dining critics, the restaurant is almost always crowded on weekends. Make reservations early and expect to pay $20 or more, depending on your beverages.

Other upscale dining places are **45 South,** 20 E. Broad St., 912/233-1881, which specializes in crabcakes and fresh seafood, and **17 Hundred 90,** 307 E. President St., 912/236-7122, a historic-inn restaurant featuring rack of lamb, steaks, and seafood.

A favorite eating place of locals for years, **Johnny Harris' Restaurant,** 1651 Victory Dr., 912/354-7810, serves some of the best barbecue and Southern fried chicken in the city. Comfortable padded booths and friendly waitresses add to the casual atmosphere. Prices are moderate.

For takeout barbecue and deviled crabs, most of the locals go to **Walls' Barbecue,** 515 E. York Ln., 912/232-9754. Basically a kitchen and a counter, there are only three tables for dine-in. Side dishes include potato salad, red rice, and vegetables for just a few dollars.

There are several dining choices on River Street, but one of the most interesting is **The Shrimp Factory,** 313 E. River St., 912/236-4229, which offers traditional seafood and an unusual concoction called Pine Bark Stew for around $10 to $15. Actually, it's a bouillabaisse loaded with oysters, fish and other seafood, and it's delicious.

Over on Tybee Island, you can get more fresh seafood at the **Oar House,** 1311 Butler Ave., 912/786-5055. A local favorite is peel-your-own boiled shrimp for $7.50 a pound. And at the **Crab Shack at Chimney Creek,** 40-A Estill Hammock Rd., 912/786-9857, steamed shrimp and crabs, low-country boils, and huge platters of fried shrimp and oysters are served in a rustic waterfront setting for around $15.

To start your day, stop at any of the trendy coffeehouses such as **Huey's,** 115 E. River St., 912/234-7385, which serves delicious beignets for moderate prices, or **Ex Libris,** 228 Martin Luther King Jr. Blvd., 912/238-2427, a

DOWNTOWN SAVANNAH

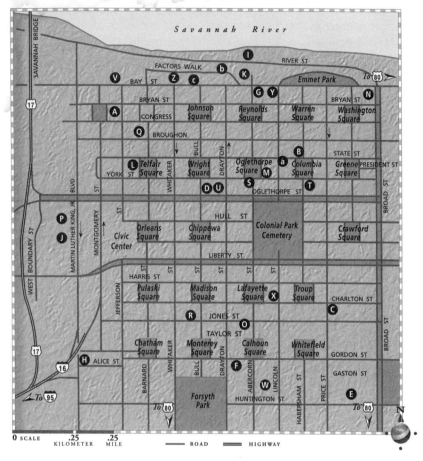

wonderful bookstore and coffee shop where you can enjoy your java and the latest novel, too.

LODGING

Savannah abounds with bed-and-breakfasts and quaint inns as well as ultra-modern hotels and moderately priced chain motels. Prices at bed-and-breakfasts range from $85 to more than $150, depending on the location. Hotels offer about the same price range, although you can book some rooms in the off-season for $50 to $60 or less. The best way to truly absorb the flavor of Savannah, however, is to stay at one of the many historic inns.

One of the most opulent bed-and-breakfasts is the 1830s **Ballastone Inn,** 14 E. Oglethorpe Ave., 912/236-1484. A former bordello, the Ballastone has 17 rooms and suites with whirlpool baths, fireplaces, and queen-size Victorian brass beds. Guests can gather for drinks at a full-service bar decorated like the one on the Orient Express.

For other luxurious accommodations, the **Gastonian,** 220 E. Gaston St., 912/232-2869, with rooms starting at $80, and the **Kehoe House,** 123 Habersham St., 912/232-1020, where rooms cost $175 and up, are excellent choices. The Gastonian, an 1868 mansion, offers 13 guest rooms decorated with nineteenth-century antiques. Each room has a working fireplace. Guests can choose between a full or continental breakfast. The Kehoe House is an elegant restored Victorian mansion that once belonged to William Kehoe, an Irish immigrant who struck it rich in the ironworks business. Rooms feature 14-foot ceilings, fireplaces, and period furnishings.

Those familiar with *Midnight in the Garden of Good and Evil* may recognize the **Hamilton-Turner House,** 330 Abercorn St., 912/233-1833, as the place where a local con man threw great parties. Some locals refer to it as the "Charles Addams House" because of its resemblance to the haunted house cartoons in *The New Yorker*. The current owners offer spacious rooms, good service, and no ghosts at moderate prices.

SIGHTS
- **A** City Market
- **B** Davenport House Museum
- **C** Flannery O'Connor Home
- **D** Juliette Gordon Low Birthplace
- **E** King Tisdell Cottage
- **F** Massie Heritage Interpretation Center
- **G** Owens-Thomas House
- **H** Ralph Mark Gilbert Civil Rights Museum
- **I** River Street
- **J** Savannah History Museum

SIGHTS *(continued)*
- **K** Ships of the Sea Museum
- **L** Telfair Academy of Arts

FOOD
- **M** 17 Hundred 90
- **N** 45 South
- **O** Clary's Cafe
- **P** Ex Libris
- **Q** Huey's
- **Q** The Lady and Sons
- **R** Mrs. Wilkes Boarding House
- **S** Nita's

FOOD *(continued)*
- **T** The Shrimp Factory
- **T** Walls' Barbecue

LODGING
- **U** Ballastone Inn
- **V** Days Inn
- **W** Gastonian
- **X** Hamilton-Turner House
- **Y** Hampton inn
- **Z** Hyatt Regency Riverfront Hotel
- **a** Kehoe House
- **b** River Street Inn
- **c** Savannah Marriott Riverfront

Note: Items with the same letter are located in the same area.

Guests are treated like White House residents at the **Presidents' Quarters,** 225 E. President St., 912/233-1600. Each of the 16 rooms is named for a president and is decorated in period furniture. Complimentary wine and an afternoon tea are provided. Rates are moderate to high.

The **River Street Inn,** 115 E. River St., 912/234-6400, features 44 rooms in a beautifully renovated 1853 cotton warehouse. Rooms face either the waterfront area or the Factors Walk promenade and start at $99.

A short distance away, the **Hyatt Regency Riverfront Hotel,** 2 W. Bay St., 912/238-1234, and the **Hampton Inn,** 201 E. Bay St., 912/231-9700, offer great locations, views of the waterfront, and the kinds of amenities you expect in upscale hotels. Rates start at $139.

On the east side of the waterfront, the **Savannah Marriott Riverfront,** 100 General McIntosh Blvd., 912/223-7722, provides 384 modern rooms and a riverfront lounge with patio dining. Rates start at $119.

For an excellent location at moderate to expensive prices, the **Days Inn,** 201 W. Bay St., 912/236-4440, is the best choice. Rooms are compact but comfortable. Facilities include a pool and a 24-hour coffee shop. Packages include carriage or trolley tours and breakfast for two. Rooms start at $79.

On Tybee Island, you can find moderately priced accommodations at the **Hunter House Bed & Breakfast,** 1701 Butler Blvd., 912/786-7515, with rooms starting at $39, or the **Ocean Plaza Beach Resort,** 15th St. and Oceanfront, 800/215-6370, with rates around $50. The two-story Hunter House offers great views and a convenient seafood restaurant. The Ocean Plaza Beach Resort provides modern rooms with oceanfront views for varying rates according to the season.

CAMPING

Located three blocks from the Tybee Island beach, the **River's End Campground and RV Park,** 915 Polk St., 912/768-5518, offers RV hookups for $20 and tent sites for $14. Facilities include a dump station, a convenience store, and a pool.

On nearby Skidaway Island, campsites are available for $15 a night at **Skidaway Island State Park,** 52 Diamond Causeway, 912/598-2300 or 800/864-7275. Daily parking passes are $2 and pool admission is $1.

About 15 minutes from Savannah, **Bellaire Woods Campground,** 805 Ft. Argyle Rd., 912/748-4000, offers campsites for $21-$27.50 in a peaceful setting in the midst of 24 acres of moss-draped oaks on the Ogeechee River.

NIGHTLIFE

Except for the St. Patrick's Day celebration, when the entire city turns out to celebrate with green beer and dancing in the streets, nightlife in Savannah is somewhat subdued.

The **Savannah Symphony,** 225 Abercorn St., 912/236-9536, performs in its regular season from September to June and offers free concerts in the squares during the summer.

Touring productions and concerts by rock and pop artists are scheduled at the **Savannah Civic Center,** 301 W. Oglethorpe Ave., 912/651-6550. And for stage productions, the **City Lights Theatre Company,** 125 E. Broughton St., 912/234-9860, performs free Shakespeare on the Square in May as well as other plays during the season. Another theatrical outfit, the **Savannah Theatre Company,** 222 Bull St., 912/233-7764, puts on musicals, comedies, and dramas in the fall and spring.

Most of the other nightlife in Savannah is centered around the Riverfront area, a kind of cobblestone Bourbon Street. One of the more popular spots is **Kevin Barry's,** 117 W. River St., 912/233-9626, where traditional pub drinks and Irish music are offered. The bar also has an excellent selection of handmade cigars. **Spanky's,** 317 E. River St., 912/236-3009, is also a popular watering hole, and **Huey's,** 115 E. River St., 912/234-7385, serves up beignets and New Orleans cooking along with music by local entertainers. For live rhythm and blues, your best bet is **J.J. Cagney's,** 17 Bay St., 912/236-0655, where a late-night breakfast is served. **Hannah's East,** 20 E. Broad St., 912/233-5757, is a must-do club where Emma Kelly, "the lady of 6,000 songs," performs jazz selections.

In the City Market, twentysomethings flock to the **Velvet Elvis,** 127 W. Congress St., 912/236-0665, for more cutting-edge music and dancing. Memorabilia includes a velvet portrait of The King, of course, and live music is featured four nights a week. For a glimpse of the famous Lady Chablis from *Midnight in the Garden of Good and Evil,* stop by **Club One Jefferson,** 1 Jefferson St., 912/232-0200. The three-story club features drag shows, dancing, and a sexually diverse clientele.

On Tybee Island, the best place for beer and beach music is the **DeSoto Beach Hotel,** 212 Butler Ave., 912/786-4542. The art deco hotel features live entertainment on a thatched-roof deck in the summer.

11
GOLDEN ISLES/
GEORGIA COAST

The first inhabitants of the necklace of islands along the Georgia coast known as the Golden Isles were the Creek and Guale Indians. They were in turn replaced by invaders from Europe. Several nations fought over these barrier islands until the British were finally triumphant in 1742 at the Battle of Bloody Marsh on St. Simons Island.

Throughout much of the eighteenth and nineteenth centuries, the islands were the homes of plantations where some of the finest cotton in the world was grown. In the late nineteenth century, wealthy Americans such as Henry Ford and his friends bought Jekyll Island and formed the Jekyll Island Club as an exclusive winter retreat. Bought by the state of Georgia in 1947, Jekyll is now an idyllic getaway open to everyone who wants to play golf or tennis, bike along moss-draped lanes, or enjoy the white beaches.

More deluxe golf courses and resorts are available on St. Simons Island as well as a historic lighthouse and a small shopping district of quaint stores and good restaurants. The southernmost barrier island is Cumberland Island, a beautiful, protected wilderness area teeming with birds, wild horses, and other wildlife. The island is accessible only by ferry.

Several towns on the mainland, such as Brunswick and Darien, offer interesting shopping opportunities and some of the best seafood on the coast.

A PERFECT DAY IN THE GOLDEN ISLES/GEORGIA COAST

There are enough activities here to last for several days. One day alone could be spent exploring Cumberland Island or Sapelo Island. Another could begin in St. Simons with a climb to the top of the lighthouse and a visit to the Museum of Coastal History. After a walking tour of the downtown shops or a bike ride out to the historic sites of Fort Frederica and Bloody Marsh, pause for lunch at the Fourth of May Cafe. In the afternoon, drive over to Jekyll Island and take a carriage tour of the historic district. Rent bikes to see the rest of the island or book a sightseeing cruise. Have a relaxed meal at the elegant Grand Dining Room at the Jekyll Island Club Hotel and end your day with a walk on the beach.

SIGHTSEEING HIGHLIGHTS

★★★★ ST. SIMONS
75 miles south of Savannah off I-95
There's an old saying on St. Simons that if you get sand in your shoes, you stay. This island town of 15,000 permanent residents has hooked many a tourist with its balmy climate, sandy beaches and interesting history. The most prominent historic landmark on the island is **St. Simons Lighthouse,** 101 12th St., where visitors in good physical shape can climb to the top for a panoramic view of the ocean and the fishing pier at **Neptune Park.**

Afterward, tour the **Museum of Coastal History,** 101 12th St., 912/638-4666, for exhibits from the island's rich heritage, or visit the **Coastal Encounters Nature Center,** 912/638-0221, which offers wildlife exhibits and educational programs for children.

For a peaceful rest, stop in at **Christ Church,** 6329 Frederica Rd., 912/638-8683. The church was founded in 1736 by the Church of England and John and Charles Wesley. The current sanctuary was built in 1836.

At **Fort Frederica National Monument,** Frederica Rd., 912/638-3639, you can walk through the ruins of the 1736 village built by Georgia's founder, General James Oglethorpe. And, at **Bloody Marsh Battle Site,** Demere Rd., you'll find a monument and a tape recording describing the decisive encounter between the British and the Spanish in 1742.

Details: Take exit 8 to the causeway (there's a 35-cent toll). Visitors Center, 530-B Beachview Dr., 800/933-2627. Open daily 9-5. (4 hours-full day)

GOLDEN ISLES/GEORGIA COAST

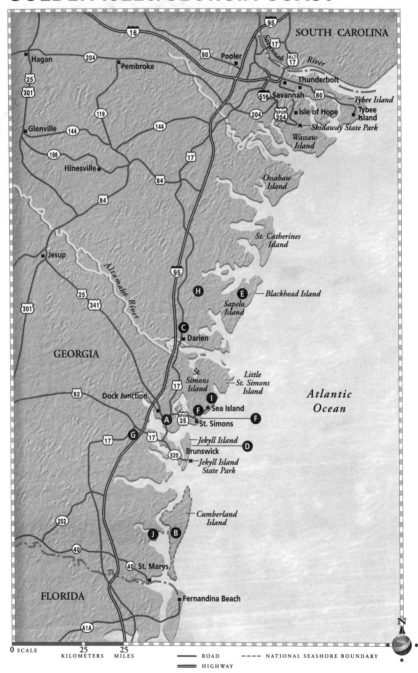

★★★★ **JEKYLL ISLAND**

About 70 miles south of Savannah

Once the playground of millionaires, Jekyll Island is now the playground for anyone who enjoys golf, beach activities, or shopping. The cottages from the Rockefeller and Vanderbilt era have been converted into craft and gift shops in a historic district where the 1887 four-story, turreted Jekyll Island Club is still the dominant landmark. Carriage rides are available at **Victoria's Carriages & Beach Trail Rides** at the **Museum Visitors Center**, 102 Stable Rd., 912/635-9500. While you're in the historic district, go into the 1904 **Faith Chapel**, 375 Riverview Dr., 912/635-2119, to see the beautiful stained-glass windows designed by Louis Comfort Tiffany.

Details: Take I-95 south to exit 6 and follow Hwy. 520 to the island. Jekyll Island Welcome Center, 45 S. Beachview Dr., 912/635-3636. Open daily 9-5. (4 hours-full day)

★★★ **CUMBERLAND ISLAND**

The largest of the barrier islands, Cumberland is a virtually untouched paradise accessible only by boat or ferry. Once owned by Thomas Carnegie, brother of Andrew Carnegie, Cumberland is now administered by the National Park Service. Wild horses believed to be descended from Spanish steeds brought over in the sixteenth cen-

SIGHTS

Ⓐ Brunswick
Ⓑ Cumberland Island
Ⓒ Darien
Ⓓ Jekyll Island
Ⓔ Sapelo Island
Ⓕ St. Simons Island

FOOD

Ⓒ Archie's
Ⓕ Barbara Jean's
Ⓓ Blackbeard's Seafood Restaurant
Ⓕ Blanche's Courtyard
Ⓕ Fourth of May Cafe
Ⓖ Georgia Pig
Ⓓ Grand Dining Room

FOOD *(continued)*

Ⓓ Latitude 31
Ⓕ Mullet Bay
Ⓗ Pelican Point Restaurant
Ⓓ SeaJays Waterfront Cafe and Pub
Ⓐ Willie's Wee-nee Wagon
Ⓓ Zach's Cafe

LODGING

Ⓐ Brunswick Manor
Ⓘ The Cloister
Ⓓ Days Inn Oceanfront
Ⓙ Goodbread House
Ⓑ Greyfield Inn

LODGING *(continued)*

Ⓓ Holiday Inn Beach Resort
Ⓓ Jekyll Island Club Hotel
Ⓕ King and Prince Resort
Ⓕ Queens Court
Ⓕ Sea Gate Inn
Ⓕ St. Simons Inn
Ⓓ Villas by the Sea

CAMPING

Ⓐ Blythe Island Regional Park
Ⓙ Crooked River State Park
Ⓓ Jekyll Island Campground

Note: Items with the same letter are located in the same area.

tury roam the island. Raccoons, turkeys and other wildlife wander through the ruins of eighteenth-and nineteenth-century mansions, alligators inhabit the freshwater ponds, and loggerhead turtles deposit their eggs on the white sand dunes. Carnegie's mansion burned in 1959, but one of the remaining houses, **Plum Orchard,** 912/882-4335, is open for tours the first Sunday of every month. Rangers also offer guided nature walks.

Details: *To reach Cumberland Island, drive to St. Mary's, I-95 to Hwy. 40 east, and catch the ferry. Ferries leave St. Mary's Thu-Mon 9-11:45; they depart from Cumberland Island 10:15-4:45. 912/882-4335. $4 daily fee plus $9.50 adults, $5.65 children, $7.50 seniors. Only 300 visitors per day are allowed. Book reservations months in advance, if possible.*

★★★ DARIEN
About 50 miles south of Savannah

Located at the mouth of the Altamaha River, Darien is a town rich in history. In 1721, a dozen years before Savannah was settled, the British built **Fort King George** on the Altamaha as a defense against the Spanish. Today, a cypress blockhouse has been reconstructed on the site, and a film and exhibits in the nearby museum illustrate the fort's interesting history.

And near Darien, **Butler's Island,** Hwy. 17 S., is the site where Major Pierce Butler established one of the world's largest rice plantations in 1788. His wife, the British actress Fanny Kemble, recorded her unfavorable impressions of slavery and colonial life in *Journal of a Residence on a Georgia Plantation.*

Details: *Take I-95 to the Hwy. 17 exit. McIntosh County Welcome Center, 105 Ft. King George Dr., 912-437-4192. Fort King George, Hwy. 17, 912/437-4770. Open Tue-Sat 9-5, Sun 2-5:30. $4 adults, $2 children. (3-4 hours)*

★★ BRUNSWICK
About 78 miles south of Savannah on Hwy. 17

Located on the mainland across from St. Simons, Brunswick is a major port and shrimping town. It is also the home of several interesting historic sites, including the **Lanier Oak,** Hwy. 17, where Georgia poet Sidney Lanier was inspired to write some of his famous poems, including *Marshes of Glynn.* At Prince and Albany Streets is the 900-year-old **Lover's Oak,** where, according to legend, Native American braves and their maidens would meet.

FORT FREDERICA

If the kids are restless, take them to the **Low Country Alligator Farm,** 6543 New Jesup Hwy., 912/280-0300, where they can observe gators and other reptiles in cages and ponds. Admission is $7 adults, $3 children.

And, while some plantations on the coast grew cotton, many grew rice. The **Hofwyl-Broadfield Plantation,** 5556 Hwy. 17, 912/264-7333, offers an education in the rice culture with exhibits, a slide show, and a scenic trail along the rice levees.

Details: *Golden Isles Welcome Center, 4 Glynn Ave., 912/265-0620. Hofwyl-Broadfield Plantation open Tue-Sat 9-5, Sun 2-5:30. (2-4 hours)*

★★ **SAPELO ISLAND**

This beautiful unspoiled barrier island is home to **Hog Hammock,** an African American Geechee community descended from slaves. Visitors take a 30-minute ferry ride to get to the island, and guided tours can be booked in advance through the **Sapelo Island Natural Estuarine Research Reserve,** 912/485-2251. You can also opt to explore the island on your own, or accept an offer from one of the locals for a private tour. For a three-hour mule-drawn wagon tour, contact **Maurice Bailey** at 912/485-2170. A full-day tour includes stops at a Guale Indian site, plantation ruins, the **R. J.**

A QUICK TOUR OF THE ISLANDS

Visitors to the Georgia coast will find a variety of manmade and natural wonders on the state's string of barrier islands. Beginning near Savannah on Tybee Island, vacationers can enjoy Coney Island-like attractions, such as video arcades, a putt-putt golf course, hot dog stands, a fishing pier, the Tybee Lighthouse, and the Tybee Island Amusement Park at 16th St. and Butler, 912/786-5917.

If you're not in the mood for noise and entertainment, seclusion is a short canoe or sea kayak trip away on Little Tybee Island. Guided trips are available from Sea Kayak Georgia, 912/786-8732.

Wassaw Island is another relatively undeveloped island that is accessible only by boat and open for day use only. Protected as a refuge by the U.S. Fish and Wildlife Service, Wassaw features seven miles of pristine beaches, miles of hiking trails, and the remnants of an 1898 fort. Seasoned sailors can rent a boat to reach the island on their own; others can use a charter boat service. Contact the Savannah Coastal Refuges office, 912/652-4415, for more information.

Ossabaw Island is worth a visit if you're interested in history or the wild hogs that inhabit the island. Some buildings from slavery times still stand and shelters are available to non-profit groups. Tours can be arranged through the Department of Natural Resources, 912/485-2251.

Blackbeard Island is named, of course, for the infamous buccaneer Edward Teach. Now designated as a wildlife refuge, the island originally was used as a source of timber for shipbuilding in the 1800s. There are miles of hiking trails, freshwater ponds for fishing, and ample locations for bird-watching. The island is a short canoe trip from Sapelo Island.

Sapelo Island is accessible by a daily ferry, but the number of visitors is controlled to protect the environment. Once owned by tobacco magnate R.J. Reynolds, the island now belongs to the state. One of the most interesting features of Sapelo is Hog Hammock, a Geechee community populated by descendants from a West African slave named Bailli. Tours of the island can be booked through the visitors center, 912/437-3224, near the Meridian dock. Paddling excursions are available through SouthEast Adventure Outfitters, 912/638-6732.

Wolf Island, 912/944-4415, is another wildlife refuge that is great for bird-watchers and anglers, but not very interesting for those who want to be entertained.

With its 10,000 acres of marshes, ponds and forests, the privately owned Little St. Simons Island is one of the better bird-watching locations on the coast. More than 200 different kinds of birds have been recorded here, as well as a variety of larger wildlife. In order to visit the island, however, you must be a guest at Little St. Simons Island Resort, 912/638-7472. Rates ranging from $290 include lodging in a rustic setting, family-style meals, and daily activities such as horseback riding, fly fishing, and canoe trips.

Reynolds Mansion, and the abandoned **First African Baptist Church.** Wildlife sightings along the way are not uncommon.

Details: From Savannah, take I-95 south to exit 11. Then take Hwy. 99 east to Landing Dr. Sapelo Island Visitors Center, Landing Dr., 912/437-3224. (4 hours-full day)

FITNESS AND RECREATION

The Golden Isles area is truly a paradise for golfers. Jekyll Island alone has three 18-hole golf courses, including the **Jekyll Island Golf Club,** Capt. Wylly Rd., 912/635-2368, Georgia's largest public golf resort with 63 challenging holes.

St. Simons Island has a reasonably priced public course, the **St. Simons Island Club,** 100 Kings Wy., 912/638-5130, in addition to the more expensive **Sea Palms Golf and Tennis Resort,** 5445 Frederica Rd., 912/638-5118, and the **Sea Island Golf Course,** 100 Retreat Ave., 912/638-5118. Greens fees can range from $50 up, but hotels often offer package deals for golf and tennis.

If you have no interest in putting around, there is still plenty to do. Water sports, of course, are very big here and the **SouthEast Adventure Outfitters,** 313 Mallery St., 912/638-6732, offers guided canoe and sea kayak trips ranging from a couple of hours to several days. Scuba diving expeditions can be booked at **St. Simons' Island Dive Center,** 912/638-6590, and the Golden Isles Marina, 206 Marina Dr., 912/634-1128, rents jet skis and offers fishing boat charters. And **Toler's Amoco,** 533 Ocean Blvd., 912/638-6775, on St. Simons rents bicycles.

On Jekyll Island, bikes can be rented by the hour or day at **Bicycle & Jogging Trails,** N. Beachview Dr., 912/635-2648. The island has 20 miles of paved bike paths that wind through the historic district and along the beach. There's also a miniature golf course. And the **Fishing Pier,** N. Riverview Dr., 912/635-3636, offers a quiet place for fishing and picnicking.

For freshwater fun, take the kids to **Summer Waves,** S. Riverview Dr., 912/635-2074. The 11-acre water park on Jekyll has a wave pool, water slides, and a children's pool. Tennis courts on Jekyll are open to the public at **Tennis Center,** Capt. Wylly Rd., 912/635-3154. Rates are $12-$14 an hour.

In Darien, would-be sailors can sign up for lessons or dolphin tours at **Blackbeard Sailing and Navigating School,** Blackbeard Cove, 912/437-4878.

All of the islands are ideal for walking, hiking, and jogging, but Cumberland Island probably offers the most interesting possibilities. Several trails wind through the forests and wilderness areas of the island, including a marsh trail and a river trail. Maps are available on the ferry ride over from the mainland.

FOOD

As you might expect, seafood is king on the coast. Georgia shrimp and crabs are fresh and succulent, and many of the restaurants catch their own fish or buy them fresh off the boats at Brunswick or Darien.

On St. Simons in the village, **Mullet Bay,** 512 Ocean Blvd., 912/634-9977, specializes in shrimp and seafood platters served in the dining room or on the charming porch. The yellowfin tuna Caesar salad is great for lighter dining. Prices are moderate to expensive. More seafood as well as steaks and chicken are available for reasonable prices at **Blanche's Courtyard,** 4400 Ocean Blvd., 912/638-3030. Inexpensive Southern-style plate lunches and sandwiches are served at the **Fourth of May Cafe,** Mallery St., 912/638-5444, and catfish dinners and other country cooking are available at **Barbara Jean's,** 214 Mallery St., 912/634-6500.

On Jekyll, fine breakfasts, lunches and dinners are served at the Jekyll Island Club Hotel's **Grand Dining Room,** 317 Riverview Dr., 912/635-2600. Prices are moderate to expensive. For casual but elegant riverside dining, try **Latitude 31,** Historic Wharf, 912/635-3301. **SeaJays Waterfront Cafe and Pub,** Jekyll Harbor Marina, 912/635-3200, is known for its low-country

Golden Isles VB

boil, and **Blackbeard's Seafood Restaurant and Lounge,** N. Beachview Dr., 912/635-3522, offers a sumptuous all-you-can-eat seafood buffet for moderate prices. Breakfast fare of muffins, waffles, and omelets is served at **Zach's Cafe,** Beachview Dr. at Jekyll Island Shopping Center, 912/635-2040. In Darien, **Archie's,** Hwy. 17, 912/233-1881, is a local culinary landmark. Heaping platters of fried shrimp and catfish are served in a casual atmosphere for around $15. Dinners only.

And, about three miles east of Crescent on Hwy. 17, look for the signs to **Pelican Point Restaurant,** 912/832-4295. The seafood is fresh and the waterfront view across Sapelo Sound is fantastic. It's open daily for dinner only for $15-$20.

If you're not a seafood lover, you can find barbecue at the **Georgia Pig,** I-95, exit 6, or fried pork chop sandwiches at **Willie's Wee-nee Wagon,** 3599 Altama Ave., 912/264-1146, in Brunswick. Prices are a bargain.

LODGING

A number of good chain motels are located along I-95 south of Savannah, but you can also find a variety of accommodations ranging from inexpensive to luxurious on the islands themselves.

Two of the most prestigious are **The Cloister,** 100 First St., 800/732-

4752, the legendary Mobil five-star hotel on Sea Island, and Cumberland Island's **Greyfield Inn,** Grand Ave., 904/261-6408, an elegant retreat in a turn-of-the-century mansion. Rates at both start in the $300 range. The Cloister features an excellent restaurant, a spa, and impeccable service. Meals and access to tennis courts, golf courses, and riding stables are included in the price.

On St. Simons, the **King and Prince Resort,** 201 Arnold Rd., 800/342-0212, offers elegant accommodations at a somewhat lower price than The Cloister and the Greyfield. Rates start at around $110 in the off-season.

Other, less-expensive choices on St. Simons include the modern **St. Simons Inn,** 609 Beachview Dr., 912/638-1101, near the village, **Queens Court,** 437 Kings Way, 912/638-8459, an older motel also convenient to the village, and the **ea Gate Inn,** 1014 Ocean Blvd., 912/638-8661, an oceanfront motel down the beach from the town with rates from $60-$80. Other hotel rates adjusted seasonally.

For historic grandeur and reasonable rates, it's difficult to beat the **Jekyll Island Club Hotel,** 371 Riverview Dr., 912/635-2600. The Victorian hotel features indoor tennis courts and a pool with scenic views of the marsh. Rates start at around $90. On the north end of the island, **Villas by the Sea,** 1175 N. Beachview Dr., 912/635-2521, offers rates from $74 up and a secluded location.

Jekyll also has several chain hotels, including the **Holiday Inn Beach Resort,** 200 S. Beachview Dr., 912/635-3311, with prices starting at $59, and the **Days Inn-Oceanfront,** 60 S. Beachview Dr., 912/635-3319, with rates around $39.

For those interested in staying at a bed-and-breakfast, some good choices are **Brunswick Manor,** 825 Egmont St., 912/265-6889, with antiques-furnished rooms for $75-$100, and the **Goodbread House,** 209 Osborne St., 912/882-7490, in St. Marys. This restored Victorian was named for Captain Walton Goodbread, who operated a ferry to Cumberland Island in the 1930s. Rooms with private baths start at $65.

CAMPING

Basic camping facilities are available in Brunswick at **Blythe Island Regional Park,** 6616 Blythe Island Hwy., 912/261-3805. Tent sites rent for $10 and sites with hookups start at $17.

One of the more scenic camping areas is in St. Mary's at **Crooked River State Park,** 3092 Spur 40, 912/882-5256, a 500-acre park overlooking the marshlands and Crooked River. Equipped cottages rent for $60 up and tent sites are $14 a night.

Better accommodations can be found at **Jekyll Island Campground,** N. Riverview Dr., 912/635-3021, with 220 campsites in a wooded area on the island's north end. Full hookups are $17 and tent sites are $12. Facilities include showers, laundry, pay phones, and a full-service store that rents bikes.

NIGHTLIFE

Most of the nightlife here is restricted to hotel lounges and a few watering holes such as **Murphy's Tavern** in the village on St. Simons Island. From fall through spring, **The Island Players,** 912/638-3031, perform musicals and plays in Neptune Park.

Otherwise, time your visit to coincide with Jekyll Island's **Country-by-the-Sea** country music festival in June, a **Beach Music Festival** in August, or the **Bluegrass Festival** in December. St. Simons hosts the **Georgia Sea Island Festival** in August with "Geechee" music and cuisine, and Brunswick pays tribute to Brunswick stew with its **Stews and Blues Festival** in October.

Scenic Route: The Georgia Coast

You can get to the Golden Isles and all the little towns along the way from Savannah very quickly by driving south on I-95, but you'll miss a lot of the local flavor if you do. The most scenic route is along Hwy. 17 from Savannah to St. Marys, about 100 miles not counting any side trips or detours you want to make along the way.

Heading south from Savannah, you'll drive through **Richmond Hill** just across the Ogeechee River. At **Fort McAllister State Historic Park,** 3894 Ft.

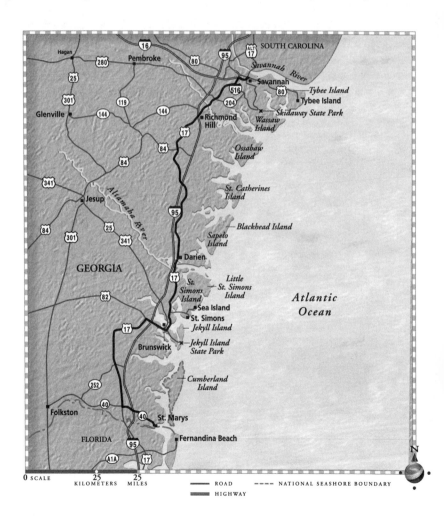

McAllister Rd., 800/864-7275, you'll see the fortifications where the Confederates took their last valiant but futile stand against General Sherman's forces. Continuing on Hwy. 17 about 33 miles from Savannah is **Shellman Bluff,** a fishing village located on the Julienton River. If you're inclined to fish, you can charter a boat at **Fisherman's Lodge,** 912/832-4671, and go out to the barrier islands. **Hunter's Cafe,** 912/832-5848, serves fresh flounder and seafood, but if you're really hungry, wait until you get to **Pelican Point Restaurant** in **Crescent,** which is about three miles east of Hwy. 17. Only dinner is served, but it's worth it to try the all-you-can-eat seafood in a rustic dining room overlooking Sapelo Sound.

Another 13 miles down Hwy. 17 is **Meridian,** where you can opt to go to **Sapelo Island** for a tour of the African American community of **Hog Hammock** in the **Sapelo Island Natural Estuarine Research Reserve,** Landing Rd., 912/485-2251.

If you continue down Hwy. 17, six miles later you'll hit **Darien,** a quiet little town on the Altamaha River. The **Darien Waterfront Park,** 103 Fort King Dr., 912/437-4192, offers a boardwalk, two fishing docks, and a picnic area. Two

RIBBON-SMOOTH BEACHES

Golden Isles VB

interesting sites worth visiting are Butler's Island, Hwy. 17 S., where the remnants of a once-prosperous rice plantation remain, and **Fort King George State Historic Site,** Hwy. 17, 912/437-4770, where you can tour a cypress blockhouse and restored fortifications of a 1721 British fort.

From Darien, head to **Brunswick** 16 miles away. Take the kids to the **Low Country Alligator Farm,** 6543 New Jesup Hwy., 912/280-0300, shop at some of the antique stores downtown, or drive out to **Hofwyl-Broadfield Plantation,** 5556 Hwy. 17, 912/264-7333, for a look at a historic rice plantation, an antebellum home, and a museum.

The last leg of your trip is the 27-mile stretch to **Kingsland** and **St. Marys.** The gateway to Cumberland Island, Kingsland resembles a turn-of-the-century town with a number of shops selling antiques and collectibles. While you're in nearby St. Marys, tour the **St. Marys Submarine Museum,** 102 St. Marys St., or pack a picnic basket and drive out to **Crooked River State Park,** 3092 Spur 40, where you can have a quiet dinner under the trees. The trip, without stops, takes about two hours. However, if you are going to stop at all the attractions along the way, allow a few extra hours.

12
OKEFENOKEE AND PLANTATION TRACE

The Okefenokee Swamp is one of the most amazing natural wonders in Georgia, or anywhere else, for that matter. The 680-square-mile wilderness area is both beautiful and frightening.

Called "Land of the Trembling Earth" by Native Americans, the swamp is actually a large peat bog fed by the pristine waters of the Suwannee and St. Marys Rivers. It is a habitat for rare plants, migratory birds, and an incredible array of wildlife from deer to alligators. There are no beavers here, however. According to legend, there was a dispute between the beavers and man centuries ago and the angry beavers broke all of their dams, flooded the Okefenokee, and left, never to return again.

The Okefenokee is accessible through three entrances. The 1,200-acre Okefenokee Swamp Park on the north, with an observation tower, wildlife shows, and boat tours, is a good place for families to start. Cabins and campsites are available at the west entrance and the Stephen C. Foster State Park. On the east, the Suwannee Canal Recreation Area provides access for boaters and canoeists along a 12-mile canal that was dug in the 1880s in a futile attempt to drain the swamp. A tour of the Okefenokee Swamp is a must for nature lovers and children fascinated with wildlife. Just be prepared with insect repellent, sunscreen, drinking water, and extra clothing, depending on the season. The nearby towns of Waycross, Folkston and Fargo are oases of civilization for city folks who can rough it only so long.

OKEFENOKEE AND PLANTATION TRACE

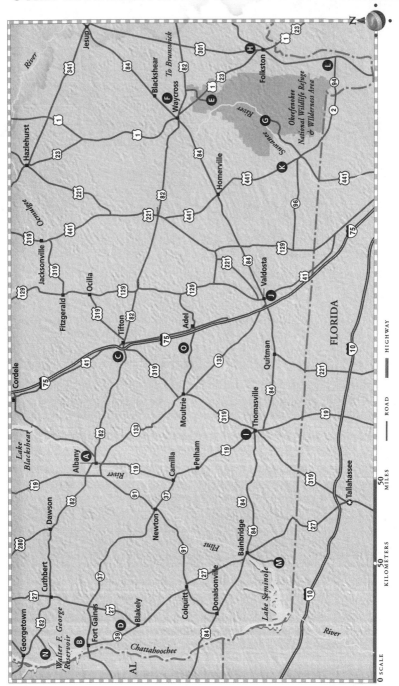

The Plantation Trace region of pine forests, pecan orchards, and cotton fields is a land once roamed by ancient Indian tribes. White settlers came to cultivate small farms, and timber barons and plantation owners followed to build grand, white-columned mansions.

In the late nineteenth century, wealthy Northerners discovered the area was an ideal place to breathe fresh, pine-scented air and escape the bitter winters. Resort hotels sprang up and great plantations covering thousands of acres were converted to quail hunting and fox hunting retreats for the elite. Most of the plantations are closed to the public now, but some, such as Pebble Hill Plantation and Melhana Plantation Resort, welcome visitors throughout the year and during special Christmas tours. The jewel of the area is Thomasville, known as the City of Roses because of its lavish rose gardens that bloom from April through November.

Those interested in ancient civilizations will find several archaeological treasures along the Chattahoochee River in Kolomoki Mounds State Park. Seven In-

SIGHTS

- Ⓐ Albany
- Ⓑ Fort Gaines
- Ⓒ Georgia Agrirama
- Ⓓ Kolomoki Mounds State Historic Park
- Ⓔ Obediah's Okefenok
- Ⓕ Okefenokee Heritage Center
- Ⓔ Okefenokee Swamp Park
- Ⓖ Stephen C. Foster State Park
- Ⓗ Suwannee Canal Recreation Area
- Ⓘ Thomasville
- Ⓙ Valdosta

FOOD

- Ⓚ Carlene's
- Ⓙ Charlie Tripper's
- Ⓘ Fallin's Barbecue
- Ⓐ Fishbones Bar & Grill
- Ⓙ Fish Net
- Ⓐ Gus' Barbecue

FOOD (continued)

- Ⓖ Holiday Inn-Waycross
- Ⓙ J.P. Muldoon's
- Ⓘ J.B.'s Bar-B-Que & Grill
- Ⓘ Market Diner
- Ⓗ Okefenokee Restaurant
- Ⓐ Plantation Grill
- Ⓛ Shirley's Cafe
- Ⓜ Wingate's Lunker Lodge Restaurant

LODGING

- Ⓘ 1848 Paxton House Inn
- Ⓕ Comfort Inn-Waycross
- Ⓐ Comfort Suites-Merry Acres
- Ⓗ Days Inn-Folkston
- Ⓐ Fairfield Inn-Albany
- Ⓗ Georgian Motel
- Ⓗ Hampton Inn
- Ⓙ Holiday Inn-Valdosta
- Ⓕ Holiday Inn-Waycross
- Ⓒ Hummingbird Perch Bed & Breakfast

LODGING (continued)

- Ⓗ The Inn at Folkston
- Ⓕ Jameson Inn-Waycross
- Ⓙ Jolly Inn Motel
- Ⓘ Melhana Plantation
- Ⓒ Morris Manor Bed & Breakfast
- Ⓐ Quality Inn-Merry Acres

CAMPING

- Ⓝ George T. Bagby State Park
- Ⓗ Okefenokee Pastimes
- Ⓞ Reed Bingham State Park
- Ⓜ Seminole State Park
- Ⓖ Stephen C. Foster State Park
- Ⓚ Traders Hill Campground and Recreation Area
- Ⓜ Wingate's Lunker Lodge

Note: Items with the same letter are located in the same area.

dian mounds built in the twelfth and thirteenth centuries are located here, and at Fort Gaines, a fort built in 1814, visitors can tour a re-created frontier village.

Other towns in the area, from Albany to Dawson, offer inviting town squares with antiques shops, quaint boutiques, and a diverse selection of restaurants. And, in Valdosta, travelers can visit Georgia's newest theme park, tour historic homes, or shop 'til they drop at the outlet malls along I-75.

A PERFECT DAY IN OKEFENOKEE AND PLANTATION TRACE

Plan on at least two perfect days in this part of the state. If you're heading for the Okefenokee, pack a picnic lunch and begin your day touring the wildlife exhibits and pioneer homestead at Okefenokee Swamp Park near Waycross. View the swamp from the 90-foot observation tower; then take a 25-minute boat tour. After lunch at one of the picnic areas, visit Obediah's Overlook and the Okefenokee Heritage Center in Waycross for a glimpse of 19th-century pioneer life. Drive to Folkston for dinner at the Okefenokee Restaurant. Then, if you're brave enough, take a night tour of the swamp at the Suwannee Canal Recreation Area.

Another great day would begin in Albany at the Albany Museum of Art and continue at the Parks at Chehaw. After lunch at one of Albany's fine restaurants, head to Thomasville for tours of the Pebble Hill Plantation, the rose gardens, and Birdsong Nature Center. End your day with a buffet dinner at the Market Diner. An alternate option would include a morning at Georgia's Agrirama in Tifton and an afternoon in Valdosta touring the historic district or playing at Wild Adventures.

SIGHTSEEING HIGHLIGHTS

★★★ ALBANY
190 miles south of Atlanta

If you're from New York, you pronounce this *ALL-bany,* but here it's *al-BENNY.* With a population of 120,000, Albany is the largest city in South Georgia. Located on the Flint River, Albany is the home of more than 40 plantations that once provided cotton, corn, and indigo to the Confederacy. Now these plantations have been converted into exclusive hunting preserves, making Albany the Quail Capital of the World. Albany offers a number of attractions, including the **Albany Museum of Art,** which has one of the finest sub-

Saharan African art collections in the South as well as nineteenth-century American and European art.

Other museums of note are the **Mt. Zion Albany Civil Rights Museum,** with exhibits dedicated to Albany's role in the civil rights movement. The museum is housed in Mt. Zion Church, where Martin Luther King Jr. preached in 1961.

The **Parks at Chehaw** offers a peaceful 800-acre environment with a 100-acre Wild Animal Park. Visitors can walk along elevated boardwalks and trails through different ecosystems and view native and exotic animals in their natural habitats.

Details: Exit 32 off I-75 to Hwy. 300. Albany Museum of Art, 311 Meadowlark Dr., 912/439-8400. Open Tue-Sat 10-5. Civil Rights Museum, 326 Whitney Ave., 912/432-1698. Open Wed-Sat 10-4, Sun 2-5. $3 adults, $2 children. Parks at Chehaw, Philema Rd., 912/430-5275. Open daily 9-7. $2 per car. (4 hours-full day)

★★★★ **OKEFENOKEE SWAMP PARK**
5700 Okefenokee Swamp Park Rd., 912/283-0583
Located 12 miles south of Waycross, this park at the northern entrance to the swamp is ideal for families with small children. Attractions include daily wildlife shows, reptile exhibits, and a reconstructed pioneer homestead. A 90-foot observation tower provides a panoramic view of the swamp. For a closer look, take the 25-minute boat tour or rent a canoe. Longer guided excursions into the swamp are also available.

Details: Open daily 9-5:30. $8 adults, $7 children. $12 admission includes boat tour. (2 hours-full day)

★★★★ **SUWANNEE CANAL RECREATION AREA**
Hwy. 121, Folkston, 912/496-7836
Serious boaters and fishermen flock to this 12-mile canal area for day trips and overnight excursions into the swamp. Guided daytime and nighttime boat tours are offered, and five-day canoe rentals are available. Call 800/792-6796 to reserve a night tour for $15. Motorists can take a five-mile scenic excursion along a nature drive to observe wildlife, or walk down the 4,000-foot boardwalk to a 50-foot observation tower. Operated by the U.S. Fish and Wildlife Service, the Canal Recreation Concession rents everything from bicycles to tents and other camping equipment.

Details: Open spring and summer 7 a.m.-7:30 p.m.; fall and winter 8-6. $5 per car. (2 hours-full day)

★★★★ THOMASVILLE
On I-75 on Hwy. 319 S.

Northern millionaires flocked here in the late nineteenth century when a medical article touted the healthy qualities of the pine-scented air. Home of author Bailey White (*Mama Makes Up Her Mind*), Thomasville and the surrounding quail-hunting plantations also figured prominently in Tom Wolfe's novel, *A Man in Full.* Wolfe, who toured several of the grand estates as research, sets part of his book on a fictional plantation called *Turpmtine.* The **Pebble Hill Plantation** is an excellent example of the grandeur of one of these hunting plantations. Built in the 1820s, the Greek Revival mansion is furnished with antiques, Native American memorabilia, and 33 original Audubon prints. Outside are lush grounds with a carriage house, sports stables, vintage cars, a reflecting pond, and formal gardens.

Other sights include the **Rose Test Gardens,** Hwy. 84, a selection of 500 varieties of roses designed around a gazebo near Cherokee Lake, and the historic 1884 Victorian mansion, the **Lapham-Patterson House.** Originally outfitted with gas lighting and indoor plumbing, the restored house is open for tours at Christmas and in April during the Rose Festival.

An overview of Thomasville's history is displayed in exhibits and artifacts at the **Thomas County Historical Museum.** On the museum grounds is a collection of vintage cars, an old farm house, and a Victorian bowling alley.

Outside of town, the **Birdsong Nature Center,** 2106 Meridian Rd., 912/377-4408, offers 565 acres of nature trails, butterfly gardens and wildlife habitats.

Details: Thomasville is located 235 miles southwest of Atlanta; take I-75 south to Hwy. 319. Welcome Center, 109 S. Broad St., 912/226-9600. Pebble Hill Plantation, Hwy. 319, 912/226-2344. Open Tue-Sat 10:30-3:30, Sun 1-5. $3 adults, $1.50 children. Guided tours $7. Lapham-Patterson House, 626 N. Dawson St., 912/225-4004. Open Tue-Sat 9-5, Sun 2-5:30. $2 adults. Thomas County Historical Museum, 725 N. Dawson St., 912/226-7664. Open Mon-Sat 10:30-3:30, Sun 2-5. $4 adults, $1 students. (3 hours-full day)

★★★ GEORGIA AGRIRAMA
I-75, exit 20, Tifton, 912/386-3344

This 95-acre nineteenth-century living history museum in Tifton features more than 40 restored structures, including farm buildings, a gristmill, saw mill, drugstore, print shop, and everything you would expect to find in a small farming community. Costumed interpreters explain what life was like for rural Georgians in the last century. Seasonal celebrations include a Victorian Christmas in mid-December and a Folklife Festival and Spring Frolic in April.

Details: *Open Tue-Sat 9-5. $8 adults, $4 children, $6 seniors. (2-4 hours)*

★★★ OBEDIAH'S OKEFENOK
Swamp Rd., 15 miles south of Waycross, 912/287-0090

More than 50 educational exhibits are featured in this example of a swamper's lifestyle in the late nineteenth century. A historic log home restored with authentic detail is the center of a homestead that includes a gristmill, farm animals, and period costumes. More than 40 exotic and native animals are housed in the Critter Center. Other wildlife can be observed from the nature trails and boardwalks in the park. Special demonstrations include a hog-butchering in mid-March.

Details: *Open daily 10-5. $4.50 adults, $3 children, $3.50 seniors. (2-3 hours)*

★★★ STEPHEN C. FOSTER STATE PARK
Hwy. 177, 20 miles northeast of Fargo, 912/637-5274

This remote part of the swamp is located on a peninsula that provides spectacular views of Okefenokee. Camping, boating facilities, and bike rentals are available, and hikers can take the 1.5-mile boardwalk trail for a close-up—and dry—look at the swamp. Be sure to explore nearby **Billy's Island,** site of a once-thriving logging town that has now returned to wilderness. Interesting trails lead past an old cemetery and an ancient burial mound. Guided boat tours are offered three times a day for $8.

Details: *Open spring and summer 6:30 a.m.-8:30 p.m.; fall and winter 7-7. $5 per car. (2-4 hours)*

★★★ VALDOSTA
230 miles south of Atlanta at exit 5 on I-75

The home of Valdosta State University, Valdosta is located in the heart of tobacco, peach, and pecan country. It is known as the Azalea City for its numerous flowering gardens. The city has three National Register Historic Districts, including **Downtown, Victorian Fairview,** and midtown **Patterson Street.** Architectural styles range from the antebellum period to the Victorian era and the Prairie and Craftsman period. Tour information is available at the **Valdosta-Lowndes Convention & Visitors Bureau,** 1703 Norman Dr., 800/569-8687.

For a look back at Valdosta in the last century, stop by the **Lowndes County Historical Society and Museum.** Exhibits include memorabilia and artifacts dating back to the early 1800s.

One of the newest attractions in Valdosta is **Wild Adventures.** The theme park features four roller coasters and other thrill rides, a safari train ride through a wild animal park, a petting zoo, and seasonal events such as Halloween Haunted Houses and Christmas in the Park.

Details: *Museum, 305 W. Central Ave., 912/247-4780. Open Mon-Fri 10-5; Sat 10-2. Wild Adventures, 3766 Old Clyattville Rd., 800/808-0872. Hours vary by season. $19.95 adults, $17.95 children 3-9 and seniors. (3 hours-full day)*

★★ KOLOMOKI MOUNDS STATE PARK
Hwy. 27, Blakely, 912/723-5296

Located near the Alabama state line, these seven intriguing mounds apparently were built during the twelfth and thirteenth centuries by the Swift Creek and Weeden Island Indians. Four are ceremonial mounds, two are burial mounds, and the other is a temple mound. A partially excavated mound allows visitors to see skeletons and artifacts. Other details about the ancient culture are provided in exhibits and an audiovisual presentation.

Details: *Open Tue-Sat 9-5, Sun 2-5:30. $4 adults, $2 children. (2 hours)*

★★ OKEFENOKEE HERITAGE CENTER
1460 N. Augusta Ave., Waycross, 912/285-4260

More examples of pioneer life in the Okefenokee region are featured at this museum. Other exhibits include a 1912 Baldwin steam locomotive train and caboose, an 1840s farmhouse, and a 1900s print shop. Other events in Waycross include the annual PogoFest in November, in which Pogo, Walt Kelly's famous comic strip possum, is honored.

Details: *Open Mon-Sat 10-5, Sun 1-5. $2 adults, $1 children. (1-2 hours)*

★ FORT GAINES
Hwy. 27 north of Blakely

Founded in 1814 on the Chattahoochee, the town of Fort Gaines remains a picturesque small town. A replica of the original fort built to protect settlers from Creek and Seminole Indian attacks has been constructed in addition to the **Frontier Village.** The village features authentic log cabins, a sugar cane mill, a gristmill, and an 18-foot oak statue as a memorial to the Creek Indians who were removed and sent to Oklahoma on the Trail of Tears.

Details: *Frontier Village, Hwy. 39, 912/768-2984. Open daily 9-5. (2 hours)*

FITNESS AND RECREATION

In addition to the hiking, fishing, boating, and biking opportunities available at the **Okefenokee Swamp Park,** the **Suwannee Canal Recreation Area,** and the **Stephen C. Foster State Park,** canoe rentals and guided excursions down the Suwannee River are offered at **Canoe Outpost,** Like Oak, Florida, 800/428-4147. For more information about Okefenokee Swamp tours, contact the Suwannee Canal Recreation Area, 912/496-7156.

Other recreation facilities include the 18-hole **Folkston Golf Course,** 202 Country Club Rd., 912/496-7155, and the **Okefenokee Sporting Clays,** Folkston, 912/496-2417, a public shooting range for skeet and clay targets. Another 18-hole golf course is located in Waycross at **Laura S. Walker State Park,** 5653 Laura Walker Rd., 912/287-4900. The park also offers swimming, fishing, and boating.

Near Fort Gaines, **George T. Bagby State Park,** Hwy. 39, 800/864-7275, is located on the shores of Lake Walter F. George. The park features an 18-hole golf course, hiking trails, tennis courts, marina, boat ramp, and swimming beach.

Serious fishermen congregate at **Wingate's Lunker Lodge,** Hwy. 97 at Hwy. 310, 912/246-0658, on Lake Seminole in Bainbridge. Accommodations include a men's dormitory, lodge rooms, and a full-service marina with all the fishing equipment you need.

Quail hunting is offered at several plantations, including the **Colquitt County Hunting Plantations,** 912/890-2131, in Moultrie; **Quail Unlimited,** 912/432-2058, in Albany; and **Myrtlewood Hunting Plantation,** Lower Cairo Rd., 912/228-0987. Deer hunting and clay shooting are available as well.

In the Valdosta vicinity, the fishing is good at **Banks Lake National Wildlife Refuge,** Hwy. 122, 912/496-3331, and canoe trips down the Alapaha River or the Withlacoochee River can be booked at the **Suwannee Ca-**

noe Outpost, Hwy. 129, 800/428-4147, just across the state line in Live Oak, Florida.

Albany offers several challenging golf courses, including **Turner Field Golf Course,** 200 McAdams Rd., 912/430-5267, and more than 50 recreational facilities at the **Albany Recreation Department,** 1301 N. Monroe, 912/430-5222. Tennis courts, baseball and softball fields, boat landings, and gyms are open to the public. Also in Albany, racing fans can watch National Hot Rod Association-sanctioned races every Friday and Saturday night from March through October at the **U.S. 19 Dragway,** 1304 Williamsburg Rd., 912/431-0077.

And, in Moultrie, **Moss Farms Diving Facility,** Fifth St., 912/890-5478, provides a state-of-the-art pool for platform and springboard diving. Six Olympic diving teams trained here in 1996.

FOOD

Restaurants are few and far between in the Okefenokee area, so don't plan on having an elaborate anniversary dinner while you're here. One of the most popular spots is **Carlene's,** Hwy. 441 in Fargo, where the locals come for an all-you-can-eat buffet of fried chicken, Hoppin' John (peas and rice), and other Southern delicacies. The restaurant, located near the entrance to the Stephen C. Foster State Park, serves three meals a day at moderate prices.

In Folkston, you can get more inexpensive country cooking at the **Okefenokee Restaurant,** Main St., 912/496-3412, and in St. George, 60 miles south of Folkston, stop in at **Shirley's Cafe,** Hwy. 121, for breakfast, sandwiches, and plate lunches every day but Sunday.

Waycross has mostly fast-food establishments, but a good buffet at reasonable prices is served at the **Holiday Inn-Waycross,** 1725 Memorial Dr., 912/238-4490.

There is no shortage of dining establishments along I-75 and in the larger cities in Southwest Georgia. Albany alone has more than 150 restaurants, from chains to privately owned cafés. Three of the more popular places are **Fishbones Bar & Grill,** 1504 Dawson Rd., 912/439-2384, **Gus' Barbecue,** 2347 Dawson Rd., 912/883-2404, and **Plantation Grill,** 629 N. Westover Blvd., 912/439-1138. Fishbones, a large restaurant with a casual atmosphere, serves traditional Southern lunch specials and fancier, more refined dinners of steak and seafood for moderate prices. Gus' is famous not only for his barbecue, but for fresh-baked pecan pie with chocolate filling. Prices are moderate. And the Plantation Grill offers seafood, steak, and pasta dishes for moderate to higher prices.

But one of the best places to eat in all of Southwest Georgia is the **Market Diner,** Smith Ave., 912/225-1777, next to the Farmers Market in Thomasville. John and Mary Graham's diner serves a buffet of four or five meat entrees with a dozen or more vegetables and dessert for less than $10. Fridays and Saturdays are all-you-can-eat seafood nights, and every Thursday is Old Timey Night, when you'll be served fried fatback, pork brains, chicken feet, chicken gizzards, and other delicacies. A couple of good barbecue joints in Thomasville are **J. B.'s Bar-B-Que & Grill,** Hwy. 319 S., 912/377-9344, and **Fallin's Barbecue,** 2250 E. Pinetree Blvd., 912/228-1071, with all-you-can-eat rib specials.

In Valdosta, you have a choice of any number of good chain restaurants, or you can dine on fresh trout or seafood at the **Fish Net,** Sportsman Cove Rd., 912/559-5410. If you catch your own fish at one of the nearby fishing ponds, the chef will cook it to order for you. More upscale dining is available at **Charlie Tripper's,** 2575 N. Valdosta Rd., 912/247-0366, or at **J. P. Muldoon's,** 11405 Gornto Rd., 912/247-6677.

Really fresh fried seafood and catfish at moderate prices are served at **Wingate's Lunker Lodge Restaurant,** Hwy. 97 at Hwy. 310, 912/246-0658, on Lake Seminole southwest of Bainbridge.

LODGING

Unless you want to camp, the best place to find comfortable accommodations in the Okefenokee Swamp area is in one of the chain motels in Waycross. Choices include the **Comfort Inn-Waycross,** 1903 Memorial Dr., 912/283-3300; **the Hampton Inn,** 1720 Brunswick Hwy., 912/285-5515; the **Jameson Inn-Waycross,** 950 City Blvd., 912/283-3800; and the **Holiday Inn-Waycross,** 1725 Memorial Dr., 912/238-4490, which features a good buffet. Room rates at the motels range from $40-$65.

The only bed-and-breakfast in the area is **The Inn at Folkston,** 509 W. Main St., Folkston, 912/496-6256, an attractive house near downtown. Rates are $75-$125. Or you can stay in one of the two motels in town, the **Days Inn-Folkston,** 1201 S. Second St., 912/496-7767, or the **Georgian Motel,** 1900 N. Second St., 912/496-7767. Rates start at $24 at the Georgian and $32 at Days Inn.

Albany has dozens of motels at moderate prices, including the **Fairfield Inn-Albany,** 2586 N. Slappey Blvd., 912/435-6589, the **Comfort Suites-Merry Acres,** 1400 Dawson Rd., 912/888-3939, and the **Quality Inn-Merry Acres,** 1500 Dawson Rd., 912/435-7721. Rates range from $46-$89. In Colquitt, the **Tarrer Inn,** 155 S. Cuthbert St., 888/803-9791, provides

12 rooms with private baths, period antiques, and hand-painted fireplaces. Breakfast is served either in guests' rooms, in one of three dining areas, or on the veranda. Rates start at $95.

If you're planning to stay a night or two in Thomasville, you may as well soak up some of the historic atmosphere. For truly elegant but somewhat pricey accommodations, the **Melhana Plantation,** 301 Showboat Ln., 888/920-3030, is the best choice. The restored antebellum home features luxurious rooms, an on-site Showboat Theater, and breakfast-all for $200. The **1884 Paxton House Inn,** 445 Remington Ave., 912/226-5197, also offers luxurious accommodations in a Victorian cottage for rates ranging from $90-$250.

Because of its proximity to I-75, Valdosta has more than its share of moderately priced motels, including the **Holiday Inn-Valdosta,** 1309 St. Augustine Rd., 912/242-3881, with rooms for $54, and the **Jolly Inn Motel,** 1701 Ellis Dr., exit 5, 912/244-9500, where rates start at $28.

In Tifton, alternatives to chain motels include the **Hummingbird Perch Bed & Breakfast,** 305 Adams Rd., 912/382-5431, where rooms with private baths rent for $60-$80, or the **Morris Manor Bed and Breakfast,** 405 Love Ave., 912/388-8329, a Queen Anne Victorian home with period furnishings. A gourmet breakfast is served.

CAMPING

One of the most unusual camping facilities is the **Okefenokee Pastimes,** Hwy. 121 S., 912/496-4472, in Folkston. Cabins rent for $35, and extra attractions include the Swamp Gas folk art gallery and a silversmith studio. Tent camping and hookups are available. Seven miles south of Folkston, **Traders Hill Campground & Recreation Area,** Hwy. 121, 912/496-3412, provides campsites and hookups on the beautiful St. Marys River. Facilities include restrooms, a boat ramp, and a picnic shelter.

In Fargo, cottages and campsites can be rented at the **Stephen C. Foster State Park,** Hwy. 177, 800/864-7275, for $56 and up for cabins and $14 and up for campsites with water and electricity hookups. Other facilities include restrooms and a dump station. The campground is an ideal location for those interested in exploring the Okefenokee Swamp.

Located near Adel, **Reed Bingham State Park,** Hwy. 37, 912/896-3551, provides 46 campsites with hookups for $14 in a beautiful setting. Four trails, including a 3.5-mile boardwalk, winds through butterfly gardens and hardwood forests around a 375-acre lake. Swimming and boating facilities are also available. Parking fees are $2.

In Bainbridge, you have a choice of staying in one of the 16 lodge rooms at **Wingate's Lunker Lodge,** Hwy. 97 and Hwy. 310, 912/246-0658, or at one of the 10 two-bedroom cottages in **Seminole State Park,** Hwy. 253, 800/864-7275, near Donalsonville. Fifty sites with water and electric hookups are also available at the campground for $14 and up. Facilities include a miniature golf course, hiking trails, boat rentals, and a swimming beach.

And, at Fort Gaines, **George T. Bagby State Park,** Hwy. 39, 800/864-7275, provides fully equipped cottages for $65 and up and lodge rooms for $42 and up. The lakeside lodge also has a restaurant that serves a nice buffet.

NIGHTLIFE

There's more nightlife than you would imagine in this part of the state. Albany, of course, has a number of chain restaurants with taverns and bars, but it also has an active **Albany Area Arts Council,** 215 N. Jackson St., 912/439-ARTS, that is a clearinghouse for cultural events; **Theatre Albany,** 514 Pine Ave., 912/439-7141, which performs six plays each season; and the **Albany Symphony Orchestra,** 2400 Gillionville Rd., 912/430-6799, Southwest Georgia's only professional orchestra with a full-time conductor.

Traveling shows and concerts are scheduled regularly at the **Albany Municipal Auditorium,** 300 Pine Ave., 912/430-5204.

In Colquitt, **Swamp Gravy,** Georgia's official folk life play, is performed in spring and fall. Call 912/758-5450 for schedule and ticket information.

Tifton's Agrirama, I-75, exit 20, 912/386-3344, also is the site for the **Wiregrass Opry,** an eclectic musical concert with gospel, bluegrass, and country music. Performances are Saturday nights from April through October, and admission is $8 adults, $4 children, and $6 seniors. Also in Tifton, the **Tift Theater for the Performing Arts,** 318 Main St., 912/386-3344, hosts dramatic and musical performances in a restored historic 1930s theater.

And, in Thomasville, concerts, plays, and musicals are performed in the **Thomasville Cultural Center,** 600 E. Washington St., 912/226-0588.

13
CARTER COUNTRY

As you might expect, the area in southwest-central Georgia where former President Jimmy Carter grew up is peanut country. It also is a land of rolling farmland and pine forests, of beautiful gardens created out of a cotton field, and historic places frozen in time.

Little has changed at the Little White House in Warm Springs since Franklin D. Roosevelt visited to soothe his legs in the warm mineral springs. In Westville, a complete 1850s village realistically portrays life in Georgia before the Civil War. And, in Andersonville, the ghosts of Union soldiers still haunt the Confederate prisoner of war camp.

Carter Country is a place where the people take their history seriously, but it is also a place of dreams. The Utopian village of Koinonia spawned Habitat for Humanity, a volunteer organization devoted to building houses for the poor.

Carter Country is also a land of incredible beauty, from the multicolored layers of Providence Canyon to the carefully cultivated oasis known as Callaway Gardens. Whether you take a tour through history along the Andersonville Trail or take a walk through the Cecil B. Day Butterfly Center at Callaway Gardens, Carter Country offers a multitude of attractions.

A PERFECT DAY IN CARTER COUNTRY

Start the day in Plains with a walk through downtown and a stop at the Jimmy

Carter Historic Site. Head for Andersonville and the National Prisoner of War Museum. After lunch at Yoder's Deitsch Haus in Montezuma, drive to Pasquan and a look at Saint EOM's collection of unique folk art. Then journey north to Pine Mountain and spend the rest of the day at Callaway Gardens. Watch the sun set over dinner at the mountaintop Country Kitchen, or put on your finery for an elegant meal at the Callaway Gardens Inn.

SIGHTSEEING HIGHLIGHTS

★★★★ CALLAWAY GARDENS
Hwy. 27, Pine Mountain, 706/663-2281
This private resort in Pine Mountain is located in one of the most beautiful settings in the state. The 2,500 acres include hiking and biking trails through flower gardens and forests, a 65-acre lake, golf courses, the Cecil B. Day Butterfly Center, and the John A. Sibley Horticultural Center. The Butterfly Center is a huge glass atrium where thousands of butterflies flutter among tropical plants. The Sibley Horticultural Center features many native plants, a vegetable garden, and a topiary garden with Alice in Wonderland creatures formed from shrubbery and ivy. The gardens are busiest in spring, when all of the blooms are at their peak, and at Christmas, when all of the gardens are decorated for "Fantasy in Lights." And, during the summer, acrobats from a college circus perform regularly.
Details: Open daily 7-7 March 22-Sept. 1; 7-5 Sept. 2-March 21. $10 adults, $5 children. (4 hours-full day)

★★★★ NATIONAL PRISONER OF WAR MUSEUM
Hwy. 49, Andersonville, 912/924-0343
This new museum near Andersonville is a powerful and shocking reminder of the horrors of war. Visitors can see the bamboo tiger cages where American prisoners were kept in Vietnam and step inside one of the cramped cells with iron shackles. Videotaped interviews with families of POWs are shown continuously on several monitors. Outside the exhibits, a stockade has been reconstructed to show what it was like for thousands of Union prisoners at Andersonville during the Civil War. Nearly 13,000 of the prisoners died from disease or malnutrition and the camp's commander was later hanged for war crimes.
Details: Open daily 8:30-5. Free. (2 hours)

CARTER COUNTRY

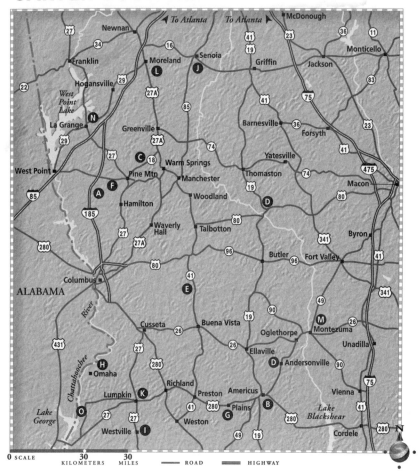

★★★★ PINE MOUNTAIN WILD ANIMAL PARK
1300 Oak Grove Rd., Pine Mountain, 706/663-8744
Kids will love this 500-acre park where hundreds of wild and exotic animals from all over the world are allowed to roam free. You can drive through or take a bus tour of the Wild Animal Safari, which includes camels, bears, lions, zebras, and other wildlife. There's also a petting zoo, and the very brave can peer into the alligator pit or visit the reptile area.
Details: Open daily 10 until dark. $12 adults, $9 children under nine. (2 hours)

★★★★ WESTVILLE
S. Mulberry St., Lumpkin, 912/838-6310

Located a 1/2 mile from downtown Lumpkin (follow the signs),
Westville is one of the state's most-visited living history centers. Iron-
ically, this 1850s town did not exist until the late 1960s when the first
house was moved to the 58-acre site. Now there are 33 buildings in
Westville, including a county courthouse, a shoemaker's shop, and
log cabins modeled after the ones the early settlers built. Craftspeo-
ple in authentic costumes work at their trades during the day and explain the process to visitors. Regular festivals are held throughout the
year, but the biggest one is the Fair of 1850 in mid-October, when
the town is filled with costumed folk cooking over open hearths,
weaving baskets, and making syrup.

*Details: Open Tue-Sat 10-5, Sun 1-5. $8 adults, $5 students and se-
niors, $4 children. (2-4 hours)*

★★★ LITTLE WHITE HOUSE
Hwy. 85W, 706/655-5870

Located in Warm Springs about 75 miles south of Atlanta, this historic house was a retreat for President Franklin D. Roosevelt. He
built the six-room house in 1933 and visited it 41 times to swim in the
warm mineral springs as therapy for his legs. The house is furnished

---

SIGHTS

- **Ⓐ** Callaway Gardens
- **Ⓑ** Habitat for Humanity
- **Ⓒ** Little White House
- **Ⓓ** National Prisoner of
  War Museum
- **Ⓔ** Pasaquan
- **Ⓕ** Pine Mountain Wild
  Animal Park
- **Ⓖ** Plains
- **Ⓗ** Providence Canyon
- **Ⓘ** Westville

FOOD

- **Ⓐ** Bon Cuisine
- **Ⓒ** Bulloch House

FOOD (continued)

- **Ⓐ** Country Kitchen
- **Ⓙ** Cross Road Restaurant
- **Ⓐ** Georgia Room
- **Ⓒ** Mac's Barbecue
- **Ⓐ** McGuire's
- **Ⓚ** Michelle's
- **Ⓑ** Pat's Place
- **Ⓐ** Plantation Room
- **Ⓛ** Sprayberry's
- **Ⓑ** Talking Bean
- **Ⓜ** Yoder's Deitsch House

LODGING

- **Ⓐ** Callaway Gardens Inn
- **Ⓙ** Culpepper House Bed
  and Breakfast

LODGING (continued)

- **Ⓑ** Days Inn-Americus
- **Ⓒ** Hotel Warm Springs
  Bed and Breakfast Inn
- **Ⓐ** Pine Mountain Motel
- **Ⓖ** Plains Bed and
  Breakfast Inn
- **Ⓝ** Ramada Inn-LaGrange
- **Ⓔ** Sign of the Dove
- **Ⓑ** Windsor Hotel

CAMPING

- **Ⓞ** Florence Marina State
  Park
- **Ⓒ** Franklin D. Roosevelt
  State Park
- **Ⓝ** Highland Marina

Note: Items with the same letter are located in the same area.

much as it was when he died here in 1945. His 1938 Ford convertible is still parked in the driveway and the portrait he was posing for sits unfinished on an easel. A path with stones from the 50 states leads to a museum with Roosevelt memorabilia such as his walking canes and cigarette holder. The nearby town has many interesting stores and antiques shops.

Details: Open daily 9-5. $4 adults, $2 children. (1-2 hours)

★★ HABITAT FOR HUMANITY
121 Habitat St., Americus, 912/924-6835

Founded by Millard Fuller in 1976, this organization has built more than 20,000 houses around the world for people who otherwise would not be able to afford them. The labor force is made up of volunteers from all walks of life, including Jimmy and Rosalynn Carter. Guided tours are conducted of Habitat's recent houses and the International Village, with examples of houses the group has built in Kenya, India, and other countries.

Details: Tours Mon-Fri 8, 10, 1, and 3. Free. (2 hours)

★★ PASAQUAN
Hwy. 137, Buena Vista, 912/649-9444

One of the most unusual sights you will see in this part of Georgia, or perhaps anywhere else, is the giant folk art exhibit created by the late Eddie Owens Martin. After an abusive childhood and a near-fatal illness, Martin began seeing visions and renamed himself Saint EOM. For the next 30 years, he created a world of colorful sculptures, paintings, and totems from other cultures, dressed in African dashikis, and attempted to turn his house and grounds into a center where time and place converged. After his suicide in 1986, his property was taken over by the Marion County Historical Society.

Details: 35 miles southeast of Columbus on Hwy. 137. Open Sat 10-6, Sun 1-5. $5 adults, $3 seniors. (1-2 hours)

★★ PLAINS
Hwy. 280, 10 miles west of Americus

The birthplace of Jimmy Carter, Plains has more visitors every year than its entire population of 700. The Plains High School that Carter attended is now the Jimmy Carter Museum, which houses exhibits relating to the former president's student days and his political ca-

BOILED PEANUTS

Visitors to Carter Country cannot drive through the flat farmland without noticing the peanuts. The little legumes are everywhere: in fields, in huge warehouses (Jimmy Carter and his family ran a peanut business before his years in the White House), and at roadside stands lining the two-lane highways.

Eventually, however, non-Southerners will encounter a strange delicacy known as boiled peanuts. These are peanuts—they can be green or dried, but the green ones are better—that are tossed into a large cauldron with salted water and cooked until tender.

Like oysters on the half shell, boiled peanuts are an acquired taste. They are soft, not crunchy, and the best ones are not overly salty. Timid souls can ask for a sample from roadside vendors. They'll be glad to oblige; just don't make a face and spit them out until you leave the premises.

reer. Tour maps at the Georgia Visitor Information Center, Hwy. 280, 912/824-7477, provide directions to Carter's early campaign headquarters at the Plains Depot, his boyhood farm, and Maranatha Baptist Church, where he still teaches Sunday school.

Details: *Jimmy Carter Museum, 300 N. Bond St., 912/824-3413. Open daily 9-5. Free. (1-2 hours)*

★ **PROVIDENCE CANYON**
Hwy. 39C, Lumpkin, 912/838-6202
Georgia's "Little Grand Canyon" is an example of how beautiful the destructive forces of nature can be. Years of erosion created this series of canyons with rainbows of stratified colors. Rare azaleas and wildflowers bloom amid junk cars left to rust. The best views of the canyon are from the three-mile rim trail. An interpretive center in the Providence Canyon State Conservation Park conducts tours and provides information on the unusual geological formations.

Details: *Open daily April-Sept 7 a.m.-9 p.m.; 7 a.m.-6 p.m. the rest of the year. $2 per car. (1-2 hours)*

FITNESS AND RECREATION

The already-mentioned **Callaway Gardens,** Hwy. 27, 706/663-2281, is an ideal destination for families or groups who don't like to do the same things. Those who simply enjoy strolling through gardens and forests can do that while others can hike or bike along miles of paved scenic trails. Swimming and paddleboating is available at **Robin Lake,** tennis and racquetball courts are offered, and golfers can tee off on one of four golf courses where fees range from $32 to $100.

In nearby **Franklin D. Roosevelt State Park,** 2970 Hwy. 190 E., 800/864-7275, visitors can hike the 23-mile **Pine Mountain Trail,** Hwy. 85 W., 706/663-4858, go horseback riding at **Roosevelt Riding Stables,** King's Gap Rd., 706/628-4533, or swim and fish in one of the two lakes.

In nearby Thomaston, the **Flint River Outdoor Center,** 4429 Woodland Rd., 706/647-2633, provides canoeing and rafting trips for all levels of experience.

Over near the Alabama state line, **West Point Lake,** a 25,900-acre body of water north of LaGrange, is a popular spot for fishing, swimming, and camping. Maps are available at the **Visitor Center,** U.S. 29 S., 706/645-2937.

FOOD

In Americus, **Pat's Place,** 1526 S. Lee St., 912/924-0033, serves burgers and sandwiches with beer and live music, and the **Talking Bean,** 142 S. Lee St., 912/924-2299, is the place to get burritos, sandwiches, and gourmet coffee at reasonable prices.

For a belt-stretching buffet, drop in at **Yoder's Deitsch Haus,** Hwy. 26, Montezuma, 912/472-2024. Fried chicken, meat loaf, and vegetables are served cafeteria style with fresh-baked bread and dessert for less than $10.

If you're on your way south from Atlanta on I-85 and you love barbecue, **Sprayberry's Restaurant,** exit 9 in Moreland, 770/253-5080, or the original location at Hwy. 70 and Hwy. 29, 770/253-4421, is a must-stop. This was syndicated columnist Lewis Grizzard's favorite barbecue restaurant. After dinner, drive over to the **Lewis Grizzard Museum,** 27 Main St., 770/304-1490, for a look at memorabilia and a collection of his books, such as *Elvis Is Dead and I Don't Feel So Good Myself.*

East of Moreland in Senoia, the **Cross Road Restaurant,** Hwy. 85 and Hwy. 6, 770/599-3003, is a good place for an inexpensive hearty breakfast or a country lunch buffet.

In Pine Mountain, Callaway Gardens offers three excellent dining choices. The **Country Kitchen,** Hwy. 27 at Hwy. 190, serves breakfast and Southern lunches and dinners in a mountaintop dining room with a great view. While you're there, check out the country store and pick up a supply of speckled grits and homemade jelly. Prices are moderate.

The **Georgia Room** at the Callaway Gardens Inn, Hwy. 27, 800/225-5292, is designed for upscale, dress-up dining, and the **Plantation Room** in the inn offers a daily Southern buffet and a Sunday brunch at moderate prices.

Also in Pine Mountain, more country cooking and barbecue is available at **McGuire's,** Hwy. 27, 706/663-2640. Thursday is all-you-can-eat rib night and on Friday a seafood buffet is served for around $15.

For lighter—and healthier—fare, try **Bon Cuisine,** 113 Broad St., 706/663-2019. Menu choices include grilled chicken and pasta at reasonable prices.

In Lumpkin near Westville, enjoy a moderately priced buffet of fried chicken, catfish, and a variety of vegetables at **Michelle's,** 109 Main St., 912/838-9991. Breakfast is served daily, too.

The village of Warm Springs offers some interesting dining choices as well as an intriguing shopping district. Get delicious hickory-smoked pork plates at **Mac's Barbecue,** Hwy. 27A, 706/655-2472, or a fancier lunch buffet at the Victorian Tea Room, Broad St., 706/655-2472. The **Bulloch House,** Hwy. 27A, 706/655-9068, also offers a buffet as well as menu items such as steak and seafood for moderate to higher prices.

LODGING

In Americus, the elegant 1892 **Windsor Hotel,** 125 W. Lamar St., 912/924-1555, is a Victorian landmark with 53 rooms, crystal chandeliers, and antique reproductions. Rooms rent for $75 and up, and gracious Southern meals of prime rib, pork loin, and lamb are served in the Windsor Dining Room.

Plains Bed and Breakfast Inn, 100 W. Church St., 912/824-7252, offers rooms in a Victorian house for $60 and up.

The **Hotel Warm Springs Bed & Breakfast Inn,** 47 Broad St., 706/655-2114, offers rooms with private baths, a huge Southern breakfast with cheese grits, and a social hour with homemade peach ice cream. Rates are $40-$160.

In Buena Vista, after viewing the eccentric folk art collection at Pasaquan, stop by the **Sign of the Dove,** 4th Ave. and Church St., 912/649-3663, to spend the night in a 1909 Georgia cottage. Each room has a private bath and a continental breakfast is included in the $75 rate. The restaurant also serves a country buffet lunch Thursday through Sunday and a seafood dinner buffet on Friday and Saturday.

ANTIQUE STORE

And, in Pine Mountain, the 349-room **Callaway Gardens Inn,** Hwy. 27, 800/225-5292, has an inn and separate cottages for $96 and up.

The quiet **Culpepper House Bed and Breakfast,** 35 Broad St., Senoia, 770/599-8182, offers rooms in a restored farmhouse for $85 and up.

For moderately priced motels, choices include the **Pine Mountain Motel,** Hwy. 27 S., Pine Mountain, 706/663-9100 for $40 and up; the **Days Inn-Americus,** 1007 Martin Luther King Jr. Blvd., 912/924-3613 for $45; and the **Ramada Inn-LaGrange,** 1513 Lafayette Pkwy., 706/884-6175, for $39 and up.

CAMPING

Rustic log cabins with stone fireplaces and 140 campsites with water and hookups are located in a nice wooded area in **Franklin D. Roosevelt State Park,** 2970 Hwy. 190 E., 800/864-7275. The 21 fully equipped cottages rent for $50 and up and campsites are $14 a night. Park facilities include two fishing lakes, a swimming pool, hiking trails, and riding stables.

In LaGrange on West Point Lake, the **Highland Marina,** 1000 Seminole Rd., Hwy. 109, 706/882-3437, provides 33 fully equipped cabins on the waterfront for $55 and up. Recreation facilities include boat and tube rentals.

West of Lumpkin on the Alabama state line, **Florence Marina State Park,** Hwy. 39, Omaha, 800/864-7275, offers 44 campsites with electric, water, and sewer hookups; laundry facilities; showers; and a concession stand. Ten cottages rent for $40 and up; campsites are $16. Parking fee is $2 per car.

Scenic Route: Andersonville Trail

Heading into South Georgia from Macon, it's tempting to stay on I-75 and avoid all of the small towns and traffic lights. But, as any veteran traveler knows, you also miss seeing the real South. With the Andersonville Trail, you can make a 75-mile detour off the interstate, drive through nearly a dozen towns, visit the home of a president and

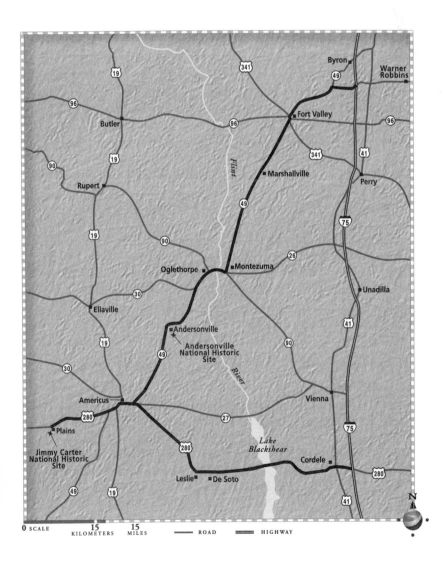

one of the most moving monuments to the victims of war you'll ever see, and still get back on I-75 to continue your journey.

Driving south from Macon, take exit 46 to **Fort Valley** and on to **Montezuma,** about 30 miles away on Hwy. 49. Along the way you'll see vast, green fields, historic houses, and a picturesque dairy farming community (just east of Montezuma) settled by Mennonite families in the early 1950s. If it's near lunchtime, stop at **Yoder's Deitsch Haus,** 912/472-2024, in Montezuma for Southern cooking Mennonite-style. If it's not lunchtime, stop and buy some fresh-baked bread for later.

Ten miles west of Montezuma is **Andersonville,** site of the **Andersonville National P.O.W. Museum,** Hwy. 49, 912/924-0343. The museum is a memorial to prisoners of all wars, from the Civil War to Vietnam. South of the museum and **Andersonville Cemetery,** the town of **Andersonville** features a historic depot and several interesting shops in a reconstructed village.

Ten miles west on Hwy. 49, **Americus** offers grand accommodations at the restored **Windsor Hotel,** 125 W. Lamar St., 912/924-1555, and elegant dinners at the **Windsor Dining Room.** Americus is also the home of **Habitat for Humanity,** 121 Habitat St., 912/924-693. The nonprofit housing group offers tours of examples of houses they have built here and in Third World countries for the poor.

From Americus, take a 10-mile drive to **Plains** and a tour of the little town where Jimmy Carter was born and grew up. Walk through the **Jimmy Carter Museum,** 300 N. Bond St., 912/824-3413, if you like, or head east on Hwy. 280 for the 20-mile trip to **DeSoto** and **Cordele.** You'll want to stop at the **DeSoto Nut House,** Hwy. 280, 912/874-1200 for a tour of the nut candy kitchen and some free samples. In Cordele, the watermelon capital of the world and the state capital during the latter days of the Civil War, browse through the historic downtown and pick up some souvenirs. The watermelon festival is held here the first two weeks in July.

From Cordele, it's only a short drive back to I-85 at exit 33. The Andersonville loop will take about two hours if you don't stop. Add two or three more hours if you intend to tour the National P.O.W. Museum or visit any of the towns.

14
COLUMBUS

With a population of 200,000, Columbus is the second-largest city in Georgia. Founded in 1827 as a frontier town on the Alabama border, the city was a major supplier of cannons and iron-clad ships for the Confederacy. One of the last battles of the war was fought in Columbus a week after General Lee surrendered at Appomattox.

The city has retained much of its Old South charm in the face of industrial progress. Many of the 100-year-old houses in the National Historic District have been restored, and brick-lined streets and Victorian gardens along the banks of the Chattahoochee River make Columbus one of the prettiest cities in the state.

When architects designed Columbus, they planned a large public green space they called the South Commons. Originally intended as a recreational site, South Commons today is a blend of the past and the future. It is now the site of the Columbus Civic Center, a restored Memorial Stadium, and Golden Park, where the minor league baseball players prepare for the big leagues.

Years ago, part of South Commons was used as a city dump and a hospital known as "The Pest House" for patients with highly contagious diseases. In 1834, a horse racing track was built and in the mid-20th century century it was used for automobile racing.

Exhibits in the Civic Center clebrates the past with the Chattahoochee Valley Sports Hall of Fame, which features a multimedia display honoring athletes

COLUMBUS

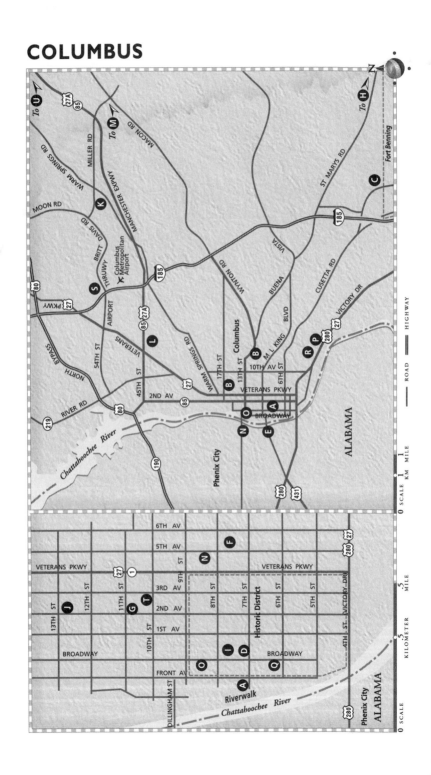

such as Olympic Gold Medal winner Harvey Glance, Master Golf Tournament champion Larry Mize and Chicago White Sox star Frank Thomas.

Columbus also is home to Fort Benning, the largest infantry training facility in the world, but it is not dominated by the military presence as it once was. The birthplace of Carson McCullers, author of *The Heart Is a Lonely Hunter*, Columbus is in the midst of an arts boom. The Columbus Symphony Orchestra plays to packed houses, and the famous Springer Opera House draws thousands to see live theater and performances by actors such as Hal Holbrook and Burt Reynolds.

Columbus also offers a variety of unique museums and art galleries, including the National Infantry Museum, the Woodruff Museum of Civil War Naval History, and the Coca-Cola Space Science Center.

Conveniently located at the end of I-185, Columbus is an ideal base for day trips to nearby natural and cultural attractions such as Callaway Gardens, Warm Springs, and Providence Canyon.

A PERFECT DAY IN COLUMBUS

Begin with a tour of the Springer Opera House and stand on the stage where John Philip Sousa, Will Rogers and Oscar Wilde once stood, then visit the historic Iron Works for a glimpse of exquisite nineteenth-century craftsmanship. After lunch at Minnie's Uptown Restaurant, see what the future holds at the Coca-Cola Space Science Center. In midafternoon, explore art exhibits at the Columbus Museum and stay for a showing of the film, *Chat-*

SIGHTS
- Ⓐ Coca-Cola Space Science Center
- Ⓑ Columbus Museum
- Ⓒ Fort Benning
- Ⓓ Historic Columbus Foundation
- Ⓔ Iron Works
- Ⓕ "Ma" Rainey House
- Ⓖ Springer Opera House
- Ⓗ Woodruff Museum of Civil War Naval History

FOOD
- Ⓘ Bladau's Goetchius House
- Ⓙ Country's on Broad
- Ⓚ Ezell's Catfish Cabin
- Ⓛ Hamilton Road Barbecue
- Ⓜ Macon Road Barbecue
- Ⓝ Minnie's Uptown Restaurant

LODGING
- Ⓞ Columbus Hilton
- Ⓟ Days Inn
- Ⓠ Gates House
- Ⓡ Motel 6
- Ⓢ Sheraton-Columbus Airport Hotel
- Ⓣ Woodruff House Bed-and-Breakfast

CAMPING
- Ⓤ Lake Pines Campground

Note: Items with the same letter are located in the same area.

tahoochee Legacy, an 18-minute documentary that offers a quick introduction to the people and history of the area. Afterward, relax over a gourmet meal at Bladau's Goetchius House overlooking the river, or book passage for a dinner cruise aboard the Chattahoochee River Princess Riverboat. Take an after-dinner stroll along Riverwalk, where you can stop to view the scenic waterfalls.

For an alternate plan, head out to Fort Benning for a tour of the base and the National Infantry Museum, where you can follow the evolution of the American foot soldier and his weapons. From there, drive north on Route 27 and stop at the Columbus Civil War Naval Museum for a look at ships and other artifacts. After a blue plate special lunch at Country's on Broad, rent a bike at Riverwalk Bicycle Rentals for a spin along the Riverwalk and around the historic district. End your day with an evening of bar food and blues at the Uptown Tap or disco dancing at Benjamin's Fine Foods & Spirits.

ORIENTATION

Columbus is located about 100 miles west of Atlanta via I-85 to I-185. Flights are available into the **Columbus Airport,** 706/324-2449, and shuttle van service is offered to and from Atlanta by **Groome Transportation,** 706/324-3939. Greyhound, 818 Fourth Ave., 706/323-5417, also offers bus service to and from Atlanta.

Because it is a planned city, Columbus is beautifully designed in grids around a 26-block historic district known as Uptown Columbus. Most of the houses, museums, and other attractions are located within walking distance in this area. Bus transportation is available, but most visitors drive, walk, or rent bikes. Bikes are available at **Riverwalk Bicycle Rentals,** 1014 Broadway, 706/322-2802, and riverboat cruises can be booked by calling 706/324-4499. Group tours can be arranged at the **Columbus Convention & Visitors Bureau,** 1000 Bay Ave., 706/322-1613 or 800/999-1613.

SIGHTSEEING HIGHLIGHTS

★★★★ COCA-COLA SPACE SCIENCE CENTER
701 Front Ave., 706/649-1470
Take a simulated voyage to the moon or watch a total eclipse of the sun in the interactive Challenger Learning Center housed in this futuristic facility. In the Omnisphere Theater, a special digital projection system allows you to visit outer space or travel through the depths of

the earth. The Mead Observatory features a research-class telescope available to both amateur and professional astronomers. Souvenirs are for sale in the Star Gazers Gift Shop.
Details: Open Tue-Fri 10-4, Sat 1:30-9, Sun 1:30-4. $6 adults, $3 children. (2 hours)

★★★★ COLUMBUS MUSEUM
1251 Wynnton Rd., 706/649-0713
This spacious facility is the second-largest art museum in Georgia and one of the biggest in the Southeast. Exhibitions include a permanent collection of American art and materials of historical significance. Be sure and watch the film, *Chattahoochee Legacy*, for an excellent overview of the area's history. Other areas include a children's room where young art lovers can touch the exhibits.
Details: Open Tue-Sat 10-5, Sun 1-5. Free. (2 hours)

★★★★ SPRINGER OPERA HOUSE
103 10th St., 706/327-3688
In the last century and into the early 1900s, the Springer Opera House was known as one of the finest entertainment venues between New Orleans and Washington, D.C. Legendary performers such as Lillie Langtry, James Edwin Booth, and Will Rogers appeared on stage during its heyday. When the theater deteriorated in the 1960s and appeared headed for demolition, a group of citizens rescued the red brick building and restored it to its former glory. In 1971, then-Governor Jimmy Carter designated the Springer as the State Theater of Georgia. Now the Springer Opera House hosts plays, lectures, concerts, and other entertainment year-round.
Details: Tours by appointment. (1 hour)

★★★ HISTORIC COLUMBUS FOUNDATION
700 Broadway, 706/322-0756
This 1870 Italianate villa is the starting point for a walking tour of the historic district. More than two dozen historic buildings are on the tour, including a **Trader's Log Cabin,** 708 1/2 Broadway, the 1855 **Pemberton House,** 712 Broadway, home of Dr. John Pemberton, inventor of Coca-Cola. The Pemberton House's adjoining kitchen is now a museum for Coke memorabilia.
Details: Tours Mon-Fri 11 and 3, Sat-Sun at 2. $4 adults. (2-3 hours)

★★ FORT BENNING
I-185 W. dead-ends at Fort Benning, 706/545-2958

The United States Army relocated its Infantry School of Arms from Fort Sill, Oklahoma, to Columbus shortly after America entered World War I. The list of Army legends who served here includes Generals George Patton, Dwight D. Eisenhower, and Norman Schwartzkopf. The base is also the home of the controversial School of the Americas, where military officers from Central and South America are trained. On the base, be sure to visit the **National Infantry Museum,** which boasts an interesting collection of historic weapons. A barracks from the World War II generation has been re-created, and visitors can trace the development of the infantryman from World War I to the Persian Gulf War.

Details: Open Tue-Fri 8-4:30, Sat-Sun 12:30-4:30. Free. Dress code prohibits sleeveless shirts and revealing attire. (1-2 hours)

★★ IRON WORKS AND CONVENTION AND VISITORS BUREAU
1000 Bay Ave., 706/322-1613

An impressive red brick structure with massive timbers and exposed ceilings, the Iron Works is an excellent example of nineteenth-century architecture. A major supplier of munitions during the Civil War, the Iron Works is now home to a 77,000-square-foot convention center with two large exhibit halls, a 665-seat amphitheater, and a 450-seat dining gallery overlooking the Chattahoochee River. The center is the scene of events such as the annual three-day **Riverfest** in April.

Details: Open Mon-Fri 8:30-5. (1 hour)

★★ WOODRUFF MUSEUM OF CIVIL WAR NAVAL HISTORY
202 Fourth St., 706/327-9798

This unique museum is home to the *Chattahoochee* and the *Jackson,* two rare gunboats used by the Confederacy. Other displays include ship models and maritime artifacts from the era of blockade-running.

Details: Open Tue-Fri 10-5, Sat-Sun 1-5. Free. (1 hour)

★ "MA" RAINEY HOUSE
805 Fifth Ave., 706/322-0756

Listed on the National Register of Historic Places, this house was the

---

CHATTAHOOCHEE RIVERWALK

Jim Cawthorne

last home of famed 1920s gospel and blues singer Gertrude Pridgett "Ma" Rainey. A postage stamp honoring her as "Mother of the Blues" was issued in 1994.

> **Details:** *Tours Mon-Fri 11 and 3, Sat-Sun at 2. $3. (30 minutes)*

FITNESS AND RECREATION

Riverwalk, a 12-mile stretch of trails along the Chattahoochee River, provides a scenic setting for walkers, joggers, and bikers. Begin your trek at the Visitors Center at 1000 Bay Ave. or rent a bike by the hour or day at **Riverwalk Bicycle Rentals,** 1014 Broadway, 706/322-2802. For more leisurely recreation, book an excursion on the **Chattahoochee Princess Riverboat,** 1000 Bay Ave., 706/324-4499.

Weracoba Park, 17th St. and Cherokee Ave., offers tennis courts, ball fields, and a playground in a shady residential section north of the downtown district.

Sports fans who are in town anytime from April to August may want to catch a game with the **Columbus Redstixx,** 100 Fourth St., 706/571-8866, the minor-league farm team for the Cleveland Indians. The Redstixx play at the **South Commons,** the site of several other ball fields used in the 1996 Olympics for the women's fast-pitch softball games. The **Georgia Pride** of the women's softball league also plays games here. In the winter, hockey fans can cheer on the **Columbus Cottonmouths** of the Central Hockey League at the Civic Center, 400 Fourth St., 706/571-0086.

Beginning golfers will want to test their skills at the **Fountain City Golf Course,** 403 42nd St., 706/324-0583, a fun, accessible 9-hole course. Golfers of all levels can find a course to challenge them at **Maple Ridge Golf Course,** 4700 Maple Ridge Trail, 706/569-0966, with five sets of tees and varying elevations.

FOOD

Like most large cities in Georgia, Columbus has its share of country cafés, chain restaurants, and a smattering of fine dining establishments. The city's culinary claim to fame, however is its barbecue. The locals prefer a spicy mustard sauce, but customers usually can request a tomato-based sauce.

Country's on Broad, 1329 Broadway, 706/596-8910, is almost too fancy to be a barbecue joint. Located in a 1930s bus depot and decorated with lots of chrome, the restaurant offers burgers, blue-plate specials, and other menu options besides smoked pork for reasonable prices.

Hamilton Road Barbecue, 3930 Manchester Expwy., 706/323-8676, serves spicy barbecue sandwiches as well as tasty breakfasts of ham, sausage, and egg biscuits. True barbecue aficionados tend to flock to **Macon Road Barbecue,** Avalon Rd. at Macon Rd., which is located in a cabin in the woods. Prices at both places are inexpensive to moderate.

For a filling country meal of a meat and three vegetables for around $6, follow the local lunch crowd to **Minnie's Uptown Restaurant,** 100 Eighth St., 706/322-2766. Meals are served cafeteria-style. Other deep-fried Southern dishes are available at **Ezell's Catfish Cabin,** 4001 Warm Springs Rd., 706/568-1149, a popular family restaurant specializing in all-you-can-eat catfish and seafood for moderate prices.

One of the few fine dining places in town is **Bladau's Goetchius House,** 405 Broadway, 706/324-4863. Located in an elegant 1839 mansion, the restaurant offers dinner choices of oysters, seafood, prime beef, and frogs' legs. Prices are moderate to expensive.

LODGING

A number of inexpensive to moderately priced motels can be found at any of the exits on I-185, but for fancier quarters near Riverwalk, the 1880s **Gates House,** 737 Broadway, 706/324-6464, features comfortable rooms furnished with Victorian antiques, private baths, a rocking-chair porch, and breakfasts with homemade breads. Rates are $85-$95.

Another fine inn, the **Woodruff House Bed-and-Breakfast,** 1414 Second Ave., 706/320-9300, offers a convenient location in the historic district for $85-$160.

The 178-room **Columbus Hilton,** 800 Front Ave., 706/324-1800, provides the modern amenities of an upscale hotel incorporated into a historic building that once housed a gristmill. Situated near the historic district, the Hilton offers a lounge, coffee shop, swimming pool, and airport transportation for $75 and up.

Two of the better chain motels in the downtown area near South Commons are **Motel 6,** 3050 Victory Dr., 706/687-7214, and the **Days Inn,** 3170 Victory Dr., 706/689-6181. Both provide basic accommodations for less than $40 a night.

For lodging near the airport, the **Sheraton-Columbus Airport Hotel,** 5151 Simons Blvd., 706/327-6868, provides double rooms starting at $60.

CAMPING

The closest camping facility to Columbus is the **Lake Pines Campground,** 6404 Garret Rd., 706/561-9675. Eighty-five sites are available with water, sewer, and electric hookups. Amenities include a swimming pool and a fishing pond.

NIGHTLIFE

Columbus prides itself on its many cultural attractions, from the plays and concerts at the **Springer Opera House,** 103 10th St., 706/324-5714, to classical music by the **Columbus Symphony Orchestra,** 101 13th St., 706/323-5059.

The ultimate in family entertainment is the **Hollywood Connection,** 1683 Whittlesey Rd., 706/571-3456, a huge complex featuring a roller rink, an arcade, miniature golf, laser tag games, a restaurant, and 10 movie theaters. Four of the theaters have stadium seating.

Bluegrass fans usually migrate to **Country's Barbecue,** 3137 Mercury Drive, 706/563-7604, while jazz lovers drop in at **Lady V's Jazz & Blues Club,** 1458 Fort Benning Rd., 706/687-5769. **Victoria's,** 5751 Milgen Rd., 706/568-3316, books local rock bands periodically. The rest of the time the neighborhood bar features karaoke, dart games and billiards. **Rae's Pub and Grill,** 3709 Gentian Blvd., 706/563-6266, also offers karaoke on Thursdays and Saturdays. One of the favorites hangouts in Columbus is **The Loft,** 1032

Broadway, 706/562-9792, which features local rock and pop bands such as the Ajax Heavies and Cornbread. For more rock music along with jazz and blues, check out the **Uptown Tap,** 1024 Broadway, 706/653-8277. And disco dancers may want to try **Benjamin's Fine Foods & Spirits,** 3396 Buena Vista Rd., 706/682-0002, where a DJ spins the best of the '70s hits Tuesday through Saturday.

APPENDIX

Consider this appendix your travel tool box. Use it along with the material in the Planning Your Trip chapter to craft the trip you want. Here are the tools you'll find inside:

1. Planning Map. Make copies of this map and plot out various trip possibilities. Once you've decided on your route, you can write it on the original map and refer to it as you're traveling.

2. Mileage Chart. This chart shows the driving distances (in miles) between various destinations throughout the state/region. Use it in conjunction with the Planning Map.

3. Special Interest Tours. If you'd like to plan a trip around a certain theme-such as nature, sports, or art-one of these tours may work for you.

4. Calendar of Events. Here you'll find a month-by-month listing of major area events.

5. Resource Guide. This guide lists various regional chambers of commerce and visitors bureaus, state offices, bed-and-breakfast registries, and other useful sources of information.

PLANNING MAP: Georgia

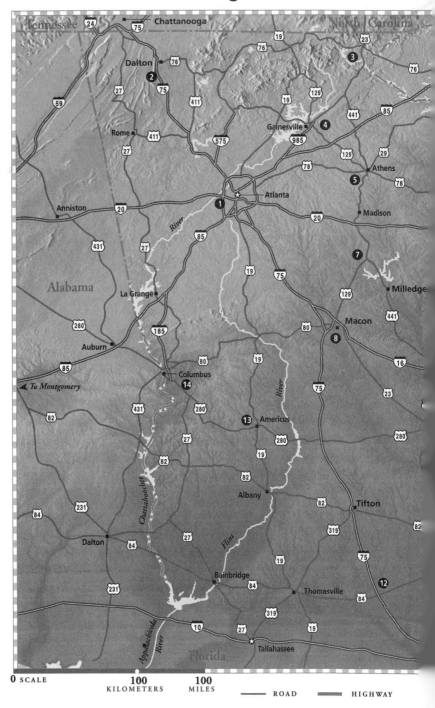

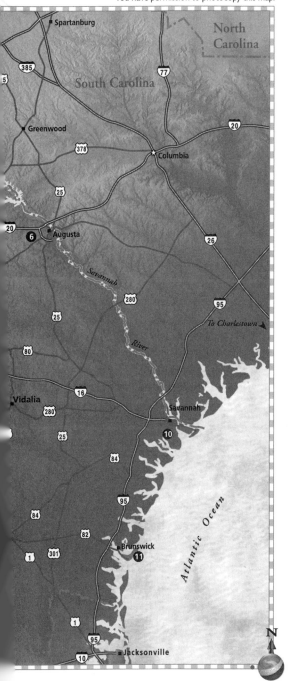

GEORGIA
1. Atlanta
2. Northwest Mountains
3. Northeast Mountains
4. Gainesville and Lake Lanier
5. Athens
6. Augusta
7. Georgia Heartland
8. Macon
9. Magnolia Midlands
10. Savannah
11. Golden Isles and Coast
12. Okefenokee and Plantation Trace
13. Carter Country
14. Columbus

GEORGIA MILEAGE CHART

	Albany	Americus	Atlanta	Augusta	Brunswick	Columbus	Gainesville	Macon	Milledgeville	Rome	Savannah	Statesboro	Valdosta	Waycross
Albany														
Americus	37													
Atlanta	166	130												
Augusta	200	198	139											
Brunswick	180	192	257	203										
Columbus	92	61	123	235	255									
Gainesville	219	183	53	135	316	176								
Macon	113	71	84	124	173	113	125							
Milledgeville	144	102	96	93	216	144	113	36						
Rome	233	190	68	206	325	147	99	152	169					
Savannah	216	206	249	125	78	255	252	167	169	317				
Statesboro	195	168	204	81	111	211	219	120	131	272	56			
Valdosta	80	120	248	221	120	172	280	154	190	310	165	162		
Waycross	113	137	239	177	59	198	281	150	166	321	103	100	61	

SPECIAL INTEREST TOURS

With *Georgia Travel•Smart* you can plan a trip of any length-a one-day excursion, a getaway weekend, or a three-week vacation-around any special interest. To get you started, the following pages contain five diverse special-interest itineraries. For more information, refer to the chapters listed-chapter names are in boldface, and chapter numbers appear inside black bullets. You can follow a suggested itinerary in its entirety, or shorten, lengthen, or combine parts of each, depending on your starting and ending points.

Discuss alternative routes and schedules with your travel companions-it's a great way to have fun even before you leave home. And remember: Don't hesitate to change your itinerary once you're on the road. Careful study and planning ahead will help you make informed decision as you go, but spontaneity is the extra ingredient that will make your trip memorable.

BEST OF GEORGIA TOUR

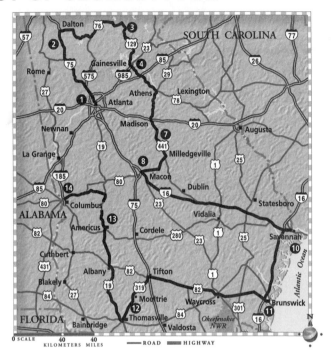

Here are some highlights from the State of Adventure, from its urban centers to its wilderness areas.

❶ **Atlanta** (ZooAtlanta, Atlanta History Center, Fernbank Museum of Natural History, High Museum of Art, World of Coca-Cola, Stone Mountain Park)

❷ **Northwest Georgia** (Paradise Gardens, Etowah Indian Mounds)

❸ **Northeast Georgia** (Dahlonega, Helen, Foxfire Museum)

❹ **Gainesville and Lake Lanier** (Chateau Elan Winery, Lake Lanier Islands)

❼ **Georgia Heartland** (Madison, Milledgeville)

❽ **Macon** (Georgia Music Hall of Fame, Georgia Sports Hall of Fame, historic district)

❿ **Savannah** (River Street, Historic Homes District, Ships of the Sea Museum)

⓫ **Golden Isles** (St. Simons, Jekyll Island, Cumberland Island)

⓬ **Plantation Trace** (Parks at Chehaw, Thomasville, Georgia Agrirama)

⓭ **Carter Country** (Callaway Gardens, National Prisoner of War Museum, Westville)

⓮ **Columbus** (Coca-Cola Space Science Center, Columbus Museum, Springer Opera House, Fort Benning)

Time needed: 2-3 weeks

CIVIL WAR HISTORY TOUR

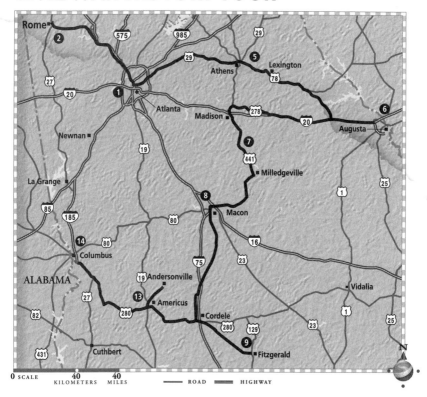

For those interested in battlefields and other historical aspects of the Civil War, this is an interesting tour of the state that was one of General Sherman's main targets.

❶ Atlanta (Atlanta History Center, Cyclorama, Stone Mountain Park, Kennesaw Mountain National Battlefield)

❷ Northwest Georgia (Pickett's Mill Battlefield, Rome Area History Museum, Chicamauga and Chattanooga National Military Park)

❺ Athens (Washington area, Washington Historical Museum)

❻ Augusta (Historic district, Morris Museum of Art)

❼ Georgia Heartland (Madison, Milledgeville, Uncle Remus Museum)

❽ Macon (Cannonball House, Rose Hill Cemetery)

❾ Magnolia Midlands (Blue and Gray Museum, town of Fitzgerald)

❸ Carter Country (Andersonville, Andersonville Cemetery, National Prisoner of War Museum)

❹ Columbus (Woodruff Museum, National Infantry Museum)

Time needed: 10 days

FAMILY FUN TOUR

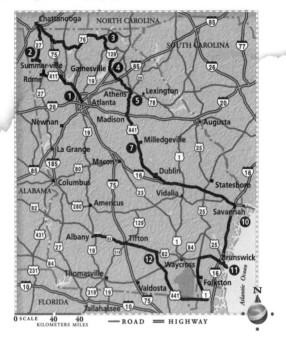

It's no fun for the family if the kids are bored. Here is a trip that should keep children of all ages entertained.

➊ **Atlanta** (ZooAtlanta, World of Coca-Cola, Fernbank Museum of Natural History, Six Flags Over Georgia, Stone Mountain Park, Sci-Trek, American Adventures and White Water Park, Center for Puppetry Arts)

➋ **Northwest Georgia** (Rock City, Cave Spring, Lake Allatoona)

➌ **Northeast Georgia** (Dahlonega, BabyLand General Hospital, Foxfire Museum, Andy's Trout Farm)

➍ **Gainesville and Lake Lanier** (Lake Lanier Islands and waterpark, Mayfield Dairy Farms)

➐ **Georgia Heartland** (Uncle Remus Museum, Parks Ferry Recreation Area)

➓ **Savannah** (Ships of the Sea Museum, Tybee Island Amusement Park)

⑫ **Okefenokee and Plantation Trace Region** (Okefenokee Swamp Park, Obediah's Okefenok, Okefenokee Heritage Center, Parks at Chehaw, Wild Adventures)

Time needed: 2 weeks

NATURE LOVERS' TOUR

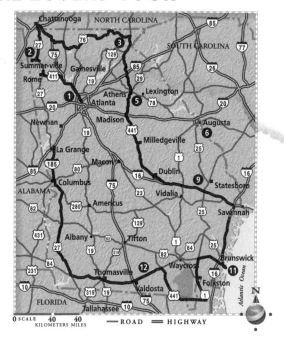

Take a trip focusing on Georgia's diverse landscape, from the remote moutons of the northwest corner to the unspoiled barrier islands of the coast.

- ❶ **Atlanta** (Atlanta Botanical Garden, Chattahoochee Nature Center, Fernbank Museum of Natural History, Fernbank Science Center)
- ❷ **Northwest Georgia** (Cave Spring, Cloudland Canyon State Park, Lookout Mountain)
- ❸ **Northeast Georgia** (Anna Ruby Falls, Tallulah Gorge, Chattooga River)
- ❺ **Athens** (State Botanical Gardens, Founders Memorial Garden, Sandy Creek Park)
- ❻ **Augusta** (Mistletoe State Park, Clarks Hill/Thurmond Lake)
- ❾ **Magnolia Midlands** (Georgia Southern Botanical Garden, Lamar Q. Ball Jr. Raptor Center)
- ⑪ **Golden Isles** (Cumberland Island, Sapelo Island)
- ⑫ **Okefenokee and Plantation Trace Region** (Okefenokee Swamp Park, Stephen C. Foster State Park, Birdsong Nature Center, Banks Lake National Wildlife Refuge, George T. Bagby State Park)
- ⑬ **Carter Country** (Callaway Gardens, Cecil B. Day Butterfly Center, Providence Canyon, Franklin D. Roosevelt State Park)

Time needed: 2-3 weeks

OUTDOOR RECREATION TOUR

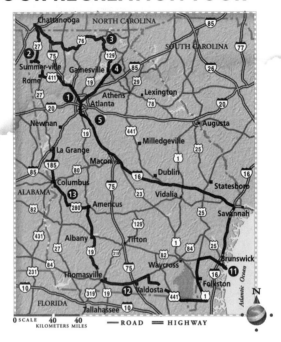

This trip offers exciting outdoor adventures from white-water rafting to wilderness hiking for those who like to do more than simply observe nature.

❶ **Atlanta** (Stone Mountain Park, Chattahoochee Outdoor Center)

❷ **Northwest Georgia** (John Tanner State Park, Cloudland Canyon State Park, Fort Mountain State Park, Lake Conasauga Recreation Area)

❸ **Northeast Georgia** (Appalachian Trail, Vogul State Park, Unicoi Gap, Chattooga River, Sky Valley)

❹ **Gainesville and Lake Lanier** (Lake Lanier Islands)

⓫ **Golden Isles** (Southeast Adventure Outfitters, St. Simons Dive Center)

⓬ **Okefenokee and Plantation Trace Region** (Suwannee Canal Recreation Area, Stephen C. Foster State Park, Colquitt County Hunting Plantations, Quail Unlimited, Suwannee Canoe Outpost, Banks Lake National Wildlife Refuge)

⓭ **Carter Country** (Callaway Gardens, Franklin D. Roosevelt State Park, Flint River Outdoor Center, Roosevelt Riding Stables)

Time needed: 2 weeks

CALENDAR OF EVENTS

January
Frontier Days, The Parks at Chehaw, Albany; 912/430-5275. (Early January)
King Week, Atlanta; 404-524-1956. (Mid-January)

February
Savannah Irish Festival, Savannah; 800/436-3746. (Mid-February)

March
St. Patrick's Festival, Dublin; 912/272-5546. (All month)
Forsythia Festival, Forsyth; 888/642-4628. (Early March)
Cherry Blossom Festival, Macon; 800/768-3401. (Mid-March)
St. Patrick's Day Festival, Savannah; 800/444-2427. (Mid-March)
Pogofest, Waycross; 912/283-3742. (Third weekend)

April
Dogwood Festival, Atlanta; 404/521-6600. (Late March/Early April)
Sheep to Shawl Day, Atlanta, Atlanta History Center; 404/814-4000. (First Saturday)
Masters Golf Tournament, Augusta; 800/726-0243. (Early April)
Hawkinsville Harness Horse Festival and Spring Pig Ribbin' Cook Off, Hawkinsville; 912/783-1717. (Mid-April)
Riverfest Weekend, Columbus; 706/323-7979. (Mid-April)
Vidalia Onion Festival, Vidalia; 912/538-8687. (Last weekend)

May
Chehaw National Indian Festival, Albany; 912/430-5275. (Third weekend)
Memorial Musicfest, Stone Mountain; 770/498-5702. (Memorial Day)

June
Country-by-the-Sea, Jekyll Island; 912/635-3636. (First weekend)
Watermelon Days Festival, Cordele; 912/273-1668. (Last two weeks)
Bluegrass Festival, Dahlonega; 800/231-5543. (Third weekend)

July
Fantastic Fourth Celebration, Stone Mountain; 770/498-5702.

Civil War Encampment, Atlanta History Center; 404/814-4000. (Last weekend)

August
Georgia Mountain Fair, Hiawassee; 706/896-4186. (Early August)

September
Kingsland's Annual Labor Day Catfish Festival, Kingsland; 800/433-0225.

Powers Crossroads Country Fair and Arts Festival, Newnan; 770/253-2011. (Labor Day Weekend)

Yellow Daisy Festival, Stone Mountain; 770/498-5702. (Second weekend)

Plains Peanut Festival, Plains, 912/824-5445. (Fourth weekend)

Riverfest Arts & Crafts Festival, Canton; 770/475-0930. (Last weekend)

October
Oktoberfest, Helen; 706/878-2747. (All month)

Cotton Pickin' Fair, Gay; 706/538-6814. (First weekend)

Georgia Marble Festival, Jasper; 706/692-5600. (First weekend)

Georgia National Fair, Perry; 912/987-3247. (Fifth Friday after Labor Day)

Sunbelt Agricultural Exposition, Moultrie; 912/985-1968. (Second weekend)

Georgia Apple Festival, Ellijay; 706/635-7400. (Second and third weekends)

Big Pig Jig, Vienna; 912/268-8275. (Third weekend)

Stone Mountain Highland Games and Scottish Festival, Stone Mountain; 770/521-0228. (Third weekend)

November
Plantation Wildlife Arts Festival, Thomasville; 912/226-0588. (Third weekend)

December
Candlelight Tours, Atlanta History Center; 404/814-4000. (First Saturday)

Dickens of a Christmas, Eastman; 912/374-4723. (Second weekend)

RESOURCES

State Offices

Georgia Department of Industry, Trade & Tourism, P.O. Box 1776, Atlanta, GA 30301; 404/656-3590

Georgia Hospitality and Travel Association, 600 W. Peachtree St., Ste. 1500, Atlanta, GA 30308; 404/873-4482

State Parks Reservations, 770/389-PARK or 800/864-PARK

City and Town Chambers of Commerce and Visitors Bureaus

Albany CVB, 225 W. Broad Ave., Albany, GA 31701; 800/475-8700

Alpine Helen/White County CVB, P.O. Box 730, Helen, GA 30545; 800/858-8027

Americus-Sumter County Tourism Council, P.O. Box 724, Americus, GA 31709; 912/924-2646

Athens-Clarke County CVB, 300 N. Thomas St., Athens, GA 30601; 800/653-0603

Atlanta CVB, 233 Peachtree St., Ste. 100, Atlanta, GA 30343; 800/285-2682

Augusta Metropolitan CVB, 32 Eighth St., Augusta, GA 30901; 800/726-0243

Brunswick-Golden Isles CVB, 4 Glynn Ave., Brunswick, GA 31520; 912/265-0620

Carrollton Area CVB, 118 S. White St., Carrollton, GA 30017; 800/292-0871

Cartersville CVB, 101 N. Erwin, Cartersville, GA 30120; 800/733-2280

Clayton County CVB, 104 N. Main St., Jonesboro, GA 30237; 800/285-2682

Cobb County CVB, P.O. Box 672827, Marietta, GA 30067; 800/451-3480

Columbus CVB, 1000 Bay Ave., Columbus, GA 31902; 800/999-1613

Eatonton-Putnam County, 105 Sumter St., Eatonton, GA 31024; 706/485-7701

Gainesville-Hall County CVB, 424 Green St. NE, Gainesville, GA 301501; 770/536-5209.

Greater Rome CVB, 402 Civic Center Dr., Rome, GA 30162-5823; 800/444-1834

Jekyll Island CVB, 381 Riverview Dr., Jekyll Island, GA 31527; 800/841-6586

Macon-Bibb County CVB, 200 Cherry St., Macon, GA 31208-6354; 800/768-3401

Madison-Morgan CVB, 115 E. Jefferson St., Madison, GA 30650; 800/709-7406

Marietta Welcome Center and Visitors Bureau, #4 Depot St., Marietta, GA 30060; 800/835-0445

McIntosh Chamber of Commerce, P.O. Box 1497, Darien, GA 31305; 912/437-4192

Milledgeville-Baldwin Co. CVB, 200 W. Hancock St., Milledgeville, GA 31601; 800/653-1804

Okefenokee Chamber of Commerce, P.O. Box 756, Folkston, GA 31537; 912/496-2536

Pine Mountain Tourism Association, 111 Broad St., Pine Mountain, GA 31822; 800/441-3502

Rabun County CVB, P.O. Box 750, Clayton, GA 30525; 706/782-4812

Savannah CVB, P.O. Box 1628, Savannah, GA 31402; 912/944-0456

Statesboro CVB, 332 S. Main St., Statesboro, GA 30458; 800/568-3301

St. Marys CVB, P.O. Box 1291, St. Marys, GA 31558; 800/868-8687

Thomasville Tourism Authority, 135 N. Broad St., Thomasville, GA 31799; 800/704-2350

Valdosta and Lowndes County CVB, 1703 Norman Dr., Ste. F, Valdosta, GA 31601; 800/569-8687

Vidalia Tourism Council, 2805 Lyons Hwy., Vidalia, GA 30474; fax 912/658-8687

Warm Springs Area Tourism Association, P.O. Box 578, Warm Springs, GA 31830; 800/337-1927

Waycross-Ware County CVB, P.O. Box 137, Waycross, GA 31501; 912/283-3742

INDEX

Map Index

AVALON
TRAVEL
publishing

BECAUSE TRAVEL MATTERS.

AVALON TRAVEL PUBLISHING knows that travel is more than coming and going—travel is taking part in new experiences, new ideas, and a new outlook. Our goal is to bring you complete and up-to-date information to help you make informed travel decisions.

AVALON TRAVEL GUIDES feature a combination of practicality and spirit, offering a unique traveler-to-traveler perspective perfect for an afternoon hike, around-the-world journey, or anything in between.

WWW.TRAVELMATTERS.COM

Avalon Travel Publishing guides are available
at your favorite book or travel store.

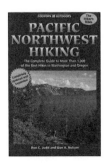

www.travelmatters.com

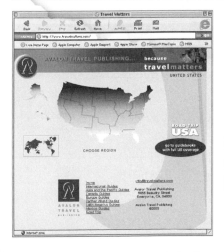

User-friendly, informative, and fun:
Because travel *matters.*

Visit our newly launched web site and explore the variety of titles and travel information available online, featuring an interactive *Road Trip USA* exhibit.

MOON HANDBOOKS

provide comprehensive coverage of a region's arts, history, land, people, and social issues in addition to detailed practical listings for accommodations, food, outdoor recreation, and entertainment. Moon Handbooks allow complete immersion in a region's culture—ideal for travelers who want to combine sightseeing with insight for an extraordinary travel experience in destinations throughout North America, Hawaii, Latin America, the Caribbean, Asia, and the Pacific.

WWW.MOON.COM

Rick Steves shows you where to travel and how to travel—all while getting the most value for your dollar. His Back Door travel philosophy is about making friends, having fun, and avoiding tourist rip-offs.

Rick's been traveling to Europe for more than 25 years and is the author of 22 guidebooks, which have sold more than a million copies. He also hosts the award-winning public television series *Travels in Europe with Rick Steves.*

WWW.RICKSTEVES.COM

ROAD TRIP USA

Getting there is half the fun, and Road Trip USA guides are your ticket to driving adventure. Taking you off the interstates and onto less-traveled, two-lane highways, each guide is filled with fascinating trivia, historical information, photographs, facts about regional writers, and details on where to sleep and eat—all contributing to your exploration of the American road.

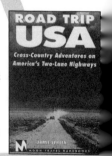

"Books so full of the pleasures of the American road, you can smell the upholstery."
~ BBC radio

WWW.ROADTRIPUSA.COM

TRAVEL✦SMART® guidebooks are accessible, route-based driving guides focusing on regions throughout the United States and Canada. Special interest tours provide the most practical routes for family fun, outdoor activities, or regional history for a trip of anywhere from two to 22 days. Travel Smarts take the guesswork out of planning a trip by recommending only the most interesting places to eat, stay, and visit.

"One of the few travel series that rates sightseeing attractions. That's a handy feature. It helps to have some guidance so that every minute counts."
~San Diego Union-Tribune

Foghorn Outdoors guides are for campers, hikers, boaters, anglers, bikers, and golfers of all levels of daring and skill. Each guide focuses on a specific U.S. region and contains site descriptions and ratings, driving directions, facilities and fees information, and easy-to-read maps that leave only the task of deciding where to go.

"Foghorn Outdoors has established an ecological conservation standard unmatched by any other publisher." ~Sierra Club

WWW.FOGHORN.COM

CiTY·SMaRT™ guides are written by local authors with hometown perspectives who have personally selected the best places to eat, shop, sightsee, and simply hang out. The honest, lively, and opinionated advice is perfect for business travelers looking to relax with the locals or for longtime residents looking for something new to do Saturday night.

There are City Smart guides for cities across the United States and Canada, and a portion of sales from each title benefits a non-profit literacy organization in its featured city.

ABOUT THE AUTHOR

Donald O'Briant is a features writer and books columnist for the *Atlanta Journal-Constitution,* where he's held a number of positions, including books editor and features editor, over the past 25 years. He is the author of *Atlanta,* a pictorial book about the city's architecture; *Looking for Tara*; and *Backroad Buffets and Country Cafes.* He lives in downtown Atlanta and is the father of a son, Chuck, and a daughter, Leigh.